KYOKUSHIN
BEGINNER'S GUIDE

Replicating Mas Oyama's Budo Karate
in the Western Dojo

KYOKUSHIN
BEGINNER'S GUIDE

Replicating Mas Oyama's Budo Karate
in the Western Dojo

by Nathan Ligo

Kyokushin Beginner's Guide, Replicating Mas Oyama's Budo Karate in the Western Dojo, was edited by Annie Gottlieb. Book design and production by Carol Majors, Publications Unltd. Cover image shows Sosai Masutatsu Oyama (center) and his uchi deshi class in 1990. Nathan Ligo is at left, beside (in the front row) Judd Reid, and (on Mas Oyama's left) Sandor Brezovai. The remaining Japanese faces (from left to right), by family name only, are Mr's Yamakage, Kato, Kamukai, Ishida, and Suzuki.

Kyokushin Beginner's Guide
Replicating Mas Oyama's Budo Karate in the Western Dojo
All Rights Reserved.
Copyright © 2014 Nathan Ligo
V1.0

This book may not be reproduced, transmitted, or stored in whole or in part by any means, including graphic, electronic, or mechanical without the express written consent of the publisher except in the case of brief quotations embodied in critical articles and reviews.

LIGO INK
www.ligodojo.com/LigoInk
ISBN: 978-0-9905522-0-8

Ligo Ink and the Ligo Ink logo are trademarks belonging to The Society for the Betterment of the Human Condition through the Training, Instruction, and Propagation of Budo Karate, Inc.

PRINTED IN THE UNITED STATES OF AMERICA

For my students
at Ligo Dojo

Table of Contents

Introduction ix
    Kyokushin's Unconquerable Country   x
    Mas Oyama's Sempai-Koohai System   xiv
    Using this Book: About the Sequence   xv
    Parents Reading this Book with their Karate Student Kids   xvi
    Runaway Spirit and Divergent Trends   xviii
    "I Don't Care About Your Kicks and Punches!"   xix
    A Cautionary Note Regarding Conflict   xx

The Sections
1. Fight to Be First   3
2. It's the *How,* Silly, Not the *What*   5
3. Follow the Rules of Etiquette   7
4. On Your Toes, Please, Not Your Heels!   11
5. The Toes-Not-Heels Dojo   13
6. Take Responsibility for Learning Even Complex Series of Motions in Just One Class, Even When Shown Just Once   14
7. OWN the Complex Series of Motions You've Been Shown   16
8. Drink Some, Spit Some? You'll Fail   18
9. BE the Ocean!   20
10. Complete Tasks That You've Been Assigned Promptly and Powerfully   22
11. The Sempai/Koohai System Brings You CLOSER to Your Teacher   25
12. Hear it Twice? It's Life and Death   26
13. Your Teacher Is Angry? It's Life and Death for Everyone, Especially YOU If You Feel Like Someone *Else* Was Responsible   27
14. React Inversely to Hardship 1   30
15. React Inversely to Hardship 2: Turn On the Animal!   32
16. React Inversely to Hardship 3: A Visibly Angry, Frustrated or Disappointed Teacher or Sempai   33
17. There's Only One Way to Do . . . Nearly Everything That You Do in the Dojo   34
18. You Need Your Teacher's Watchful Eye to Motivate You?   36
19. You Ask Yourself, "Am I Important? Does My Teacher Value Me?"   38
20. The Deepening of Human Relationships   40
21. Sempais and Koohais are Friends   45
22. The White Belt's Job, Even, to Bring Spirit   46
23. Are You Doing All This Hard Work to Be Mediocre?   48
24. Train Yourself to See the WHOLE Dojo, Understand Dojo Priorities   49

25. Challenge vs. Command	51
26. The Implicit Challenge: You Got It! Respond to ALL Challenges!	53
27. Always Answer, Always Answer Promptly	54
28. Do Not Disappoint / Inconvenience Your Sempai!	56
29. Encourage Your Koohais, Don't Be the Koohai That Needs Encouraging	58
30. How Do You Pay for Your Karate Lessons?	60
31. Treat New Students Delicately? No! Slow Motion is Akin to the Assassination of Learning for the New Student	61
32. Easier Training When Sensei's Not Looking?	63
33. When Will THAT Dojo Get Stronger?	64
34. There's Really Only One *How*	66
35. Weak *Osu* Has No Meaning, Unheard *Osu* Might As Well Not Have Been One at All, Not Even Trying *Osu* Means You Might As Well be Home	68
36. How and When to Bow in the Budo Karate Dojo: The "Two, Three, One"	70
37. Think Three Times Before You Speak: If That's Hard for You, Shut Up!	74
38. Be Strong to Become Strong	75
39. Hang the Dog, Leave Him at Home, Drive Him Out of the Dojo!	76
40. Example First, Words Second	81
41. Get Your Sempai's Back, Get Your Teacher's!	82
42. Respond to ALL Challenges	84
43. Imitate Someone Strong, Not the Other Way Around	86
44. Parallel Lessons: The Surface and the Esoteric, Identify the Task at Hand, Fulfill It, Support Its Delivery in the Eyes of Your Koohais	88
45. Karate IS Your Teacher's Karate	93
46. How Hard Do I Hit?	96
47. Unified Action Makes Karate Budo	98
48. Don't Let Yourself Be the One Who . . .	100
49. It's Your Dojo, Not My Dojo: If That Was in Your Living Room, Would You Walk Right Past It?	101
50. Grow Your Dojo, or Get Out of the Way	102
51. When Do I Gain Enough Seniority That I Don't Have to Follow One of These Principles Anymore?	104
52. Know the *How,* Know Your Teacher's Words For It, SHOW That You Know It	105
53. How Often in a Week Do You "Do Karate"? That's All? Okay, So No Excuse! Do It Right All the Time That You Do It!	107
54. "I'm Gonna Buy Me Some Karate!"	110
55. Your Teacher Has Been There, Your Teacher Has to Know 10 Things to Teach You One	110
56. Your Teacher Sees You in High Definition	112
57. Most Injuries in Karate Are Really Just Karate's Normal Aches and Pains	114
58. It's YOUR Responsibility Not to Get Hurt	116
59. Train Twice Per Week?	116
60. Everything You Do Is FOR EFFECT: Show That You Did What Your Teacher Asked, but Be Careful!	118

61. Learn to Reassess Yourself, and Take the Opposite Path: Stop, Drop, and Roll　119
62. Budo Karate is For Every Body　121
63. Disappointed? Yes, But If You Show it, You Blew It Again　122
64. Succeed Consistently, You Can't Buy a Break by Showing Strength Every Once in a While　125
65. If Someone Drops the Ball, Make Sure It's Your Koohai: This is the Sempai-Koohai Machine for Strength in the Budo Karate Dojo　126
66. Volunteers?　128
67. "Long Stance, Please. No, Long Stance!" The H-Type Student's Ball and Chain　130
68. Your Teacher ALWAYS Remembers　131
69. The ACB Ease, Not the ABC Lock　133
70. Your Teacher Can Read YOUR Mind, Learn to Read Your Teacher's　136
71. Telepathy? Hyper-Empathy?　138
72. "Channel" Your Teacher's Teaching　140
73. Karate Teachers Have to Teach Your Parents, Too?　142
74. You Carry the Dojo, Dummy! If the Dojo's Carrying You, You're in the Wrong Dojo　143
75. Which Path Do You Really Want to Take?　144
76. Be Powerful, Be Confident the First Time, Too!　146
77. Seiza, Lines, Fudo Dachi, Raise Your Hand, Listen to Lecture: The How-To's　147
78. Coddle Your Koohai?　151
79. BE a Karateka, Don't DO Karate　152
80. Budo Karate Remakes You, Americanized Karate Teaches You a Skill　153
81. To Fight For Correct Training Attitude IS to Defend Your Life After All　154
82. Leaps of Faith, Pride Resistance vs. Shame Resistance, and the Full-Contact Fight　157
83. Concepts Not Rules: Use Your Heart, Not Your Head　159
84. Hold the Lines, and Hold the Lines!
—The Sympathy Failure Conundrum　160
85. The Sinkhole, The Buzz Kill, The Drain, The Moss-Covered Stone　162
86. Monkey See, Monkey Do　164
87. Roll On, Role Model!　164
88. The Higher Your Rank, The More Your Responsibility　165
89. Beginners, Don't Fret!!　167
90. Class Instruction vs. Individual Instruction　167
91. Sensei, I Have to Pee!　169
92. It's YOU, Silly, Not Your Teacher!　170
93. It's Probably YOU, Not the Other Guy　171
94. There's Always Someone in the Dojo More Challenged than You　173
95. Provide No Refuge for Pride in the Dojo　174
96. Grasp Your Teacher's Priority, Understand Your Teacher's Intent, See the Dojo through Your Teacher's Eyes　176

97.	BE the Karateka! No Pain, No Gain	179
98.	If Training Doesn't Force You to Face Your Limitations, It's Not Budo	181
99.	Revealing the True Object of Budo Karate: Fight to Be First, But . . .	182
100.	Harder Training is Easier Training?	183
101.	The Condition of Your Uniform	184
102.	Oh My God, I Think I'm the Sinkhole! I Can't Seem to Figure My Way Out!	185
103.	The Importance of Consistent Training	186
104.	Bully vs. Victim	187
105.	Dissent and Complaint	188
106.	Addressing, or Discussing, Your Sempais: ALWAYS Use Their Title Correctly	190
107.	Responding to All Types of Criticism	192
108.	Wouldn't You Rather Be Corrected for Doing Too Much, Rather Than Called Out for Not Doing Enough?	194
109.	There's Nothing Wrong with a Bit of Ferocious Dedication to Your Dojo	195
110.	The BS Dojo	197
111.	Stealing Karate: No Thieves Welcome Here, Please!	199
112.	Pronunciation, Enunciation	199
113.	Charging to the Front of the Curve	200
114.	You ARE the Dojo!	202
115.	Careful, or Your Dojo Will Weed You Out!	203
116.	Dojo Decorum and Sempai-Koohai Interaction AS IF THEY WERE KATA	206
117.	The Minimum Standard	210
118.	Panicking? One Look Back at Cultural Differences	211

Epilog

The Establishment of Budo Karate Culture	217

Appendixes

Appendix 1: The Dojo Oath	223
Appendix 2: A Sample Complex Exercise Chart	225
Appendix 3: A Sample What/How Chart	229
Appendix 4: The Techniques of Mas Oyama's Kihon Series	231
Appendix 5: Our Moment in History (For the Kyokushin Instructor)	235
Appendix 6: Could It Be That It's NOT Desirable to Replicate the Way Things Were in Mas Oyama's Dojo?	241
Appendix 7: A Photograph That Should Inspire Us	245

Introduction

This book is intended to prepare the beginning student, and to better *empower* the intermediate one, for learning Budo karate in the Kyokushin dojo of the West. Such preparation is beneficial because of the cultural differences that exist between Japan, where Budo is an inherent part of the national persona, and your Western country where some of the ideals integral to Budo karate training are not always so easy to grasp. Read this, and you will be better empowered to learn karate *as it is best learned.* Adopt the principles contained within—avoid the pitfalls away from which this book will warn you!—and the attitude with which you train will have a better chance of developing into something that would have fit in Mas Oyama's world headquarters dojo. In short, your karate training experience will be more rewarding, and you will be made stronger by following the more authentic path.

This book presupposes that your dojo is one in which students of all levels train together in one class, and that there is, therefore, some attempt made to adopt Mas Oyama's sempai-koohai (senior-junior) system. The advice contained within is written for the beginning student looking up, although the advanced student—or the teacher!—wanting to make his/her dojo stronger might certainly benefit. The book is separated into 118 one- or two-page essays, each with a title designed to conjure the section's content at a glance, so that the student who has already read might later review with ease. The best use of this book will be to read it when you begin your training, and then to revisit it two or three times during your first and second years of training. Since each essay can be devoured in a matter of minutes, the ongoing student might also opt to review one or two principles at each sitting, and just continue to revisit the book regularly.

The stark beginner should be cautioned about becoming intimidated by the strict nature of some of the advice contained within. "Get with the program, or go find a different dojo!" for example. Budo karate students in the West start and continue and fumble along in their Budo karate training all the time without following the type of advice contained in this book. Any part that you don't understand — or that might not apply in your dojo, where your teacher might do some things differently — will become clear to you as you train. One point made handily within is that karate IS WHAT YOUR TEACHER DEFINES IT TO BE in the relatively closed world of YOUR dojo. Some concepts that I promote here, therefore, might not fit within your dojo; the extent to which they do will depend on your teacher and which parts of what's presented here he/she chooses to promote.

Kyokushin's Unconquerable Country

America.

Kyokushin's unconquerable country.

At least Mas Oyama considered it to be, and it is critical that we consider what it might mean to us in the West that our founder, Mas Oyama, at the very least believed the American personality, and to a lesser degree the Western one, to be the one in the world that was the most *inhospitable* to Japanese *Budo*, the *Martial Way* of Japan.

In recent years I heard an interview with Mas Oyama that was recorded in America during his final visit to this country, where he first began Kyokushin's amazing overseas expansion 40 years earlier. It was late autumn of 1992, less than two years before his death, and he was here for Shihan Michael Monaco's tournament in Rochester. Australia's Shihan Cameron Quinn was interpreting. The interviewer asked Mas Oyama what he thought of America.

"Uh oh," I thought, "this ought to be good!"

And it was.

Brilliant!

Mas Oyama responded by saying how a young Japanese woman he'd been traveling with had been brought to tears by how beautiful a country it was, i.e. by its landscape. It was quite masterfully said, since the uninformed listener would have heard, in Mas Oyama's words and tone, how much he admired America.

And Mas Oyama had nothing personal against America or Americans, but I can personally attest, since I had lived and trained in Mas Oyama's daily presence for nearly two years immediately before this (from early 1990 up until the start of 1992), that Mas Oyama *despised* the influence that "the American spirit" was having, even on his Budo karate at home *in Japan*. If the Budo karate spirit was matter, for Mas Oyama the American spirit was antimatter. For six years before Japan I grew up a student of his nephew, Sensei[1] Seong Soo Choi in North Carolina, *knowing* that Mas Oyama had given up on ever replicating the Budo karate spirit in this, the world's last superpower. In his residential program in Tokyo, where I was finally admitted at the age of 19, I was told that Mas Oyama had said repeatedly that he would never admit another American. He believed America to be a lost cause. Let us remember that Mas Oyama watched as even his earliest *Japanese* students that he sent to America to introduce Kyokushin in the '60s and '70s—students he'd loved like his own sons!—were apparently so altered by America that they ultimately betrayed him and struck off on their own.

Happily, I do believe that Mas Oyama had some hope for America in the end.

I know better than anyone that he put a great deal of personal effort into ME and my development while I was his only American student, and, although he was daily lecturing how "American spirit" was the force most likely to undo his life's work, I know that he was not directing that criticism at me personally. He loved the times that I broke through and demonstrated attitude that he would have considered unexpected given that

---

[1] "Sensei" is used here to match the Japanese tradition described throughout this book, but "Sensei" Choi was actually "Master" Choi to us, since we used the English term for what probably should have been "reverend teacher" when it was first translated from Korean. Mas Oyama, originally Baedal Choi, fully accepted Japanese culture when he became a dual Japanese-Korean citizen. My very first teacher, Master Choi, had no Japan connection.

I was an American, and I constantly sought to show him that I was aware. I do believe that in his daily lectures, Mas Oyama was waging a war to make ME understand the importance of Budo *as a product of Japanese culture*, and the importance of understanding that certain attitudes contained within American culture were destructively inhospitable to it. At the very least, the bottom line for me has always been that we cannot take Budo karate for granted without very careful attention paid to the cultural differences between Japan and the cultures of the West.

Readers in other Western countries should not let themselves off the hook. *Your* culture also differs from Japanese culture, and *your* culture has also been influenced by America. Many of you will have the advantage of having at least some impulse similar to Mas Oyama's, since American *culture* is having such an incredible influence on ALL the cultures of the world, and in both good and bad ways. Karate teachers and students in most foreign counties will be able to identify, like Mas Oyama, ways in which America's influence is ALSO influencing their young people in negative ways. Democracy is good, Coke and McDonald's hamburgers are bad. You get the point.

Mas Oyama certainly did.

So, what's our responsibility?

What is important for us to keep in mind as we begin our study of Budo karate?

First, I believe that far from being something to be ashamed of, it is our DUTY to understand and embrace the fact that we might be disadvantaged. We live in an era where so much fracturing has occurred in the Kyokushin world that it's easy for us, no matter whom we're affiliated with, to find someone to compare ourselves to such that we can feel pretty good about our own level of achievement. When Mas Oyama's Kyokushin was one unified whole, everyone had no choice but to compare themselves to the whole wide world of Kyokushin. Now, however, the whole world of Kyokushin, for many of us, can be (if we allow it) a much smaller world indeed.

"We are good at what we do! We do it better than those other guys, we must be doing something right!" no longer necessarily holds as something to be proud of in the various small slices of the Kyokushin world.

This statement might cause some readers to take pause, but I would hold that it is our responsibility as karateka, really no matter where we're training, to accept the fact that our karate *is not good* compared to what it should be. As "enlightened" Americans, is it not more patriotic, after all, to accept our deficiencies? Isn't it only by doing so that we might truly open the doors to embracing ways in which we might improve? Of course we have learned to do some things well in the Budo karate dojos of the West, and even, for that matter, in the dojos of America.

Of course we can be proud of the achievements we've made!

But all one needs to do is to watch a present-day kata competition in a North American tournament to see how far we truly have yet to go. I'm not boasting about my own kata—far from it!—but I have had enough exposure to some folks who actually have a very good understanding of kata, for example, to know that there really aren't, on the North American continent, very many people who are teaching kata in a way that reflects its true meaning. The way kata is taught on this continent, it might as well be something isolated and apart. People learn to fight, and people learn, separately, the mysterious dance called kata. You can beat someone up with the kind of karate learned separately from kata, but a mastery of self-defense? Your ability to defeat five attackers, all of them able, and half of them armed? Not yet, not with this North American Kyokushin. Not unless the five attackers are very wimpy indeed.

If Mas Oyama were here today to focus on the West, and on breaking the back of trends that are counter to the development of a more authentic Budo karate, I know in my bones that he would be doing so, also, by trying to bridge the cultural gap that he didn't have enough time to bridge during his lifetime.

Americans will never be Japanese, Canadians will never be European, a people's culture is going to be their culture no matter what. However, the American example is certainly proof that cultures do spill, and can be spilled, across international borders to influence the development of foreign cultures. Sometimes this happens naturally: Coke and the McDonald's hamburger, for example, piggybacking on democracy. But there is also a *path of least resistance* element to cultural exchange. Negative aspects of culture tend to trickle downhill, and that's the final point that I believe it's important for us to embrace.

Whereas American pop culture will spread automatically because it's light, and free, and fun, and easy, that element of Japanese culture that is Budo will NOT spread automatically into Western culture because it's NOT light, or free, or fun, or easy. We absolutely have to understand that it's NOT natural. It won't come automatically. We have to go and get it. We have to fight for it.

To adjust and improve our practice of Budo karate, as I believe it is our duty to do, we have to work at it. We have to study. Sure, much of it will emerge through the blood, sweat, and tears spilled in hard physical training. But I would attest that, while that might be enough in the dojos of Japan, here it won't ever be.

In America, we spill American blood, American sweat, and American tears. It's my opinion that in order to really grasp Budo karate, we need to do some learning of how to spill, not even a few *Japanese* tears—because there's also now an America-influenced pop Japanese culture that's not so comfortable with Budo either—but a few *samurai* tears, some samurai sweat, and some samurai blood. At least, if we VALUE doing so, we will gain some insight into Budo karate that we wouldn't otherwise have had.

It's my firm opinion that we would gain some insight that would please my teacher and yours, Mas Oyama.

Does this book advocate spilling blood?

Well, only in a manner of speaking. The book is not about warfare and we don't tend to spill much actual blood in karate training. Rather, it's about how a beginning practitioner of Budo karate might best approach his/her training. It's about developing attitudes and personality that are best receptive to the most authentic way in which you can experience Budo karate in your own Western dojo.

Mas Oyama's Sempai-Koohai System

Mas Oyama wrote that karate is not Budo karate, and therefore not Kyokushin karate, without the sempai-koohai (senior-junior) system.

This is an important point for us in the West to consider, since the sempai-koohai system is an inherently cultural element that does not, for the most part, exist in the West. In the Budo karate dojo, our sempais (seniors) take an active role in guiding our learning as they tell us what to do, and we do it without question. In return, we fight to show them, through our attitude (the focus of much of this book) and determination, how committed we are to learning from them what they have already learned before us. Our sempais feel, therefore, obligated both to help us learn, and to behave both in the dojo and beyond in a way that should inspire us to follow their example and become, with time, better human beings.

In the Japanese system, our *sempai* is any student who began his/her karate training earlier than we did. Our *sensei*, in that sense, is also our sempai. Karate students on their second day of training may have their very first koohais if there are any new students who join the dojo that day. Of course, there is a significant difference between our sempais who started training one day earlier than we did, and our sempais who started training years, or even decades, earlier than we did. So many of the concepts I deal with in this book have to do with the relationship between sempai and koohai that an earlier title I considered was "Replicating Mas Oyama's *Sempai/Koohai System* in the Western Dojo."

The reader should stay mindful of two things.

First, karate is NOT Budo without the sempai/koohai system, and, second, THE sempai/koohai system, i.e. Mas Oyama's, is not just whatever you want it to be. Your dojo might have sempais and koohais who interact in a certain way based on the traditions established in your dojo. Please understand, however, that your sempai/koohai system, some generations of teachers removed from Mas Oyama's, is not necessarily the sempai/koohai system Mas Oyama intended.

I look up to people who, however much they may know, are willing to admit that there's still so much left for them to learn. I try to live this way myself, and in the case of the sempai-koohai system of Mas Oyama, I *know* that I am an American, and therefore inherently disadvantaged. I know that so clearly, however, precisely *because* I have had a closer, long-term sustained view of the sempai-koohai system in use in the environment in which it was created than most other karateka of the West. Please be patient with me as I do my best to present that which I have learned.

Using this Book: About the Sequence

Please read the first 15 sections of this book first.

"Of course we read books from the beginning," you might say, but the point is that the sections in this book can be read out of order, with the one key exception that many of them presuppose an understanding of the first 15 or so. If you are a true beginner, and you've acquired a copy of this book, I encourage you to read those first twenty pages before you even come back for your second training! My intent is that they — and the others — will empower you, both by starting you off on the right foot, and by steering you clear of progress-impeding pitfalls that I see American students of Budo karate finding they have fallen into.

We live in a computer age, and you will see that many, if not most, of the sections are "linked" to others. Some assume that you understand content contained in another section—almost all of them assume that you've read the first 15!—and others will refer you to later sections that will help you to deepen your understanding of the point already presented.

And please don't fret!

You do NOT need to master all of this material to start training, or even to continue to train for some time. You will see that all the material contained within contributes to helping the reader understand one single approach, one single attitude. Even after reading the very first essay, *Fight to Be First*, you will ALREADY have a notion of what that attitude is. Yes, you'll get more as you read more; it will become more and more clear to you, but read 15 of these, and I think you'll already be able to see where it's all going.

More than that, though, don't worry for this reason, too: You do not have to master this material, ever!

You just have to *prioritize* the attitude described within. I do a lot of describing here of what makes bad karate. But don't let that make you worry! *Prioritize* the concepts contained within and you won't be one of the ones who propagates bad karate. Prioritize these concepts and you'll stay ahead of the curve!

Parents Reading this Book with their Karate Student Kids

If parents are concerned about the strict wording of some of these sections, please understand first that they are written, also, to accommodate the adult student. But also please consider that one reason to be strict in our expectations towards students' training attitude is so that your child's teachers won't have to be so strict in class. Although the book focuses on instilling a certain attitude in the individual, please consider that the overall goal of doing so is to raise the bar, and instill a certain training attitude *within the majority* of those who train at the dojo, so that the instructors and sempais won't have to play disciplinarian.

It is certainly true that the more your child's classes lack discipline—the less the kids try to train with the attitude described here—the harder their teachers in the Budo karate dojo will have to be. Of course, in the right environment, acquiring the right attitude should be automatic. Taking for granted that that environment already exists in your child's class, however, is a mistake worth considering. After all, simply by introducing YOUR child to the class, you are lowering the class's average. Every new adult student lowers the class average, too, since so many of the routines are foreign to every beginning student.

ANY preparation, therefore, any discussion of how any student is supposed to conduct himself or herself in class, ups the average and empowers both your child and also his/her dojo. Your child's teacher will certainly appreciate any small amount of assistance you can give.

Let's consider your child's soccer league.

I'm sorry to resort to a stereotype, but how willing is the average American parent to fight for the victory and team spirit of his/her child's athletic teams?

That's all we ask here.

What's often missed in the mind of the beginning karate student, or the minds of the parents of the beginning child karate student in America, is *the team element* of karate training.

If the norm at your child's dojo is that everyone stays revved up to the point where they all work hard and don't let their attention stray, that becomes the environment in which *your* child has the best chance of developing the habit of learning in that accelerated fashion. By helping your child to understand even a bare minimum of the concepts contained within, by cheering for your child on the way into class, and by sharing encouraging words with him/her those nights that you pick your child up and he/she has a long face because the teacher was cross, you are in fact working together with your child's teachers in the best interest of your child. By understanding the concepts here as if you, too, were a student at the dojo, you can help to create an environment at your child's dojo that can be LESS strict, one in which *strict* is automatic, because a majority of the students behave that way naturally, so that kids can focus their energy on fun rather than on discipline.

Of course, this is exactly where the discipline you really want for your child is the easiest to come by!

If discipline comes automatically, so kids can focus on fun, isn't that better than classes in which instructors have to constantly knock heads together to demand discipline and nobody has fun?

Do understand, though, and I caution:

If your child's Budo karate instructors are any good, they won't let your kids have too much fun if they're weak, as a group, in terms of discipline. They would be bad instructors if they did. Do you want a play-group monitor or a karate teacher?

In the Budo karate dojo, you can be assured you'll be getting the latter. For more on this, please see #73, *Karate Teachers Have to Teach Your Parents, Too?*

Runaway Spirit and Divergent Trends

Strong spirit or powerful attitudes (such as those described within) in the closed environment of the dojo will *run away* and become the norm if the majority adopts them. That means that if enough people set off on the right path, it will be next to effortless for newcomers to fall into place. If all their role models are behaving correctly, newcomers will have no doubt about how they're supposed to behave. The adoption of powerful attitude, in this case, happens automatically.

This is where any dojo's karate should be. This is where every instructor should endeavor to bring his/her dojo. Negative trends in the majority can also, of course, run away and become the norm. I've watched this occur in various eras of my own dojos' development. It's critical that every student carries his/her own weight and understands what his/her role is supposed to be. Hence, I've written this book to offer you all a leg up, a gentle nudge in the right direction.

Do your teacher a favor, and take the advice contained within to heart.

The difficulty in the West, of course, occurs before the dojo's powerful *norm* is successfully established. When newcomers have powerful role models to compare themselves to, AND weak role models to compare themselves to at the same time, they are presented with an unconscious choice of how they are supposed to behave. One serious pitfall that occurs is that this newcomer comes to believe (subconsciously) that it's normal in the dojo to be powerful *sometimes*, and not powerful other times. Indeed, with this book, I seek to empower new students with the ability to identify, from day one, which behaviors it would behoove them to emulate, and which ones should be avoided.

Indeed, some sections of this book — we could probably go through with a red highlighter and mark them! — address situations in which students have already fallen into deviating trends. Each time I write one of these sections, I find myself feeling embarrassed, because in them I confess to folks beyond my own branch that I know these situations and that I know these students, too. Shouldn't I be the type of instructor that's so inspiring that my students should never find themselves lost down an environment-damaging divergent path in the first place?

Believe me, I ask myself that question time and time again. I ask myself, "Where have I failed these students?" How painful it is to write a section in which I feel I have to complain about failed students in order to highlight for students who haven't yet begun how better to avoid the same pitfalls!

Students who read this who have already formed habits of on-again-off-again strength that don't belong in the Budo karate dojo can also clearly see that they are on the wrong path, and perhaps that new insight—arriving better late than never!—will help me to help them to move themselves onto the right path.

It's all about the average.

It's all about the majority.

Every student should fight to improve the average of his/her dojo, and that fight starts with themselves. How convenient that, in this one case, we can be both ultimately selfless (by thinking only about our classmates' well-being), and ultimately self-serving, at the same time, that is, because WE are the biggest beneficiaries of training with strong classmates!

"I Don't Care About Your Kicks and Punches!"

Seriously.

I mean it!

Your kicks, your punches, your kata, your fighting ability, all of that will come, and all of that will come ten times better if your make it your priority to adopt the training *attitude* presented in this book.

Please.

Change your thinking, or, if you're just starting, set your thinking out on the stronger path from the very beginning. Read and understand these concepts that piece together to define what it means to train in Budo karate. Instead of just *doing karate* like so many Westerners do, if you can *become the Budo karateka*, there will be no comparison in terms of your progress . . . and yes, I do mean in terms of your kicks and your punches, and your kata, and your fighting ability, as well!

In a later section of this book I discuss the parallel lessons of the Budo karate dojo. There's almost always a surface lesson and an esoteric, a *secret* lesson. If you follow the deeper one, the one that lies behind the kicks and the punches, your kicks and your punches will be ten times more than they would have been otherwise.

Of course I care about your physical technique!

I care so much about it that I've written this book.

Understand the concepts presented within. They're written so that the ten-year-olds in my dojo can understand (if even with a little help). Do your best to adopt those concepts altogether as one unified training personality, and make it yours. Read them, and then say, "Ah ha! This is how I'm going to move forward! This is how I'm going to learn the kicks and the punches of karate!"

Do, and I promise you, you won't be disappointed. Don't, and I promise you that your Budo karate teacher will be.

Do you want to see your teacher happy?

Show your teacher that rather than caring only about the physical of karate, show him/her that first and foremost, you're caring about the principles described here in this book.

Do you want to be the best you can be?

Remember that your goal and that of your teacher are one and the same. Please your teacher and you'll also be on your way to mastering karate.

A Cautionary Note Regarding Conflict

See Case A and Case B, on facing page.

In Case A the students' performance falls short of the teacher's expectations, but in Case B, the students' performance does fall into better line, but the two are not completely lined up (as it should be, since the teacher should always be there to *challenge* the students to perform better). Consider, however, that in case A, the students are likely living unhappy days because their teacher's efforts to improve their performance have likely reached a fever pitch, one that's potentially uncomfortable for teacher and student alike, particularly if the discrepancy persists over time.

As you read, you will find that in several of the sections of this book I refer to actual experiences that I've had, in my own dojo, in which uncomfortable conflict arises because students find themselves in the

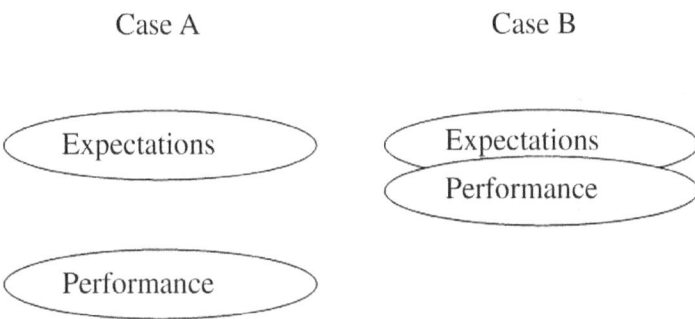

Case A situation. If the students would only hold themselves to a slightly different standard, however, and move into the Case B situation—or if I am able to move them there!—that conflict would completely disappear. Of course, I would be a poor teacher if I lowered my expectations too far below the Budo karate standard.

Before you read one of those sections and panic, however, thinking, "Oh my gosh, I don't want to practice an art in which that kind of conflict exists!" please consider that that's exactly why I've written this book:

To save all my future students—and myself!—from that exact situation.

It seems that when you squeeze a Japanese student, Budo seeps out like wine from grapes. I saw this happen all the time, because my own birth in the Kyokushin world happened in Mas Oyama's dojo in Japan. Apparently the same cannot necessarily be said, however, about the Western student, certainly not the American one. Squeeze the American student and it's not often Budo that spills forth automatically.

Remember that your teacher will never ask you to sprout wings and fly. He/she will never ask you for rocket science. If you've fallen below an expectation, as in the diagram, it's likely instead that you're missing something very simple, but that just hasn't occurred to you yet.

I certainly wish I'd written this book earlier.

Read, however, and I think we will tip the majority to where we will remove all future conflict.

Remember that you need not master all of this material to move yourself in line with your Budo karate teacher's expectations. The concept described within is actually one single concept. Read only the first section of this book (see #1, *Fight to Be First*), and you will already start to know what that concept is. The more you read, the clearer it will become, but it would be a mistake for you to put too much pressure on yourself, and think that you have to memorize it all. There will be no written test.

Just read and relax.

Train hard in the dojo, ask questions if you have them, and I think you will see that the combination will yield positive results.

The Sections

1. Fight to Be First

This is the central attitude of training in the Budo karate dojo. You might hear it referred to as "having strong spirit."

It's not something someone will give you. It's the attitude that even the white belt must endeavor to BRING to the dojo from his/her first week of training. It is a requirement of participation, not something you'll get over time by waiting for it to come. Ask yourself: What's the best way to ensure I'm not last?

Answer: Fight to be first.

Consider: Your teacher asks you to line up for class. Everyone fights not to be last, by racing to be the first one to get to their places. Who wins? Well, probably no one. Almost everyone gets to their places at about the same time. This is a UNIFIED powerful action. Good for you! You're practicing Budo karate. The important thing is not *being* first—it's that everyone uniformly fights to be.

What if 1/3 of the students take their time? What if another third doesn't know where to go and waits, always, for someone to tell them? This is a MIXED action: Some are strong, but most are weak. There is a range of motivation, some eager, some not. This class will fail. It does not resemble training in the Japanese dojo. Ask yourself: How do I ensure that my kiai is not the quietest one?

Simple! Fight to make it the loudest.

How do I ensure that I'm not the one that didn't hear the instruction? Answer: Fight to be the one that heard and understood it best. How do I ensure that I'm not the weakest student? Answer: Fight to be the one that understands this book better, and fight to be the one who shows it in the dojo. Again, how do I ensure that I'm not the weakest student? Answer: Fight to be the strongest one. Remember 99% of strength is *how you behave*, not how physically gifted you are. Behave strong by fighting to be the best at adopting the training personality presented in this book, and you will excel beyond the students who are athletically gifted but are too sure that they know too much to try to adjust their thinking.

Try this one:

How do I ensure that I have the closest relationship with my teacher and can therefore learn the most? Answer: Fight to be best and to follow the rules of etiquette. Fight to show the strongest spirit by following the ideas in this book. Fight to *channel* your teacher's teaching.

Remember, karate IS fighting, after all!

Remember that actually BEING first is far less important than fighting to be. In Budo karate, succeeding has little to do with outdoing your peers. It has EVERYTHING to do with staying at the front of the curve with peers who are likewise struggling to stay at the front of the curve.

Of course karate training is learning how to fight! If you don't fight to be first, fight to be loudest, fight to be strongest, fight to be the best at EVERYTHING in the dojo, you are not practicing Budo karate, you are practicing Americanized *play* karate, and in the Budo karate dojo you are in the way of progress.

And guess what else!

You are ALSO not learning how *actually* to fight should you ever have to defend yourself. Your fight to be first, as a student, IS one and the same as your learning also how to actually fight. See #81, *To Fight For Correct Training Attitude IS to Defend Your Life After All.*

Change your attitude, even today, fight to be first in all things, and you'll be fine. Don't worry if this seems intimidating to you. Perhaps you try it, and it's hard, and then you feel like you're going to have to be constantly exhausted trying to keep it up.

But then you're not exactly seeing the point.

Make it a priority, that's all.

Train from the heart, allow yourself to feel ashamed if you realize in some particular exercise that you're the last one, or slipping behind. This is an attitude that you can adopt in one single changing of the mind. Realize what your role in the dojo is supposed to be and this concept will be yours forever. You won't have to fight a lot to fulfill it. You'll just have to fight a little.

Deny the concept, though? Fail even to try to adopt this way of thinking?

If you do, you'll not only have to fight a lot, but you'll also burden the students around you, and the chances are that you won't be successful in the end. Your teacher will be working against you, rather than working to support you.

Develop this as a priority, though, fight to be first in all things that you do in the dojo, and you'll be a great success.

2. It's the *How*, Silly, Not the *What*

Your teacher will guide your training by telling you *what* to do in the dojo, and almost in the same breath he/she will tell you *how* to do that thing. Only the first-day white belt student should be all-consumed with *what* he/she is supposed to do. By the time you are working towards your first colored belt, certainly, you must be paying more attention to *how* your teacher tells you to do the task at hand.

Train your ear to hear the *how* louder than the *what*, and you'll be on the right track. Here's an example:

Your teacher asks the class to begin *Taikyoku sono Ichi* (this is a kata made up of twenty motions), and, in almost the same breath, your teacher says, "Make sure you have long stances." The kata (and its correct sequence of movements) is the *what* and "with long stances" is the *how*. The Budo karate student hears the *how*, "long stances," louder than the *what*, *Taikyoku sono Ichi*, because he/she knows that's what his/her teacher will be watching for. The Budo karate student gets stronger, faster. And so does his/her dojo.

The beginning Budo karate student might make a mistake in the memorization of the sequence of moves, but at least when that student does so, he/she has a long stance, because he/she understood that to be the teacher's priority. The weaker student fights so hard to recall the movements, the *what*, that he/she has disregarded the *how*, and fumbles just like the first student, but with a tall, short, awkward stance to boot. At least the first student *looked* strong when he/she misstepped by SWEATING and doing the parts of the exercise he/she *can* do in a powerful way.

If you think you might be the weaker student described here, remember that a priority adjustment is a one-second choice, not something you have to learn how to do over time. Make a decision, today. DECIDE to listen for the *how* from now on. Congratulate yourself when you hear it. Celebrate by showing your teacher and your classmates alike that you heard, by doing it *how* you were asked to do it.

Of course, if you're learning a new, complex motion or series of motions for the first time, you have to learn the motions before you can start practicing them. The practiced student learns the motion or exercise in one lesson, or even in the first half of one lesson. As soon as possible, then, that student can forget about the *what* and start concentrating on what his/her teacher is asking for in terms of *how* to do the motion or the exercise correctly.

The white belt's practice of karate involves the highest percentage of memorization. You have to learn a series of motions by imitating them. However, this is not really karate training. Training doesn't begin until you're comfortable enough with *what* to do that you can focus on *how* to do it better. From the very first training, therefore, you should start shedding the mentality of "trying to figure out what I'm supposed to do." Instead, try to HEAR what your teacher is telling you in terms of *how* to learn, and then *how* to practice.

It is a tragic sight to see in the dojo when a student gets stuck in white belt learning mode, and is, months later, still trying—and mostly failing!—to memorize things. Training doesn't start to be pleasurable until you get a handful of the motions down and can begin training in them. Otherwise, it's one big headache. See #6, *Take Responsibility for Learning Even Complex Series of Motions in Just One Class, Even When Shown Just Once* and you see how easy it can be.

Budo karate or the dumbed-down Americanized version?

Concentrate only on the *what* and you are failing. Train yourself to hear, AND DEMONSTRATE that you heard, the *how* and you are practicing Budo karate. It's that demonstration of effort that employs, and therefore *develops*, your strong karate spirit.

Remember that you can show that *you're trying to do* the motion *how* you've been asked to do it, even when you can't quite do it that way yet. Rome wasn't built in a day, nor was anyone's karate technique mastered in just one day. The important thing is showing your teacher *you're fighting to do it the way he/she asked you to*. It's the *not* trying, whether deliberate or because of confusion, that leads to failure.

"Hajime!" ("Begin!") your teacher says, "Make sure you keep your guard up!"

What did you hear?

"Begin" was the *what*. Keeping your guard up was the *how* your teacher wants to see that you do it.

What are you going to be sure to SHOW your teacher that you're doing? Beginning the exercise? Showing him/her that you're doing the right one?

If so, you blew it.

Instead, take that part for granted:

Show your teacher you've got your guard up at all times, and you'll be showing your teacher how strong you are.

3. Follow the Rules of Etiquette

Following the rules of etiquette is a requirement for entering the dojo for the first time, not something that you learn to do over weeks and months of training. Answering with "Osu!" (Long o, silent u!) and bowing might feel awkward to the new student, but, in the dojo, you only look funny when you DON'T do them, or when you do them sheepishly, not when you do them powerfully and correctly.

The rules of etiquette are a finite list. This means there are not hundreds of them. There are only a handful, so there's no excuse to feel intimidated and succumb to frustration for not getting them right.

Your teacher and your sempais will seem friendly when you follow the rules, but will seem unfriendly over time if you don't. Of course you want a friendly teacher, so follow the rules. Once you've been around long enough to know better, your sempai will consider you *rude* if you don't follow the rules, and he/she will consider you *strong* if you do, so please do your best! In this sense, remember that making everyone happy and successful is in *your* hands.

Although many of these rules will have their own section, the most important ones are listed here. Remember it's the *how* you do them that's important, not simply doing them (see #2, *It's the How, Silly, Not the What*), so be sure to read the essay on each one. Following these rules (below) without doing them correctly is tantamount to not doing them at all. Of course, if you're not doing them at all, you might as well stay home.

1. Always answer your sempai with "Osu!" promptly, and powerfully (Long o, silent u!). Answer "Osu!" even if the instruction wasn't verbal (e.g. even if the instruction came as a gesture or an actual physical correction). There should be no long pause after your sempai speaks and before you answer; your sempai shouldn't have to wonder if you're going to answer or not. You can't say "Osu!" too many times, but you can say it too few. You can even answer "Osu!" mid-sentence when your teacher is addressing you or the class if, for example, your teacher pauses in his/her speech. This is not interrupting, it's affirming that you're on board. Just make

sure you don't say "Osu!" *on top* of your teacher's speech, i.e. don't interrupt. Answering with "Osu!" in response to a command is actually more important than fulfilling the command, so make sure "Osu!" comes first. See section #35 for pronunciation and a further explanation of "Osu!"

(Did you notice the *what* and the *how* here in the very first sentence above? "Answer with 'Osu!'" is the *what*, answer "always," "promptly," and "powerfully" is the *how*. If you're answering with "Osu!" but not doing it promptly, powerfully and always, you are missing the point.)

2. Answer "Osu! Sensei, I'll fix it!" or "Osu! Sempai, I'll fix it!" when you are being corrected, or when you make an error, or otherwise inconvenience your teacher or sempai. "Osu," by itself, is not enough for the Western dojo trying to establish the Budo karate system, because there absolutely *must* be a verbal expression of determination to correct the error (i.e. in order to be an effective role model for junior students), and the Western student doesn't always know how to express this determination with his/her tone in "Osu!" alone. In Mas Oyama's dojo we used "Osu! Shitsurei-shimashita!" ("Osu! I was very rude to make that mistake!") Although this might be new to your Western dojo, it's not something I've made up; it was the tradition established in Mas Oyama's dojo.

3. Always bow twice when entering and leaving the dojo, in two divergent directions, once towards the room, and once to the students in the room, and even when there's no one there! (In this case "the dojo" refers to the room where you actually train, not the facility, i.e. don't bow like this entering the lobby; only bow to any sempais that happen to be in the lobby.) Bow correctly. See section #36 for detail about bowing.

4. Always stand up and bow and say "Osu!" to your teacher or sempai when he/she enters or leaves the room (or area) that you're in, and, likewise, bow and say "Osu!" when YOU enter or leave the room (or area) where your teacher or sempai is. Even if you're not leaving the room where your sempai is, but you're leaving your sempai's presence by going to the other side of the room, the rule applies: You have to excuse yourself, not just walk away. Always bow and say "Osu!" when you *greet* your sensei

(or sempai), no matter where you happen to be. Do it correctly. See section #36 for detail about bowing.

5. Stand correctly when it's time to stand, sit correctly when it's time to sit (always sit first in seiza), sit comfortably correctly when it's time to sit comfortably (only when invited to "relax, and sit comfortably" from seiza), raise your hand correctly when raising your hand (straight arm, tight fist!), listen correctly (maintain eye contact!) when it's time to listen. See section #77 for detail.

6. Respond "Osu, Onegaishimasu!" when beginning an exercise (your instructor has just said, "_____ keiko o hajimemasu!") and answer "Osu, Arigatou Gozaimashita!" when an exercise is over (your instructor has just said, "_____keiko o owarimashita.") In English: "We begin _____training!" "Osu! Please extend this favor to me!" and "We now complete _____training!" "Osu! Thank you for the guidance you've given me!"

7. Relentlessly fight to improve your attitude as described by this book. One who is not trying to do so will be easy to spot, and your teacher will consider it rude. Developing this attitude is more important to your teacher than your kicks and your punches. Make your attitude one of "staying on your toes." See section #4, *On Your Toes, Please, Not Your Heels!* Make your dojo the *Toes-Not-Heels Dojo* (see section #5). At all costs, *Don't Let Yourself Be the One Who* . . . (stands out for being less determined, less correct, less spirited, etc.). See section #48.

8. Take responsibility for learning even complex series of motions in just one class, even when shown just once. See section #6. Fight to *own* the complex series of motions you've been shown. See section #7.

9. Always complete tasks that you've been assigned promptly and powerfully. See section #10. Respond to ALL (even subtle) challenges your teacher/sempai issues as if they were commands. See section #25.

10. SHOW that you heard and complied with all instructions both by answering with "Osu!" AND by promptly and powerfully fulfilling the challenge in a way that SHOWS your teacher or sempai your desire to improve, and shows your koohai your humility and willingness to make the correction. Make sure the correction is a powerful one that both your teacher (making the correction) and

your koohais (looking to you as a role model) can see. See section #60.

11. If you hear a correction twice, it's life and death that you make the correction immediately because you clearly failed to make a sufficient correction the first time. I.e. in this case, *overcorrect* to make sure you're never told a third time. See section #12.

12. If your teacher or sempai is angry or frustrated, it becomes life and death for EVERYONE, especially YOU, even if you feel like you're not the one who caused the frustration, and YOU, as well, have to SHOW that you are determined to fix whatever the problem is. After all, it's your job to influence your classmates, either by example or by command. If your teacher is frustrated with another student and you remain indifferent, you are part of the problem. See section #13.

13. Always answer your teacher or sempai, always answer promptly. Was it an e-mail or a telephone message? Same thing, you have to answer powerfully, and promptly. See section #27.

14. Do not disappoint or inconvenience your teacher or sempai. Look for ways to make your teacher or sempai's task easier. See section #28.

15. Encourage your koohais, but don't be the koohai that needs encouraging. See section #29.

16. Properly maintain the condition of your uniform. Take responsibility for maintaining the condition of the uniforms of all your classmates. (This means make sure they *wear* their uniforms correctly, and make sure you convince them to take better care of them if they're not.) See section #101.

17. When addressing your sempais, or mentioning your sempais in third person, ALWAYS use their title, and always use their title properly. See section #105.

18. Do not touch your sempai or teacher unless invited to do so. One's teacher, for example, might slap a student on the back to congratulate or encourage, but the koohai should never do so to the sempai. Even when shaking hands, we use a two-handed handshake after a tournament fight, but the second hand should only touch the back of your opponent's hand, never his/her arm or shoulder. A koohai

in the dojo should never tap a sempai on the shoulder to get his/her attention. Yet the sempai might do so to get the koohai's attention (if necessary).

19. When handing something to, or receiving something from, a sempai, always bow and use two hands. The sempai may use one, but the koohai must always use two.

You'll note that my purpose here has not been to describe all the proper routines of the training itself. The Japanese training is definitely made up of traditional sequences, e.g. how to "bow in" at the beginning of a training as a class, a sequence of the motions of kihon, etc. but I have not given you those here, and traditions will differ from dojo to dojo. Those of you who have read traditional lists of rules of Kyokushin etiquette might have been surprised by some I listed here as *rules*. Understand that it is my purpose to create the proper attitude in the *Western* dojo, and since some of these attitude elements are not intuitive for the Western student, you would do well to institute those that I've listed here as rules. I.e. these points of behavior that indicate and propagate internal attitudes should not be considered OPTIONAL, and students who do not follow them ought to be corrected on the spot.

4. On Your Toes, Please, Not Your Heels!

We know from fighting that the competitor who's rocked back on his heels is generally getting beaten, while in most cases the winner has kept his weight rocked forward towards the front of his feet. If you don't believe it, stand normally and then rock your weight back onto your heels (you can pick up the fronts of your feet if you want to; 100% of your body weight will rock back onto your heels). Now try to jump. You will find it quite difficult. Now stand normally and rock your weight forward onto the fronts of your feet, even lifting your heels slightly if you choose. Try to jump now. It's much easier, right? To win a fight, control of one's balance is the most important thing, but one also has to be able to spring to a new location in an instant. Therefore, the fighter that *stays on his/her toes* is the one who wins.

The important point here, however, is to apply this concept to one's ATTITUDE towards training in the dojo. The student that is, figuratively, *on his/her toes* is crisp, powerful, and alert. That student is fighting to be first, loudest, strongest, and most correct (see #1, *Fight to Be First*). He/she is fighting to be the one that best follows instructions. He/she is fighting to concentrate on the *how*, not the *what* (see #2, *It's the* How, *Silly, Not the* What). He/she never misses the rules of etiquette.

On the other hand, the student that's *on his/her heels* in class, i.e. in terms of attitude, is slow, and slow to react; has heavy eyelids, is missing instructions and not following the rules of etiquette, and is failing to demonstrate a priority of concentrating on the *how*, rather than the *what*. This student's technique is weak and off balance. This student is the one who has to be told the same things night after night, probably because he/she hasn't adapted his/her priorities to be in line with his/her teacher's.

The *stay on your toes* attitude is not something you learn in the dojo. It's a requirement for beginning your training; it's a decision that you make. It's a white belt requirement for simply walking in the door. Without it, you are not practicing Budo karate, you are fooling yourself and practicing fantasy karate, and if you like that way better, perhaps you should consider another dojo.

I realize that that's fairly blunt, but I'm trying to emphasize a critical point. It's not your dojo's job to teach you attitude. Attitude is what you bring with you when you enter the dojo. Sure, a *disadvantaged* student might have to learn attitude, but are YOU the disadvantaged student?

Imagine you're a public school student and in math class. Some students are alert and eager and fighting to have the highest grade in the class. Others, though, aren't even trying. They have their heads down on their desks and they are rude to their teacher when confronted. Please understand that this is not your math class. This is karate. To even come to karate, you are required to have a positive, fighting attitude.

Remember #1, *Fight to Be First*?

Ask yourself: How do I make sure I'm not the one on my heels? Answer: Fight to be the one who's the most alert, the most crisp, the loudest, the most powerful, the best at hearing instructions and acting on them, the best at concentrating on the *how*, the best at following the rules of etiquette.

I was always amazed at the students in Japan who would try so hard to kick so high that they'd flip over and fall on their heads. The Western student tends to think that that's a failure. He/she falls down for trying too hard and is ashamed. The Japanese student, on the other hand, is ashamed for NOT trying hard enough, even at one's personal risk.

This is the proper Budo karate attitude. Be willing to stand out for doing too much. Be willing to go over the top.

Do, and you won't be sorry. You will get so strong!

5. The Toes-Not-Heels Dojo

Consider the aerial views of these two dojos, where the H's represent students who are on their heels (in terms of attitude), and the T's are students who are on their toes. Each dojo has 18 students:

```
Case A:     T T T T T T        Case B:    T H T H T T
            T H T T T T                   H T H H T T
            T T T T T T                   T T H T H T
```

Notice that in Case A, all the students are on their toes, except one. This student is probably the newest student, or the youngest one, or the one who has a learning disadvantage, or the one who's got a bad attitude, or the one whose parents made him/her come when he/she wanted to stay home playing video games. In Case B, notice that half of the students in the room either have some kind of bad attitude, or are just not fully engaged, which IS a bad attitude, since *not being engaged* is not allowed in the Budo karate dojo.

Case A is the Budo karate dojo, Case B is the Americanized fantasy karate dojo. Since it is a requirement for white belts, even from their first day, to fight for an *on their toes* attitude, Case A is what everyone, collectively, must fight to achieve. If your class feels like Case B, it's appropriate to disapprove of, or even be angry at, those classmates who are not fighting to fit in to the proper model. It's important for everyone to understand, in such a situation, that the fastest way to fix the problem is to take responsibility for one's self first. Fight to be even stronger, even crisper, even louder when answering with "Osu!" If you already are being strong and crisp, and yet some of your classmates are still failing to be so, you must feel inclined to make your own techniques even stronger and crisper, even if into realms that you haven't pushed yourself into before. If that still fails to have an effect, you should feel inclined to use your words (as sempai), or other means, to *push* your classmates into getting with the program. Those that deliberately resist should make YOU angry. If your teacher is, so should you be at any student that's being thus resistant.

This is the Budo karate spirit. It is YOUR dojo, after all, and the progress that you will make depends on your dojo average.

In Case B, consider that it's the failing student who decides to make his/her own attitude match the *average* attitude of the class, or, worse, the attitude of the H's. Instead, the winning student identifies the best of the T's in the room, and then fights to be even stronger.

Take a moment, finally, and consider the H in Case A. Imagine for a moment that this is the child with a severe learning disability. How great an advantage this dojo has given that student, because the students to his/her right, left, front and back are all setting strong examples! Now, imagine that this disadvantaged student is one of the H's in Case B. Where is he/she to look for the example to follow? Of course that student *should* look to the T's, but if he/she is a disadvantaged student already, the odds are he/she will be looking to the H's.

Case A, Budo. Case B, fantasy.

Understand that it's YOUR responsibility, even if you're a beginner, to make your dojo resemble Case A.

Start with yourself.

Despise the attitude that allows the H-type student to behave in a way that so lowers the standard of *your* dojo.

Make yourself the T.

Insist on it.

See #33, *When Will THAT Dojo Get Stronger?*

6. Take Responsibility for Learning Even Complex Series of Motions in Just One Class, Even When Shown Just Once

The proper attitude for learning karate is to fight not to make your teacher repeat him/herself (see #12, *Hear It Twice? It's Life and Death*). This includes simple (but not unimportant) things like *how* you're supposed to perform a single motion better, but it also includes entire, complex *series* of motions you've been shown even once (such as new kata).

Of course when you learn your first kata as a white belt, it takes being shown several times, because the white belt has to learn *how to learn* the kata, and even what a kata is, for that matter, as well as the motions of the kata itself. However, once you've learned the sequence and motions of a few kata (by the time you're testing for your first colored belt), and if you open your mind to the learning process, complex series of motions become easier and easier to learn. Most basic kata, after all, are just new patterns of motions that the student generally already knows, or, at the very least, has become familiar with in another context. Therefore, the karate student beyond white belt must take responsibility for learning the kata after being shown it only once, in just one class.

This is achieved by taking responsibility for the kata, immediately upon seeing it for the first time, and by deciding, right then and there, that "I will not embarrass myself by coming into my next class still not knowing what I've been shown in this one." If you are confused by a kata today, you have until your next class to become not confused. The student who places the burden of making him/her not confused on the shoulders of the teacher is the H-type student, the student on his/her heels.

But don't fret! Of course complex series of motions are sometimes confusing, especially for beginners! The point is, though, that the T-type student, the student on his/her toes, will take responsibility for sorting it out before the next class. Here's how:

> *Responsibility is achieved through individual review after class, at home, or before the next class to evaluate how much of that kata one knows or doesn't know, and then by being sure to ask one's sempai (not sensei!) to show him/her those parts of the kata that weren't learned the first time, before class, so as not to force the teacher to teach, again, how to do the same thing one was already taught.*

Students who assume such responsibility immediately even improve the quality of the learning experience when seeing a kata for the very first time. The H-type student who takes for granted that he/she will be shown the kata again (and again) if he/she doesn't get it the first time can stay rocked back on his/her heels for class after class and not learn the kata. The T-type student, however, who holds him/herself to task, and knows that he/she has to have it all sorted out by the next class, pays better attention the first time through, picks up more early on, and learns even *how to learn* a complex series of motions in one single exposure.

If a student has a colored belt, and fails to learn a complex series of motions that he/she has been shown, it is appropriate for that student's classmates to let him/her know that his/her performance is substandard, and that he/she needs to *buckle down* and *get with the program*. To not take such responsibility is to lower the standard of the dojo below that of the Budo karate dojo, and one's classmates should be not remain complacent.

7. OWN the Complex Series of Motions You've Been Shown

This section address the intensity and confidence with which students who have *learned* an exercise must *perform the first couple moves of that exercise* from that point forward.

One common early hurdle that must be crossed in every beginner's karate learning experience is figuring out that *how one learns* changes as one progresses. For example, a first-day student can virtually only imitate and try to copy what the other students are doing. Taking that first leap to where he/she can perform a complex series of motions by looking inward to what he/she *knows*, instead of looking outward and copying *what someone else knows*, is a necessary step that some students have a surprising amount of trouble with. I have seen beginners, particularly kids, who develop their ability to copy over their first weeks and even months of training to such an extent that it's difficult even to tell that that student doesn't know the exercise for him/herself until that day when you ask that student to do it on his/her own.

Lo and behold, with no one to copy, he/she's completely lost!

Remember that training is NOT memorizing. It's not struggling day after day to learn the *what*. Learning the *what*, rather, is what you have to do in one class or two, before your training in that exercise actually begins. Training means performing the exercise over and over again to master it. But your practice doesn't even begin until you can at least do it once without interrupting the flow of the class to sort out how you're supposed to do it.

It's therefore very important that the colored belt student *owns* what he/she's learned, and even when shown only once (see #6, *Take Responsibility for Learning Even Complex Series of Motions in Just One Class, Even When Shown Just Once*). This means, in the case of a complex series of motions, *performing it powerfully the first time in any class when called upon to do so*, rather than performing it, as may be the habit formed when you first learned it, in slow motion a couple times, tentatively, as if to recall what comes next. Once you know an exercise, there's no such thing in the Budo karate dojo as *trying to remember* it the next time you do it, even if weeks later.

OWN the techniques you've learned, and SHOW that you own them each and every FIRST time you're called upon to show them. After all, if you know the exercise, but show doubt the first time through, you are, in effect, teaching your koohais that they are always going to be allowed a warm-up round. Do you get a warm-up round in a self-defense situation?

"Hang on! Let me practice first!" you say to your attacker?

Of course not! In the dojo, you have to do the exercises that you know expertly the first time. Doing so IS training for self-defense, where you have no choice.

Imagine two cases, and you'll see what I mean by *own*:

In Case A, the student exudes confidence that he/she knows the moves of the exercise. That student might not be good at them, but at least he/she can follow along confidently without interrupting everyone else with his/her confusion. So can the majority of the students in the group. Therefore this class's training (i.e. as opposed to memorizing) begins from the very first execution of the exercise.

In Case B, on the other hand, the student comes in to class each day to perform the same exercise and displays doubt or lack of confidence that he/she knows the sequence of motions. This is an H-type student: he/she is on his/her heels, taking a passive approach to learning. Day after day before the training even begins, the teacher must reteach the exercise to bring the group to a level at which it's no longer an exercise in memorization and it becomes, instead, training.

What's more important, the *how* or the *what*? (See #2.)

The student who doesn't *own* the exercise, the one who unknowingly forms a habit in which his/her first day's doubt is at the core of his/her training attitude, rather than confidence, insists on being retaught the same exercise day after day. That student in fact forces the class to focus on the inferior *what*, and is denying everyone else the chance to focus on the far more important *how*.

I've seen it happen before that enough of the students in the room unknowingly resist *changing gears* to where it's no longer a exercise in memorization, and, since that group has enough of a majority, it can go on like that for days, much to the frustration of the minority T-type students who were long ago ready to move on.

See #6, above, and take responsibility for the complex series of motions you've been shown. It takes just a little bit more work when you first see something new. But then, all of a sudden, you'll find your training ten times more enjoyable.

The first moves of all the kata that you know?

Do them powerfully, knowingly.

Perhaps you could practice just doing your katas' first moves to make sure you never blow it at the start. Have someone call out the names in random order. You do the first two or three movements of each kata, powerfully, to prove to yourself that you own them and will never miss the beginning of any kata you know.

8. Drink Some, Spit Some? You'll Fail

The proper attitude for learning in the Budo karate dojo is to DEVOUR what you're being taught like you're ravenous. Drink it down like you're dying of thirst! The student who does so is the student on his/her toes, he/she is the student who is fighting to be first to ensure that he/she is never last.

Imagine the teacher handing the students a full glass of water, and the water is what's being taught. The student who gulps it down and says "Osu! Sensei, may I have another glass?" is the strongest student.

Now consider the student who cautiously sips, tastes each sip, and then decides whether or not to swallow depending on whether he/she likes the taste or not. Consider the student who spits out some of what the teacher is teaching. This is the student who is on his/her heels, the student who is not fighting to be first, the student who is failing, the student who would prefer the fantasy karate dojo to the Budo karate dojo.

Now, consider the following critical point.

Imagine the bad teacher who's teaching bad karate, bad attitude, or, worse, unethical behavior. In this case, what's the student's responsibility?

Easy! Find another teacher!

However, now consider the more likely situation.

This author HOPES that 98% of what I teach is positive. However, I'm also human, humans are not perfect, and sometime during many hours of time spent with my longest-term students, I will likely demonstrate some poor choice or another, thus setting a poor example. Now here's the part that is difficult for the Western student of Budo karate to grasp. If you have a well-intentioned teacher, it is your job as student to gulp down the teacher's EVERYTHING and say "Osu! Sensei, may I have another glass?" even if you question, privately, what's being offered. Just as it's absolutely critical that the student quit learning from a teacher that that student has determined is *not* well-intentioned, or *not* ethical, it is also absolutely critical that the student gulp down everything the well-intentioned teacher offers, BECAUSE . . . and this is important enough to give it its own paragraph:

Some of the lessons of Budo karate are esoteric. (See #44, *Parallel Lessons: The Surface and the Esoteric, Identify the Task at Hand, Fulfill It, Support Its Delivery in the Eyes of Your Koohais*.) We, as students, don't always grasp immediately why we are being told something that our Budo karate teacher tells us, because there are often lessons behind the lessons, and when our teacher has been at something for 30 years longer than we have, probably he/she knows a thing or two that's hard even for us to conceptualize. Remember that the Western way of learning is often quite different from the Eastern way. Sometimes, the proper response is to just say "Osu!" and take the lesson that we didn't understand home with us, file it away, and consider it from time to time, until one day, BOOM, the student says, "Eureka! Now I understand why that was so important! Now I understand why my teacher was telling me something that seemed bizarre to me at the time!"

How can the student who spits out the parts of the lesson he/she didn't like ever benefit from these oh-so-critical eureka moments?

The choice in Budo karate regarding a teacher is to follow or not to follow. Following partially is failing Budo karate at the very core. Take a leap of faith! Let yourself go. Follow the teacher like his/her word is the end-all. Your teacher is advising you on karate, after all — that, and on any life advice that might be called for by what happens in class in the dojo. (Don't worry, your teacher is not your marriage counselor, and he/she is crossing a line if he/she tries to be!) One day, once you achieve a certain level, or a certain degree of separation (once you've moved away to another city and started your own dojo, for example), it will occur to you that, "Hmmm, I liked 98% of what Sensei taught me, but he is human, and after all these years, after all these classes, I realize that I still don't get (or like) that other 2%. I don't think I'll live that way myself, I don't think I'll teach my own students that way."

This would be the correct type of learning experience you might have in the Budo karate system.

On the other hand, one day you might decide, "I can't follow this teacher because he/she's asking the unethical." In that case, you have only one choice: Find a new teacher. This would, likewise, be the correct choice in that circumstance.

Following partially, though, knowing that you're following partially, and lingering on, and trying to take from your teacher only those parts that you want to take?

That, on the other hand, is a poor choice.

In this case, you are stealing, and now YOU are the one who's being unethical.

Be careful, though! Your teacher's got lessons behind lessons behind lessons to teach. Of course he/she's got to consider the good of the dojo over you as an individual. But don't be afraid to ask if you feel like you're still not getting it. *Channel* your teacher's lessons (see #72), and the odds are you'll be able to figure out that it's YOU that didn't grasp something, rather than that it was your teacher that was asking the unreasonable.

9. BE the Ocean!

Consider the drawing (facing page) in which the squiggly line is the surface of the ocean, and the star represents a location at the ocean's depths.

My Taikyokuken (Tai Chi) teacher (a Zen and Tai Chi master in Japan named Sensei Yamaguchi Hakuei) recently explained to me that if we take this diagram to represent life, most people live their lives on the surface. They have good days and bad days, healthy days and sick days, strong days and weak days. On the diagram, the good days are the crests of the waves, the bad days are the troughs. However, he said, "Those of us who are training have a chance during our training to experience the depths of the ocean."

Whether it be through Zen meditation, or Tai Chi, or through Budo karate, when training *flows* like it's supposed to, when the group is a group of mostly T's (see #5), when the majority have the proper spirited attitude, when everyone is following the rules of etiquette and focusing on the *how* rather than the *what*, when everyone is *channeling* their teacher's teaching, we all get a chance to experience a temporary release from the concerns of life. On the diagram this is represented by the star in the depths of the ocean. Here we get to visit when training runs the way it's supposed to.

*

In theory, the student who regularly visits this release from life's concerns also learns how better to handle the hardships of life. At the surface, the waves become calmer. That person, therefore, becomes stronger in life, as well as in training.

It's very important, in the dojo, to understand what you're missing if you're training with an incorrect attitude and thus denying yourself — and even your classmates! — the chance to experience the ocean. If you're resisting what's being asked of you (see #82, *Leaps of Faith, Pride Resistance vs. Shame Resistance, and the Full-Contact Fight*), if you're the H-type student, if you're weak on the rules of etiquette so your teacher always seems like he/she is disapproving rather than approving (see #11, The *Sempai/Koohai System Brings You Closer to Your Teacher*), you are denying yourself one of the key experiences through which Budo karate students become stronger in life, not just stronger in the fight. You are, in fact, denying yourself the ocean.

Remember this diagram from the introduction?

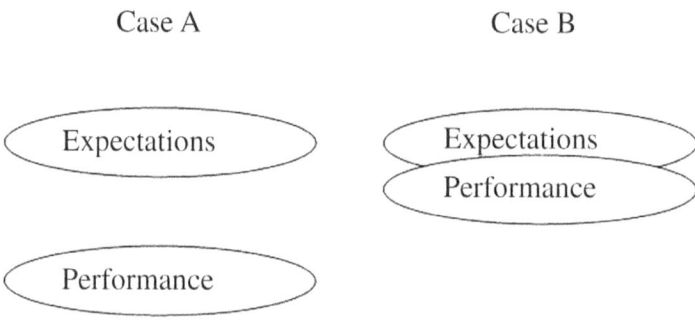

The Case A situation is one in which the student is denying him/herself the ocean, and the teacher is always battling to help the student *see the light*. In Case B, the student realizes that the teacher is not asking for rocket science, and that "Oh! It's in MY power to exist harmoniously in my own dojo! I just have to prioritize what my teacher is asking me to prioritize!"

10. Complete Tasks That You've Been Assigned Promptly and Powerfully

It is a central part of the Budo karate system that the koohai fights to complete any task that the sempai challenges the koohai to perform, and to do it promptly and powerfully. The rule can be summarized this way:

> *If your teacher asks you to do something, do it. If your teacher asks you to do something and it's hard to do, fight harder and get it done. If your teacher asks you to do something, but, try as you might, you can't do it, make sure you communicate that fact to your teacher before your teacher finds the task undone, or sees you not doing it. If you teacher asks you to do anything unethical, leave that teacher.*

In this sense, the worst response is to not only not do what you've been asked to do, but also not to say anything about it. It looks to the teacher as if you ignored the challenge completely. Then you've shown a lack of desire, and, therefore, a lack of respect. The Japanese student would say that "you have weak spirit."

This concept both falls into the realm of a rule of etiquette, and is an important ingredient in the recipe for becoming strong. It's rude, of course, to ignore your teacher's request, but it also makes you stronger to undertake the challenges and assignments your teacher gives you, and it makes you stronger to fulfill them. It's part of the learning process. It's part of the strengthening process. Your teacher will find challenges for you that will make you stronger, and will do his/her best to avoid asking of you what is impossible so that you don't spend too much time disappointed.

If, on the other hand, you allow yourself to not fulfill the tasks or challenges you've been assigned that are ones you actually could have done, it is you who condemn YOURSELF to dwell in a realm of disappointment. That alone will make you weaker, and it will be of your own doing! It's remarkable that, in the West, we encounter students who seem to like to reside in defeat, when victory is so near!

Let's consider an example or two.

Your teacher announces in class that all students should participate at least two times per week (two classes). Most students do. For several of the students, however, it's hard to make it in that particular week twice due to work or family concerns. The Budo karate spirit is that that student fights to find a way to make it in. However, if it does turn out to be impossible, he/she should communicate the fact to the teacher, for example by phone or text message, "Osu! Sensei, I did really try to find a way to make it in a second time this week, but it looks like I won't be able to. I will endeavor to make it up next week, and come in 3 times!"

The timing of such a message, of course, is critical. It has to come BEFORE the end of the week. If it's not delivered until the following Monday, the teacher spends the weekend believing the student ignored the challenge.

Another example.

The teacher challenges an adult student to straighten up the locker room, and then leaves for the night. The student will clean the locker room promptly and powerfully, i.e. before going home, and he/she will do it perfectly. Sometimes the task might be very hard, because that student also has a prior social arrangement after class to meet someone. If the student truly can't buckle down and get it done and be a little late, he might show strong spirit by coming in early the next morning before work to get it done. The situation turns bad, however, if the teacher comes in the next day and finds the task undone, and the student has failed to communicate anything to the teacher. In this case it looks like the student ignored the teacher's challenge.

Your teacher might say, make sure you learn this kata by your next class. Your teacher might say to the class, "Be sure you get your dues in on time." He/she might say, "Make sure you keep your guard up while sparring." All of these are tasks, big and small, that your teacher has asked of you. In the Budo karate system, all must be taken very seriously. The student who thinks, "These are things I'm supposed to get over a period of time," is following the Americanized model, and failing in the Budo karate sense. All challenges, all assignments, must be taken to heart and the koohai must SHOW that he/she took them to heart.

In another section (see #20, *The Deepening of Human Relationships*), you will read that the sempai/koohai relationship is intended to be a very close, very serious one (i.e. it must be taken very seriously). You must therefore take the things your sempai asks of you very seriously, or you are denying yourself one of the core exercises of Budo karate training. One of the ways through which you become strong through karate training is by perfecting your relationship between sempai and koohai. If you like the kicks and punches, but *spit out* that part of the training, you're either in the wrong dojo, or your dojo is not a Budo karate one.

One final note:

Between sempai and koohai, regarding *tasks* like "clean the dojo" or "teach tonight's class": Yes, the koohai always has to do it, but the sempai must show, first and foremost, strength of character and willingness to do these tasks as well. That is, the sempai must show a sense of internal resistance towards asking the koohai to do something when it's not necessary. Is the sempai asking so that the sempai can take care of something that's more important for the dojo? Is it because the sempai wants to teach the koohai? Or, on the other hand, is it so the sempai can be lazy and make it to the ballgame? (Of course, it's different if the sempai has worked so hard for so long for the dojo that he/she rarely gets the chances to relax that the koohai gets regularly.)

Tasks that you've been assigned, you should fulfill alone and with determination. If your sempai asks you to do something, it's weak spirit to turn around and ask *your* koohai to do it for you, unless that was your sempai's intent. Take note! Was the assignment one of delegation, or was it a task that YOU were meant to do individually?

Students who cannot fulfill a task, on the other hand, should indeed ask for help—it is in fact their duty to ask for help—from their koohais, or advice from their sempais, before simply leaving the task undone.

11. The Sempai/Koohai System Brings You CLOSER to Your Teacher

Students who are struggling with the rules of etiquette, or students who are having trouble following instructions, or relaxing enough to concentrate on the *how*, or who are resisting the flow and staying on their heels in class, can easily become confused and think that the sempai/koohai system is designed to create distance between them and their sempais, or between them and their teacher. This student who is mistakenly insisting on the wrong track can easily come to believe that his/her sempais—or even his/her teacher!—is haughty and unfriendly. That student might come to believe that the rules of etiquette are there so that the sempai or teacher can feel superior.

But this student should look again.

Imagine the case where the teacher is welcoming students outside the dojo before class. One student, the T-type student (see #4, *On Your Toes, Please, Not Your Heels!*), gets out of his/her car, jogs energetically towards the dojo (being sure to look both ways before crossing the street), and, when he/she gets to a reasonable distance from his/her teacher, stops in his/her tracks with both feet parallel and facing his/her teacher, bows powerfully, and announces "Osu!"

In this case, the teacher's response is probably, "Osu! Hi, _____! What's up? It's good to see you!"—that is, a very friendly response from the teacher. The teacher is, after all, grateful that the student has such spirit to take the leap of faith and follow the instructions that have been given regarding the rules of etiquette.

Now imagine another case in which the colored belt student (i.e. one who should know better) climbs out of the car, walks across the parking lot and when he/she sees his teacher, waves like one would to one's friend on the playground, and says, "Hi, Sensei!" In this case, the teacher as likely as not frowns at the student, or scolds him/her for not bowing properly, or for not bowing at all, and for not saying, "Osu!" If this is that student's experience day after day, of course that student is going to be at risk of thinking his/her teacher unfriendly and haughty. "Oh, so the sempai/koohai system is there so that the teacher can condescend and make me feel small," that student might think.

Oh, but this student is so much off on the wrong foot!

Your teacher will always be strict with you, but your teacher always, first and foremost, wants to be friendly with you, too! But, as in the second case above, where it's the student's incorrect attitude that prevents the teacher from being friendly, you would be wise to consider whether your teacher seems friendly towards you, or not. If not, look hard at how YOU are falling short in something your teacher has asked you to do. If you figure it out, you'll be in for a great surprise! All of a sudden, your teacher will start smiling at you when he/she sees you!

If you can't figure it out, ASK!

See #20, *The Deepening of Human Relationships*, because this gets even better!

12. Hear it Twice? It's Life and Death

One very common mistake made by beginners is to make too small a correction, when asked, so that the teacher has to repeat him/herself. This is particularly true of the H-type student (see #4, *On Your Toes, Please, Not Your Heels!*). However, the Budo karate spirit is to never make your teacher or sempai repeat him/herself because of your weak response. One easy example is the zenkutsu-dachi ("long stance," we tend to call it in English):

It's called a "long stance" for a reason: It's supposed to be long, and deep. But sometimes the beginning student's stance isn't long enough, so the teacher reminds the student, "Long stance, please!" The student answers, "Osu!" and makes his/her stance longer by an inch, but it wasn't a big enough correction, since the stance was more like eight inches too short. So the teacher says, "No, *long* stance!" and the student responds, "Osu!" and makes his/her stance another inch longer. How many times in this situation does the teacher have to tell the student to make a long stance? Eight!!! How rude! How weak! Of course, this is not the Budo karate attitude. It's the Americanized version in which the standard is far too often the student's looking to the teacher to *make* him/her strong.

So, here's the rule:

If you hear it twice, you should already be embarrassed (the Japanese would say "ashamed," although *ashamed* in Japan is how one feels, not how someone tells one one should feel), and you have to make a giant correction the second time to make 100% sure you've shown your teacher your strong desire to make whatever correction is necessary. You have to make *hearing it twice* like a cowbell ringing in your head. Make *hearing it twice* like an alarm. When that alarm bell starts screaming, make a MAJOR correction, make an *overcorrection*. The one you just made was ALREADY too little, and too late.

Remember, to the teacher, your one-inch correction looked weak-spirited. Then if you demand your teacher's attention while he/she begs you seven more times for the proper correction, your teacher thinks it especially rude, because you are preventing him/her from focusing on the rest of the class.

At that point, it's selfish as well.

Best policy is to fight to be first in all things that you do in the dojo. When you're asked for something, some correction or assignment, make sure it gets done powerfully and promptly. If you misjudge, however (and all beginners will until they learn their teacher's expectations), and make a correction that's too small, and if your teacher then repeats him/herself, make 100% sure that your SECOND correction is a huge one.

See #13 immediately below, as this discussion continues.

13. Your Teacher Is Angry? It's Life and Death for Everyone, Especially YOU If You Feel Like Someone *Else* Was Responsible

Please be sure to read #12, *Hear it Twice? It's Life and Death*, before reading this section.

Please understand that it is your teacher's job to maintain a certain standard of training.

In my case, since I trained under Mas Oyama for two years in Japan, I tend to compare classes that I teach to that very high standard. Western students are often confused by the cultural divide into thinking that "we can't possibly match the Japanese standard." On the contrary, however, if you were to understand and embody the principles set out in this book, you would most certainly match it. See #83, *Concepts Not Rules: Use Your Heart, Not Your Head* in which I make the point that it shouldn't be about a long list of rules; all of what's presented in this book is really a detailed presentation of one single concept. Embrace that concept and matching trainings at Mas Oyama's world headquarters will be easy.

However, if you want to understand your teacher, it is important to understand that keeping classes to a certain minimum standard of training is a matter of principle for your teacher. It is a matter of conscience. When Western students resist that standard and—unknowingly, of course!—try in numbers to do something less, the teacher's job is to do whatever's necessary to keep the standard up. I myself do not, but my first teacher, Mas Oyama's nephew, used to beat us with a shinai (split bamboo sword), both to toughen us, and, sometimes, to drive home certain understandings that we were slow to acquire.

And *we loved him for it* because we were able to figure out the lessons that he was putting himself at risk to teach us!

Imagine your class today has become a H-type class (see #5, *The Toes-Not-Heels Dojo*), and your teacher is visibly frustrated.

First, please understand that if your karate teacher is any good, he/she will even blow his/her top, if he/she has to, to get through to students who are unknowingly resisting progress, and therefore unknowingly asking their teacher to lower the dojo's standard. How frustrating it is when the teacher blows his/her top as a last resort to try to get through to a thick-headed student, who—still!—instead of figuring out that the teacher is frustrated because of something that student is doing, acts like there's something wrong with the teacher for blowing his/her lid!

I've been there, believe me, and it's not a fun place to be! So, help your teacher out:

Understand not only that if your teacher has gotten angry, it's in the service of the effort to maintain a standard that you or some other student in the room is resisting, but also that he/she has done so at some personal risk. That is, by keeping after that thick-headed, still-resisting student, the teacher has put even his/her own dignity at risk to follow his/her conscience and uphold the standard of training demanded by his/her sense of duty. There is no loss of dignity, of course, in the eyes of the students who get it and sacrifice to support their teacher; there is only a loss of dignity in the eyes of the student who *doesn't get it* and tries to turn his/her shortcomings back on his/her teacher.

And that is exactly the key point to consider.

Your teacher has willfully put him/herself in jeopardy in order to defend the team standard, and that's YOUR standard. This means that your teacher has put him/herself at risk FOR YOU and for the sake of YOUR training, because you've come to the dojo to learn Budo karate, not the dumbed-down Americanized version.

As a student in a Budo karate dojo it is your job, therefore, to *get your teacher's back*. Of course, like soldiers on a battlefield (the origin of Budo is *Bushido*, the warrior's code), you should get all of your dojo-mates' backs, starting with your teacher (the would-be commander on the battlefield), and then his/her lieutenants, and then everyone else (see #24, *Train Yourself to See the WHOLE Dojo, Understand Dojo Priorities*). But if your teacher is angry or frustrated, it becomes EVERY student's job to rise up and fix whatever it is that has occurred. Develop a sense that YOU should have fixed it long before it forced your teacher to get riled up.

Is it a dojo-wide failure?

Then everyone has to buckle down, or get revved up, or whatever it takes to get with the program. Start training harder, sweating more, shouting louder, listening better, concentrating on the *how* better, fighting harder to be first, etc. If the teacher is frustrated, it's likely that the class is dropping the ball in terms of one of the key concepts presented in this book. Figure out what it is, and turn up the heat!

Is it, on the other hand, one individual's failure?

Is it one or two thickheads in the room? In that case, turn up the pressure on those individuals. Train harder beside them to make them stand out as being a step behind, encourage (or scold) them verbally, get your teacher's back by making it 100% clear that in spite of the teacher's having gotten angry, you understand that it was the thick-headed student who's responsible. (See #41, *Get Your Sempai's Back, Get Your Teacher's!*)

You are not out of place, in the Budo karate dojo, to raise your own voice to scold one of your koohais who is showing bad attitude, even in the middle of your teacher's lesson. All the better! If you raise your voice to scold the student with weak attitude, you've gotten to it *before* your teacher had to, and good for you! Your teacher will be grateful!

On the contrary, you ARE out of place to remain indifferent if your classmate is struggling to learn the way. Step up to the plate! Fix it, even if it's not you!

See #84, *Hold the Lines, and Hold the Lines!—The Sympathy Failure Conundrum*, regarding sympathy failures.

See #s 14, 15, and 16 regarding having inverse reactions to challenging situations.

14. React Inversely to Hardship 1

In my own corner of the Western world, this concept has historically been one of the hardest to punch through. Yet it is a critical aspect of Mas Oyama's Budo karate.

It's very easily stated, but, apparently for some, much harder to implement. Jocks on football teams do it all the time. It's a very common phenomenon for sportsmen, even in American culture. And yet it seems to be hard to come by in the dojo, for some reason. Simply stated, it's "When the going gets harder, or when the environment becomes a challenging one, you have to start fighting harder to overcome," and in the karate sense, since it's all ultimately about life and death, that inverse reaction has to be to the umpteenth degree.

Back to the football team:

It's halftime and you're down by two touchdowns. Why does the coach either give inspirational speeches or—in other cases—shout and throw things in the locker room? Exactly to get the team *psyched up*, right? To get them to pull out their best, the most animal of their animal nature perhaps, in order to get them to work together—fight!—and pull out the victory.

Anyone who knows my particular situation knows that the nonprofit that I run works, also, with disadvantaged kids. Perhaps, in my corner of the world, it has to do with a certain class's tendency to be demoralized in the face of hardship rather than buckling down to overcome. I do notice a motivational divide. Some students do naturally buckle down when the going gets rough; others tend to crumble.

Please recall the lesson of #5, *The Toes-Not-Heels Dojo*, and understand, therefore, how important it is that every able student in the class form a habit of fighting like badgers to succeed anytime *the going gets rough*. The best way to help the student who tends to roll over in the face of hardship is to surround that student with fighting spirit, not targeted *against* that student, but parallel to him/her, so that that student learns to *get riled up* by proximity. Of course if there's only one H-type student in the room, the one who's rolling over, it will be very easy to surround that student with energy. But if half of the students are H's? Of course it becomes a bit harder.

This is why it's absolutely critical that every student who understands, and has the ability to get riled up in the face of hardship, does in fact get themselves riled up to the umpteenth degree whenever the going gets rough. Take responsibility for yourself first—make sure your own attitude is where it's supposed to be—and then those around you will be afforded the best possible advantage.

One complicating factor for the Western student, one circumstance where the Western student seems to fail to recognize a situation in which one is supposed to have an inverse powerful response, is not when something is hard and *challenging* (like 100 push-ups), but rather when an environment is *challenged*. If you are a brown belt and most of the other students in the room are brand-new white belts, it is a challenged environment. Therefore it's harder to train hard, right?

Of course it is! It's harder—so you have to turn up the steam and work harder to raise the standard.

I have brown belt students today (ten-year-olds) who find themselves in this situation and, instead of getting riled up, match the confused attitude of the white belt average. In other words, these students—who still have a big lesson to learn before I'll give them black belts!—don't see themselves as any different from the white belts. They don't yet have any concept of what it means to be a leader in a group.

If a task is harder, the Budo karate system is to fight harder and overcome.

If a training environment is challenged, rather than seeming hard and challenging, it might seem dull, or uninteresting—yet it's harder to train properly, right? What if a baby is crying in the lobby? What if the tap dancing class upstairs starts a ruckus? These are distractions, by which the H-type student, particularly, tends to be distracted, and the group average generally takes a major hit. So, then especially, the Budo karate student has to clue in, and realize that it's his/her job to fight harder. Maybe you're fighting to be first, and it's easy to be first because everyone else in the room is weak and confused. If that's the case, you're fighting to be first in comparison with the wrong folks. If the class average is really that bad, fight to be first against the strongest students you know, who aren't even in class that night. Why would you want to make your training match students who are less than you?

See #43, *Imitate Someone Strong, Not the Other Way Around*.

See #15, below, since the discussion continues.

15. React Inversely to Hardship 2: Turn On the Animal!

Consider the beginning student who can comfortably do 30 knuckle pushups in a set.

Consider now two opposite ways that that student might respond psychologically to being asked to do 60. Either the student is dismayed as soon as he/she hears the nature of the challenge, and is so distressed by the assumption of failure that that student doesn't even perform well the 30 he/she can do comfortably, OR, on the other hand, the student gets riled up, growls like an animal, and goes *over the top* blasting out the first 30, and riding the adrenaline well into the next 30, and then improvising and figuring out a way to get the job done even for the last few.

This is a NECESSARY ability to have in the Budo karate dojo.

More than that, it's more attitude than it is ability, i.e. students can DECIDE to behave this way in the face of challenges, and decisions can be made in an instant. It's not something that you have to learn, and it's definitely not something that's going to fall on you from Heaven if you wait long enough.

In the preceding section, I referred to disadvantaged teenagers who may (or may not) have a tendency to buckle in the face of hardship. Now consider the child (or adult) at the other end of the spectrum, the proverbial spoiled rich kid, who's never been asked to do anything for him/herself. The point is that anyone, from any walk of life, might lack the natural tendency to *turn on the animal* and overcome hardship. Yet, in the Budo karate dojo, everyone has to learn it. Everyone has to DECIDE to have it.

I promise you that, if I'm your teacher, I will give you regular opportunities to face your physical, mental and spiritual limitations. Help me out, though, if you please: Those times that I do, recognize the fact that that's where I've taken you intentionally and *turn on the animal!* Help me to establish that response, too, as the norm.

In Mas Oyama's dojo, of course, it was.

In your dojo it can be, too. It just takes YOUR understanding that that's where you're supposed to go.

The challenge at hand is a hard one?

Let that be your signal like a cowbell ringing in your head, and turn on the animal!

16. React Inversely to Hardship 3: A Visibly Angry, Frustrated or Disappointed Teacher or Sempai

This section is really a continuation of #13, *Your Teacher Is Angry? It's Life and Death for Everyone, Especially YOU If You Feel Like Someone Else Was Responsible* peppered by your new understanding of #15, *React Inversely to Hardship 2: Turn on the Animal*, so please make sure you've read both of those sections.

If you have, you'll probably already know what I'm going to say here.

Go back and consider, one more time, the *Sensei has blown his top* scenario. Remember that your teacher has done so to defend YOUR dojo, and YOUR standard of training. Your teacher has done so as a matter of principle, because he/she is bound to do so by conscience. Your teacher has put his/her own dignity at risk FOR YOU.

Now, the question is, how are YOU going to respond to whatever has made your teacher angry, frustrated, or disappointed?

Yep, you got it: *Turn on the animal!*

Like an angry badger, pound whatever it was right into the dojo floor, drive whatever it was right out of the dojo! Start with yourself, and then move on to your classmates, and provide no refuge in YOUR dojo for whatever it was that occurred that's enough below your teacher's standard that he/she had to resort to such measures!

In Japan this was often done with one's fists. In my corner of the world, I cannot encourage that per se. At the very least, though, understand that it's your duty to isolate the H-type student. Accentuate his/her weak behavior by proximity to your strong behavior. Surround him/her with strong spirit to encourage change.

If it's more than just one student, break the trend by focusing first on yourself.

React INVERSELY to hardship.

Take responsibility YOURSELF and fix the problem even if it doesn't seem at first like it's your problem. If it's a problem in YOUR dojo, it actually is your problem, is it not? It's certainly your responsibility.

Your alternative is to leave your teacher alone to handle YOUR dojo's problems all by him/herself.

I can tell you as a teacher who does struggle to maintain a high standard, that the dojo in which the sempais don't understand this aspect of their responsibility can be a very lonely place indeed.

If you see your teacher frustrated with other students, are you going to think, "That has nothing to do with me"?

If you do, you wouldn't fit in Mas Oyama's Budo karate dojo either.

It has EVERYTHING to do with you. If your teacher's having to do all the work to win over hearts and minds, it's *your* heart and mind that are still in the wrong place. You should have positioned yourself to have fixed the problem BEFORE it ever frustrated your teacher in the first place.

17. There's Only One Way to Do . . . Nearly Everything That You Do in the Dojo

Consider the meaning of *improvisation*.

For you kids, it means being creative and doing something the way that works for you. It means doing it your way because that's the way you like to do it. In the case of music, it means playing around with the notes written down and coming up with your own variation.

What are the exercises that we do in the dojo in which you are supposed to improvise? When are you supposed to do it your way?

The answer: Full-contact fighting.

That's it. That's really just about the only time.

Nearly everything else we do in the dojo has a specific, unified way in which it's supposed to be done. Even light kumite, light-heavy kumite, and heavy kumite (See #46, *How Hard do I Hit?*). The only time you really break free in my classes, for example, is when you fight for real.

The way you stand has to match the way everyone else stands, that is, the *textbook* fudo dachi. The way you sit, again, *textbook* and the same as everyone else. The way you punch? The way you kick? The shape of your stance? The length of your stance relative to your height? The tempo of your kata? How you bow?

Everything.

There's only one correct way to do it all, which means that everyone should look nearly the same when they do most of what they do in the dojo.

Now, let's take a step back, because I fear that I may have lost a reader or two.

Consider the H-type class from *The Toes-Not-Heels Dojo* section (see #5). I will reproduce it here, but be sure you've reviewed that section.

```
T H T H T T
H T H H T T
T T H T H T
```

Worse even than this class, in which half the students are on their heels (the H's) and half the students are on their toes (the T's), imagine the class in which everyone is doing a basic motion or holding a basic position (a long stance with a middle punch, for example), and every single student is doing it differently.

Of course, if that's the standard in the class, there's not a student in the room who understands and is confident that there is only ONE correct position for a long stance with a middle punch. If a class that's 50% heel- and 50% toe-type students makes it next to impossible for the H's to figure out where they're supposed to be in terms of attitude — the *how* — how on Earth are students even supposed to figure out that there's a standard for the *what* if *everyone's* doing the position differently?!!

Of course, luckily, my dojo's average, with some sempais in the room, is generally better than that. As a beginner, though, it will help you to progress faster if you understand that nearly everything we do has only one way to do it. Compare yourself to the others in the room who are best at doing whatever it is you're doing. Consider your own technique in the mirror when you have a chance, because the beginner doesn't always know when his/her body is doing something differently than he/she thinks it is. Compare your technique to your teacher's. Make sure you've heard *the how* of the technique (see #2) and that you're fighting to be the best (see #1, *Fight to Be First*) at applying it to your own.

A warning, though!

Remember that there's generally only one correct way to be when you're in some *position* (that is, when you are still, not moving). And, also, there's generally only one correct way to perform any *motion*.

Make sure you apply this concept to both.

You're practicing one-two punches from fighting stance?

There's only one correct fighting stance for this exercise. And when you take that stance, as a beginner, you're not moving. Also, though, there's only one way to perform the motion(s), only one correct path for the motion(s), once you throw the punches.

One step further?

What's your position once any one of your punches is complete and your fist has hit the target (your opponent's sternum, for example)? Yes, you're right: you *do* hold that position (you're stationary, with no movement) for a millisecond before pulling it back again (movement again). Every still interval, no matter how short, in any complex motion has only one correct position; every moving moment that makes up a complex motion also has only one correct path, tempo, and destination.

Fight hard to make what you do MATCH what the best of your sempais is doing. Make sure you're not influenced by those in the class whose motions are awkward and incorrect. Do your best to make your technique match your teacher's.

18. You Need Your Teacher's Watchful Eye to Motivate You?

Everyone should want to impress their teacher.

I'm aware that in American public school, kids can become the target of retribution by other kids if they're perceived as trying too hard to impress their teachers.

But we're not in public school.

Not merely *trying*, but FIGHTING to please your teacher is the Budo karate way. (Of course one has to be humble, but in the dojo, there are no points earned for resisting the teacher, or being disrespectful, like there might be in public school. On the contrary, your progress is based on your ability to understand, and demonstrate that you understand, your teacher's priorities.)

No question, there's a certain rush you get by fighting—and sometimes winning—the battle to impress your teacher. Therefore, sometimes students prefer to attend classes that their teacher is teaching, rather than those taught by their sempais.

So, what about the student who *avoids* classes *not* taught by *Sensei*, the student whose morale and performance are weak in classes in which *Sensei* is not present?

Oh, but how disrespectful this is to the teacher who is not present!

Your dojo needs you MORE when your teacher is not present. Your sense of duty and dignity and support for your dojo should be MORE turned on when your teacher is NOT in class.

The only way the dojo can become strong is if your teacher doesn't have to babysit every single student all the time. If you need your teacher's watchful eye to be strong, where is the strength really coming from? Is it present in you, or is it just something you can show because you get a rush out of showing off?

It is MORE critical to *fight to be first* (see #1) when your teacher is NOT present.

A hint:

At times your teacher will stay away from class because the dojo ALSO needs to develop in this way. That is, the dojo needs to learn strength that's independent of the teacher as well. Be careful, though: In my dojo, whether I'm there or not, I always get a report from the instructor who taught the class. I know who's winning in my absence and who's not. About the proudest I ever am of a student is when I hear that he/she is a strong leader or role model in my absence.

Careful though! Before we turn the page, let's briefly consider the opposite case.

What if *Sensei* is on a tear, trying to win over hearts and minds to the Budo karate way—rather than the Americanized anything-goes way of doing karate—and, as a result, *Sensei's* classes are not really all that fun. Maybe *Sensei* is upset lately, because the attitudes of this recent class of students have fallen below his standard.

I can't know what's in my students' hearts all the time, but I have *sensed* situations in which weak-minded students will actually AVOID my classes, because they prefer to be left alone and just do their workout.

Oh, but how great a miscalculation *this* is!

First of all, if there is an instructor or sempai in my dojo who is making classes fun for that type of student when I'm *not* around, that should-be role model is failing in his/her duty.

Remember that you can only succeed in the Budo karate dojo by channeling your teacher's teaching. There is no karate in your dojo that's independent of your teacher. There's only one way in every dojo, and that's your teacher's way. If the going gets rough, what are you going to do? Hide? Of course not: In the Budo karate system, you have to *turn on the animal*, and work HARDER to succeed in the challenged environment. (See #15, *React Inversely to Hardship 2: Turn on the Animal!*) If your teacher is battling to win over hearts and minds, it's your DUTY to get your teacher's back in that struggle. It's your duty to be there spilling sweat to show your support. (See #41, *Get Your Sempai's Back, Get Your Teacher's!*)

Ducking and hiding to *do it your way* is a purely American phenomenon.

I've had students before who want to have a black belt in karate, and another in tae kwon do, and another in kung fu. That happens in the U.S. environment because it's hard to find good teachers. If this student is in MY dojo, however, he/she is in my dojo to TAKE, not to learn, and I hope this student reads this, figures out the error in his/her ways, and either gets 100% behind the program, or leaves for good, and goes down the street to try to buy a fantasy proficiency in a style that is more easily bought.

19. You Ask Yourself, "Am I Important? Does My Teacher Value Me?"

When we're kids, we are always important to our parents, even if we behave badly. As adults (and as karate students!), however, whether or not we are important to any social unit depends on us. We make ourselves important by how we behave, and by the choices we make. I recall (and lament) one particular student who quit training, finally, because that student didn't feel valued, apparently (by me). What that student failed to see, however, was the extent to which that student was resisting the teaching! As a high-ranking student, he/she had, in fact, virtually negated his/her own value by STILL failing to adopt the attitude presented in this book.

"But I was giving all I could, Sensei!"

My response:

"No, actually you weren't. You were giving only what you wanted to give, and by doing so, you were asking me to lower my standard for everyone in the dojo, because you were an important role model. The fact that you weren't giving the bare minimum of what was expected of you as a leader made you a burden. You negated your own value by being unable to take the required leap of faith. Read this book carefully. Read it with a highlighter and highlight the attitude points in which you find that you were falling short. You'll be surprised, and enlightened. Your highlighter will run dry and, hopefully, you'll pull yourself together, and come back to training, and do it right this time."

Of course I *liked* that student. I wished the best for that student. But whether or not that student was important to my dojo community was in that student's hands, not mine. Loving and caring for the weak is one thing, but coddling the one who CHOOSES not to make strong choices when that choice affects other weaker students? That's another matter. In the Budo karate dojo there is no choice, because everyone, unanimously, has to fight to raise the average of the dojo.

Are you, as an individual, important to your dojo?

In a Japanese sense, from the inside looking out, no. No individual is, and no individual should think themselves important, or lament the fact when he/she realizes that he/she is not. American people tend to think themselves important in a group. Japanese people tend to think themselves not. American people tend to feel threatened when they realize that in the Budo karate dojo they're expendable. (Did you feel threatened when you read this section?) Japanese people tend to celebrate the fact because it sets them straight as to their place in the world, thus freeing them up to grow and get stronger from a starting point that's more realistic.

It's a cultural difference.

From the outside, though, from an external perspective, how important you are depends on you, and it is the Budo karate expectation that you fight to make yourself important to your dojo.

Whether your dojo *keeps* you or *lets you fade away* depends on you. If you resist the teaching, and deny the dojo your strong spirit, because you come in on your heels and don't hear instructions, don't follow rules of etiquette, and concentrate always on the *what* and ignore the *how*, if you do all these things chronically, then no, you are in fact NOT important to your dojo, you are in the way of progress, and you can go to the other dojo down the street where karate might be the game that you seem to want to play.

On the other hand, however, if you are a strong student—and what I mean by that is if you have a good attitude as described in this book!—of course your dojo will want to keep you. Of course you are making yourself important. Of course your teacher values you!

Will your dojo have your back in a crisis?

Of course it will! A dojo is a family, and like a family your dojo will be there for its members.

BUT, you do have to remember that it's also a *strict* family, that people earn their way into this family by showing their dedication. If you're committed, your dojo will help you when you need it. If you're constantly missing the boat, however, there'll be no one there to help you when you might need it because you've already worn your dojo mates out having to carry you day after day. Compare your performance to the principles outlined in this book. Are you fulfilling them? If so, you're developing a small army of folks who will be there for you. You're developing bonds *stronger* than family. See #20, *The Deepening of Human Relationships*.

But if you're not on your toes, if you're the one that needs coaxing all the time?

Follow your teacher's flow (see #72, *"Channel" Your Teacher's Teaching*) and you will make yourself very important indeed. Resist your teacher's flow, on the other hand (see #11, The *Sempai/Koohai System Brings You CLOSER to Your Teacher*), and you're more likely just a burden.

Of course all white belts are a burden in the beginning, and students of all levels are a burden SOMETIMES, and that's fine. It's the sempai's job to be patient as well.

To be clear, it's the student who's NOT TRYING, or the one who's chronically resisting the teaching, that I'm referring to here. The student who remains a burden for months on end should go back and study this book, work with a highlighter, re-gather his/her energy, and try again the right way.

Remember, it's not important to master the material contained in this book; it's just important to prioritize it. If you believe you *are* prioritizing, though, and your performance is really that bad, then perhaps you need to adjust how you define prioritizing, and how it is related, in your world, to tangible choices that make a difference.

20. The Deepening of Human Relationships

Aside from learning self-defense (some would say learning to fight!), what is the purpose of learning Budo karate?

There are many, but we can easily list the most important ones:

1. The development of physical, mental, and spiritual health. 2. The development of physical, mental, and spiritual *strength*. 3. The strengthening of human character *leading to the deepening of relationships between people.*

Wait, what was that third one again?

What does the deepening of relationships between people have to do with karate?

Mas Oyama would have had an answer for you.

It was one of his most cited reasons behind his push to carry his karate to twelve million people worldwide. "World peace" has become a cliché, but Mas Oyama taught that through the training of Budo karate, we could strengthen human relationships, improve character, and therefore move world populations towards peace.

How could this possibly be achieved?

Well, it starts in the dojo, and in the dojo it starts with your relationship with your teacher.

You've gathered by now that the dojo is meant to be a place where we do everything stronger, a place where we take the important things more seriously, a place where we exclude the mundane, the distraction, the petty. Among the most important things to treat MORE seriously in the dojo are our relationships with our sempais and our relationships with our koohais.

Look at the rules of etiquette used in the dojo. In what situation are you supposed to use them in a fashion that's less than serious?

None. There is no such situation.

So, clearly, just in terms of the surface gestures of respect shared between people, the dojo is a stricter environment than your everyday life outside of the dojo.

But take that a step further and consider this entire concept of correct Budo karate attitude as described by this book.

It's almost unthinkable for many Americans to ALWAYS use their eyes and ears before blurting out a question (see #37, *Think Three Times Before You Speak: If That's Hard for You, Shut Up!*), to ALWAYS do what they're asked to do (see #10, *Complete Tasks That You've Been Assigned Promptly and Powerfully*), to ALWAYS stand up for somebody else (see #13, *Your Teacher Is Angry? It's Life and Death for Everyone, Especially YOU If You Feel Like Someone* Else *Was Responsible!*), to ALWAYS fight to be strongest so that everyone gets strong (see #1, *Fight to Be First*), etc.

Compared to the American system, the Japanese system of human interaction is already strict, but the Budo karate system, based on the do-or-die code of the samurai, is HYPER-strict, is it not? (Perhaps let's use "serious," not "strict." The sempai/koohai system is something that you volunteer, something that comes therefore from within, not something that's imposed. If it feels imposed, it's because YOU are not yet carrying your weight; you're the H. See #4, *On Your Toes, Please, Not Your Heels!*)

It's a system that, if you implement it perfectly, you can then use as a model, and actually redefine the standard to which you hold all the other relationships of your life. You can identify, straightaway, the limits of seriousness to which you might develop a non-dojo relationship, and you can see the extent to which any one of your everyday relationships probably falls short of what it actually could be. If nothing else, you can at least learn how to be that much more attentive and polite to *everyone* with whom you interact.

By practicing the sempai/koohai system, therefore, and by succeeding, we in fact empower ALL of our life's human relationships.

The difficulty, in the Western dojo, is that the average Western student tends to fumble through the implementation of the sempai/koohai system. It's not in our blood like it's in the blood of the Japanese, and it's hard to practice something perfectly with other people who, likewise, don't practice perfectly. Hence (and this should be blindingly obvious to most of you) the importance of everyone fighting to be best at the sempai/koohai system to keep everyone at the front of the curve, and, hence, the importance of maintaining the *Toes-Not-Heels Dojo* (see #5) in Budo karate attitude and the sempai/koohai system as well. The average American student thinks the kick or the punch is important, but that the "Osu!" is optional.

But this is wrong.

It's the other way around!

Everyone must unanimously fight in the Western dojo to perfect the sempai/koohai system, and YOU, first and foremost, must fight to perfect it first in your relationship with your teacher.

Does that mean hugging your teacher and holding his/her hand? Should you leave an apple on your teacher's desk? Does it mean having long, in-depth conversations with your teacher about your personal life?

Of course not!

It just means to read this book, make it your goal to adopt the attitude described within, and fight to be first all the time in all the things that you do to interact with your teacher. Sounds hard?

Oh, but how many hours per week do you *do* karate? (See #53, *How Often in a Week Do You "Do" Karate? That's All? Okay, So No Excuse! Do it Right All the Time That You Do It!*) It's limited, right, the amount of time you spend in the company of your teacher, and your sempais, and your koohais?

Since it is, it's your duty as a Budo karateka, even from white belt level, to treat *those* relationships, those between sempai and koohai, in a hyper-serious way, all the time, whether inside the dojo or out. It's here, in this crucible of picking and choosing this particular handful of relationships in your life, and disciplining yourselves to make those specific relationships hyper-serious, that, through karate training, you can deepen your ability to relate to others.

Like soldiers who face death together on a battlefield, a bond is formed between those who experience hardship together. And it is undeniable: we all face hardship together in the dojo. (See #109, *There's Nothing Wrong with a Bit of Ferocious Dedication to Your Dojo*.) But consider the importance of receiving some guidance in *how* to develop that stronger bond between people, rather than just leaving individuals to figure it out on their own. Isn't the entire purpose of this book to present for the beginner the model attitude that one might develop in the dojo?

Ask yourself this question:

Is it better practice for all of us to have stronger *but equal* relationships? Or is it actually better practice to have stronger *and hierarchical* ones, that is, relationships in a structure where everyone looks *up* with respect to those who have more experience, and reaches *down* with kind but strict expectations to lift up those who have less? Of course, the hierarchical relationships of the dojo challenge us MORE than would the average happy-go-lucky friendship picked up in a bar, at a garden party, or on a playground.

Do you know what it means to "train with a disadvantage?" Consider running with leg weights on, so your feet become lighter when you take them off. Since in the West where it's drilled into our Democracy-influenced personalities that all of us are equal—when due to our behavior, or natural abilities, and the choices we make, we're really not!—why not consider this practice *in an artificially induced hierarchical setting* a similar kind of *training with a disadvantage*? What's the harm? Do so, and you might discover that there actually is some inherent benefit — if not even pleasure! — to treating some folks who are more experienced with a little bit of reverence, and taking a little bit of extra notice in those who are less so?

I could go on to say how important it is that the teacher (or sempai) live a life that is pure enough, or at least well-intentioned enough, so that students will be comfortable allowing such a strict human relationship to develop. Remember, the choice in Budo karate is to follow or not to follow, never to follow partially (see #8, *Drink Some, Spit Some? You'll Fail* and #44, *Karate IS Your Teacher's Karate*).

Take a moment and imagine the dojo in which the students *do* karate in the dojo, and say "Osu!" to their sempais, but once they're outside of the dojo, they just slap each other on the back, without deference, and say, "What's up, man! Let's grab a beer!"

This is a failing Budo karate dojo. It is a slipping, Americanized imitation.

The correct language here is, drenched in sweat after a hard workout, "Osu! Sempai, some of us are going out. Can we invite you for a beer?" — and that only if you feel like your performance in your training life has been exemplary. Even if your teacher or sempai wants to relax with you, the correct sempai can't, won't, and should not if you're blowing off *the Way*, taking only the parts of it that come easily, and if you're not handling your in-dojo relationships as strictly as you can.

Remember that the dojo that enacts a sempai/koohai system that its members don't carry outside of the dojo into their daily lives (for example, when interacting with dojo-mates outside the dojo) is an imitation. Every member of every Western dojo ought to read this, and do the best they can to rise to the challenge, EVEN in cases when your sempais are less dedicated to *fighting for the cause* than you are. Stay humble, of course! — but it is okay for you to outperform your sempais in a quest to follow the correct way. That, too, is part of the Budo karate system.

Change, remember, starts with the individual, and Mas Oyama would smile down from Heaven, eternally, to see this particular change successfully enacted in Western Kyokushin, even when it's initiated by next generations in long-established dojos.

21. Sempais and Koohais are Friends

Of course you should be friends with your sempais!
Of course you should be friends with your koohais!
But be careful! I can only make this claim because of a nuance of translation. The Japanese would say "No!" because the Japanese word *tomodachi* (friend) means equal, whereas the sempai-koohai relationship is NOT equal, and to treat a sempai as one's equal is to show disrespect.

Perhaps consider — as we cross the cultural divide — that being strong friends doesn't always mean being *friendly* in the taken-for-granted, happy-go-lucky, chummy sort of way. In the sempai/koohai system, you will develop strong *brotherly* (or *sisterly*) bonds, because of the common, powerful, strict, and challenging thread that bonds you: your common, tireless pursuit of self-improvement through the rigors of Budo karate training. To degrade all that hard work you do by allowing yourself to become happy-go-lucky chummy with your sempais, or with your koohais, whether in or out of the dojo, is to betray the entire sense of what you're pursuing.

To do so would be a symptom of the failing Americanized attempt.

Why not fight for something more?

Did you come to the dojo just to learn how to beat someone up?

If you're in my dojo and that's the case — if you still haven't grown up, in other words — I hope you'll move on. You're in the way of progress.

If, on the other hand, you're in the dojo to learn a lethal self-defense ability AND a code of character improvement so that hopefully you'll never have to use that lethal ability you've practiced, then, to be true to your practice, you must also base your powerful friendships with your dojo-mates on powerful adherence to the principles that bind you.

Be very strict.

Let's look at two examples of how the Budoka should of course behave. Which one is more important?

1. Always answer with "Osu!" whether inside the dojo or out. Always stand up from your barroom table (that is, even if you're *out on the town*) to greet your sempai with "Osu!" (and a bow) when he/she arrives.
2. Always get your sempai's back if your sempai is physically attacked and his/her life is in danger. Always be willing to fight to protect your koohais if they're physically attacked and their lives are in danger.

The jock, the thug, or the student who only cares about fighting would say, "#2, of course! The second one is more important!"

But he/she would be wrong.

Both are *equally* important.

Failure in either would be a breach of the code.

Which one, after all, is a life-and-death battle? The bar fight, or the struggle to strengthen character through the sempai/koohai system?

BOTH ARE!

Success learning kicks and punches might teach you to fight, but it's success in *the code* that makes you survive when your life, or the lives of your loved ones, are in danger from the many other *nonviolent* threats you or your family will face in life.

See #81, *To Fight For Correct Training Attitude IS to Defend Your Life After All.*

22. The White Belt's Job, Even, to Bring Spirit

One would think this would be a no-brainer, but somehow, in Western culture, it seems that the first-day/first-month white belt student often comes in with a built-in *signals-crossed* training demeanor, at least compared with the Japanese first-timer.

It's difficult, perhaps, because you have to take a leap of faith and overcome your shame reaction to shouting (and shouting unusual words, like "Osu!"); and also because you're participating in a new athletic activity, and it's natural to be cautious doing new motions so as not to hurt yourself, particularly if you're not athletic or if it's a motion to which you're completely unaccustomed.

Perhaps therein lies the difficulty.

What are the things that you CAN do, even in your first class, to display an "I'm going to show my new teacher and my new sempais how eager I am to learn what's being taught!" attitude?

Kiai'ing (issuing the karate shout we use when executing many techniques) is certainly one. So, a piece of advice:

From your first day, shout your head off, at those times when the whole class is. Shout till your throat hurts. You might feel like a idiot for the first few classes, but look again!

It's the ones who are afraid of their own voice who embarrass themselves, because in the dojo doing things powerfully is the correct way.

It may seem counterintuitive, but if you shout like a madman (or woman) in the Budo karate dojo (at the right times), you are showing your desire and your spirit. Consider this diagram we've looked at several times already, and make sure you've read *The Toes-Not-Heels Dojo* section (see #5).

```
T T T T T T
T T T T T T
T T T T H T
```

That's you in the third line, the H. You're a brand new student, and you don't know yet what's going on. In terms of the unified energy that's so important in the Budo karate dojo, you are the sinkhole.

But don't fret.

You are the beginning student and every beginning student runs that gauntlet, but the apparent difference between the Japanese first-timer and the American first-timer is that the Japanese one doesn't want to be an inconvenience to everyone, so he/she shouts his/her head off, throws wild punches that he/she doesn't know yet but that make his/her uniform pop and the sweat fly. The Japanese newcomer is 100% sure that if anyone's not going to hear an instruction, it's not going to be him/her. The American one, on the other hand, is also ashamed/embarrassed to be in the way, but instead of being powerful, he/she tends to be timid, slow and quiet, as if thinking that it's more polite to fade into the woodwork.

In the Budo karate dojo, it's not.

If you're shy, you're the sinkhole, and your lack of bravery is a drain on your new classmates.

Beginners, be the ones who shout the loudest, be the ones who train the hardest even if you fall down, be the ones who don't miss instructions!

You don't understand yet what "Osu!" means?

No problem.

Be the loudest one answering with "Osu!" anyway!

Take the leap of faith!

See #35 for pronunciation and a further explanation of the word "Osu!"

23. Are You Doing All This Hard Work to Be Mediocre?

Take a leap of faith.

Listen carefully to the *how* your teacher cites (See #2, *It's the* How, *Silly, Not the* What). Read and understand the principles outlined in this book.

Would you rather train hard a couple of times per week and be mediocre after a couple of years, or would you rather do the same training and be exceptional?

Of course, all my students tell me they'd rather be exceptional when I ask them this question. And yet, *being exceptional* is not going to fall on you from Heaven! Whether or not you reap the benefits of the training as you could is up to you.

Karate students can *do karate* for years and not become good at karate if they don't train properly. If you don't listen to and act on your teacher's advice, it's possible for you to spend a whole lot of time and not get anywhere compared with the student next to you who's carefully paying attention, and carefully doing his/her best to enact the teacher's advice.

Which one hurts more — safe, careful H-type training, or the animally intense T-type training?

Again, it's counterintuitive, perhaps, for the Western karate student, but going over the top *means* that you're propelled by the excitement of it all, and it actually hurts LESS, and you make more progress at the same time.

At the opposite end of the spectrum, you've got to drag yourself along, and so does your teacher (have to drag YOU along), and so do all of your dojo-mates.

If you could spend three years and get black belt, or three years and get blue, which would you choose?

Of course, that might be an imperfect example, because in the Americanized system there are black belts . . . and then there are black belts. Do you want to be the exceptional one, or the mediocre one? How would you feel about having the black belt that's the same as a blue belt in someone else's dojo?

Listen carefully, read carefully, ask questions when necessary. Take those leaps of faith and you will avoid the mediocre.

See #74, *Which Path Do You Really Want to Take?*, which argues that those who resist the teaching and take the mediocre path don't just reach the destination *later*, but they actually reach it *never!*

24. Train Yourself to See the WHOLE Dojo, Understand Dojo Priorities

For the Western student it takes another leap of faith, perhaps, but natural T-type students do this all the time.

In the dojo, YOU are responsible for how things run. That is, you are just as responsible as everyone else (including your teacher), and your responsibility increases as your rank does. It's therefore important for you to learn to ignore yourself a little bit and see your WHOLE dojo as you train.

The H-type student tends to see only what that student him/herself is doing. If that student is working with a partner, that student tends to see his/her partner, but little else. Sometimes, in fact, this student becomes so intent on what's going on in this limited sense that he/she isn't even aware of his/her teacher.

To be a leader, however, you have to train yourself to see what you're up to as *less* important than 1. how what you're up to is affecting the group, AND 2. how any of your classmates are either positively or negatively affecting the group. You have to see the whole picture in terms of the dojo average.

I'm sorry to make so many of my Western students panic, but you have to *turn on your radar*. You have to perceive, and be aware of, more in the dojo than just you. This is easier than it might seem. All you have to do is adjust your priority, and that awareness will kick in.

"I care more about the common energy of the group," you tell yourself, "than I do about my own progress," and lo and behold! You will start to see the whole group, rather than just your own hardships. This is a natural ability to have, not some impossible magical skill that I'm asking you to learn.

"Me, me, me. What am I going to get out of this training?" you ask. If you do, you're failing. Please reconsider. Ask instead, "MY dojo, MY dojo, MY dojo. What can I give to my dojo?" Do so, and one moment to the next you will have changed from the dumbed-down Americanized version of the fantasy karateka, and become the real McCoy! You will have taken your first step towards becoming the Budoka.

Helping you to understand a simple set of priorities will help you to better participate in making your dojo a strong one. Consider the following sequence:

1. sensei (or sempai)
2. dojo (or group)
3. koohai
4. self

To begin, let's look at #2 and #4, dojo and self. Which is more important, keeping harmony in the dojo, or dealing with a personal concern?

We've already answered that question.

You don't have to be Japanese to understand humility. Yet students have trouble with that one all the time. We do a lot of work in the dojo in lines, or grids (i.e. how the students line up). If you really haven't seen a karate class, consider the marching band. Everyone is in straight lines and moves as a unit. If one guy totally didn't know how to play his drum, as long as he kept his place in his line (or in his grid), at least he wouldn't be underfoot. Now consider a dojo full of karate students practicing kata. New students, very often in the Western dojo, are so wrapped up in themselves that they lose their position in line and get *underfoot*, thus breaking the harmony of the group.

Your not knowing the motion hurts that harmony a little. Your not knowing it AND being in the wrong place, thus throwing off someone else, hurts it a lot more.

Now let's look at #3 and #1, koohai and sensei. You know you are responsible for your koohais. You see one doing the wrong thing, so you start correcting him/her. Yet, in the process of doing so, you managed to ignore your teacher's latest instruction. It's always fun for me when a sempai in my class snaps at one of his/her koohais (a child who is misbehaving, for example) right in the middle of one of my sentences to the class. Which was the bigger distraction to the dojo's energy?

Well, it depends on what the kid was doing to make him/herself a nuisance, but if whatever the child was doing was not distracting anyone (other than the sempai), since the sempai was more concerned about his/her koohai than about his/her teacher, it was in fact the sempai that caused the grater distraction.

It is a little tricky, because there is another, slightly different priority list that goes like this:

1. self
2. koohai

Notice that self, here, comes first. The order is reversed. This is the order in which you have to focus in terms of *being a strong leader*, as all sempais must be. Make sure YOU are powerful, and in the right place, and doing the right things in the right way FIRST, and then, SECOND, take care of your koohai who's not. But if you are overly concerned with your koohai, and thus get yourself out of place, you've interfered with your dojo's energy (see the first priority list), and so you have to adjust.

I'll caution you that even I, as I read back over this section, see how difficult this might seem to a beginner, particularly if that beginner is trying to memorize the priorities and then decide on a case-by-case basis which is which, and which is more important. Of course that's too much for anyone to conjure up on the spur of the moment.

Remember that it's important to prioritize, rather than memorize. Don't try to *learn* all that you're supposed to do. Just feel, in your heart, which is the more important thing: you or your dojo, you or your teacher, your koohai partner or the overall energy of the dojo.

I think then all the rest should fall into place.

Do remember, though, that seeing your whole dojo is only half of the challenge. You also have to know what to do if, when you see your dojo, you see holes in the grid. To answer that question, see #29, *Encourage Your Koohais, Don't Be the Koohai That Needs Encouraging*.

25. Challenge vs. Command

Consider case A and case B:

Case A, your teacher tells the class, "You guys should always endeavor to train two times per week, but it's far better if you train three or more." And Case B, your teacher says instead, "You are required to train two or more times per week, or you won't get your next belt."

The Western karate student tends to pay greater heed to the second one, whereas the first one sometimes gets completely ignored.

One is a challenge, and the other is a command. One uplifts; the other has the potential to degrade.

Take a step back, and consider:

The purpose of karate training is for YOU to become stronger by setting up and overcoming challenges for yourself. Yes, you overcome one if your teacher TELLS you to come two or more times per week and you actually do so, but that was only half of the strengthening process.

Do you want to be mediocre, or do you want to be exceptional? If there really is a difference between Budo karate and the embarrassing dumbed-down American version, which one do you want to practice? If you want to be exceptional, you also have to learn to set challenges for yourself and to HEAR challenges your teacher issues and succeed in the face of those, too.

In the Budo karate dojo it is your DUTY to do so. It is not optional, it's part of the code. If you ignore challenges, you are the H-type student, both in terms of your own personal strength, and in terms of your responsibility to act as a role model.

Now let's look at it from the other direction.

Which one is more gratifying for your teacher? Do you think your teacher really likes bossing weak students around?

Of course your teacher doesn't! That's the worst part of the job, that's the part that shows your teacher how mired he/she is in a Western environment in which the students might never get what Budo karate is meant to be.

But, oh, how much pleasure comes for the teacher when he/she challenges students to make choices that will lead to their strength, and thus to the strength of the dojo, and those students HEAR the challenges, realize that it's something serious, and then charge forward to fulfill them!

This is the Budo karate spirit.

A good rule of thumb?

Pay very close attention when your teacher is speaking. Try to pick out the challenges, the *advice* or encouragement that doesn't sound like an order. Your teacher at that moment is likely watching the eyes of the students in the room for the one who clues in to the challenge. Your teacher is wondering which one is going to rise to the occasion.

In the Budo karate dojo, EVERYONE should.

Everyone?

YES, everyone!

Learn to hear challenges like orders. If you try to fulfill a challenge, and then try harder, and still can't manage it, communicate it to your teacher so he/she knows you didn't ignore him/her completely (see #10, *Complete Tasks That You've Been Assigned Promptly and Powerfully*). Shall we add *respond to all challenges* to the list of dojo etiquette rules in #3?

Perhaps it wouldn't be a bad idea.
Also read #26, just below, as the discussion continues here as well.

26. The Implicit Challenge: You Got It! Respond to ALL Challenges!

Any time a classmate is training harder, doing more, kicking higher, or sweating more in your proximity, they are issuing an implicit challenge—one not stated in words—that the Budo karateka should never ignore. Think about it:

Fight to be first! (See #1.)

If you are fighting to be first, and someone ups the average next to you, you have to feel it as a challenge and rise to the occasion. This is an attitude decision you have to make when you enter the Budo karate dojo. "I will not be outdone! I will not be left behind! I will not embarrass myself by being less beside someone who is more!"

Compare Mas Oyama's dojo to the Americanized one. In Mas Oyama's dojo everyone is unanimously charging towards the front of the curve. See #113, *Charging to the Front of the Curve*. Therefore, if anyone charges out to the front by kiai'ing louder, or kicking higher, or doing more push-ups, everyone else FEELS that as their being left behind, and they redouble their efforts to charge forward. But what about the Americanized dojo?

I see it myself all the time: one slow-motion student training contentedly next to one that's in overdrive. The slow-motion student doesn't recognize what's going on right next to him/her as anything that has any bearing on what he/she is doing. What if they're both brown belts? That's one thing—one brown belt failing to respond to the unspoken challenge of his equal. But what if the revved-up student nearby is your koohai?

Even then, in the American dojo—in my own!—I see students who are not concerned that they are being shamed by the stronger spirit of the koohai next to them. It's somehow as if the *shame sensors* they would have been born with if they were Japanese have been removed.

But all it takes—I hope!—is for that to be pointed out to each and every (particularly new) student in a way that makes it sink in, and the American student, too, can bridge the cultural divide and respond to this type of challenge as well.

Is the brown belt student who's blind to the implicit challenge issued by the more spirited student training next to him a Budo karateka?

Sadly, no.

And yet you came to the Budo karate dojo to learn Budo karate, right?

Then you have to turn your shame sensors on. Fight to be first. Don't allow yourself to be the one who gets left behind. Respond to ALL challenges, even the implicit ones!

Apparently, having *challenged myself* to write this entire book in 10 days (thus achieving the empowerment by which I was actually able to complete it, cover to cover, in 29), it seems that I considered this particular concept so vital that I wrote it twice! See #42 as well, *Respond to ALL Challenges*.

It IS that important, so I've decided to leave in the repetition.

27. Always Answer, Always Answer Promptly

This is so much fun for me!

Writing this book is, first because I can see how much it will improve training for those new students who read it, but also because I get to share experiences that I have with beginners from MY perspective, so many of you will get to chuckle at how easy some of this stuff is, and shake your heads at how much of a disruption it can be when the beginner is rocked back on his/her heels.

Imagine the case where I ask a student to move from one side of the room to the other.

Very eagerly, the student runs to the other side of the room, gets there, stands up straight and at attention, and then shouts "Osu!"

What was wrong with that?

The student was eager, right? He/she ran powerfully to do what the teacher asked him/her to do, right?

Did you figure it out?

Exactly! By running FIRST and waiting until the task was complete to answer "Osu!" NEXT, the student demanded and consumed the teacher's attention (and the attention of the sempais in the room) for the time it took the student to run across the room. Instead of moving on to the class's next "beat," the song actually missed one. The teacher thought, "He/she didn't answer 'Osu!'" Half the sempais in the room probably shouted out, "Say OSU!" to remind their koohai what he/she missed. (See #29, *Encourage Your Koohais, Don't Be the Koohai That Needs Encouraging*.)

See how simple an error? See how harmful the result of not correctly understanding the proper priorities? The dojo average was lowered, after all.

The solution? The rule?

Always answer immediately when your teacher or sempai addresses you. Simple.

What about this case? You'll laugh:

The teacher asks the student a question, but the student has to think about it before he/she comes up with the answer.

The teacher asks the question, and the student says, "Hmmmm . . . uhhh . . . hmmmm." Meanwhile, the momentum of the class is being held hostage. The weaker students have diverted their attention, and the other beginners have the idea reinforced for them that answering their teacher promptly and powerfully is optional. The collective energy falls.

So what's the correct way?

The teacher asks the question and the student has to think about it so he/she immediately says "Osu! Sensei, I have to think about it for a second!" The teacher chuckles (so do several other people in the room), and the teacher says, "Okay! Good, I'll come back to you in a few minutes!" and goes on with the lesson, no momentum lost, no damage to the collective energy.

What if you don't know the answer at all?

In Japan we used to hear this all the time: "Osu! Sensei, I'll find out for you as soon as I can and report back!"

What about answering telephone messages, e-mails, letters, notes and text messages?

You got it!

It is a matter of etiquette, just like bowing and answering with "Osu!" If you don't answer these nonverbal, non-immediate communications, and if you don't do it promptly, you have disrespected the sempai who sent you the message, and you have betrayed that key element of karate training cited in #20, *The Deepening of Human Relationships*: that the relationships between sempai and koohai MUST be treated as something MORE than the average relationship.

Mas Oyama went so far as to say that karate is not karate without the sempai-koohai system executed properly. By not promptly answering an e-mail or text message sent by your sempai, you are not betraying him/her . . . you're betraying the Budo karate ideal.

The electronic message requires some thought and some time to write, and you don't have that time right now?

No problem, respond immediately, "Osu! Sensei, I'm taking this very seriously! May I respond by tomorrow?" But even to this, of course, you have to apply the #1, *Fight to Be First* mentality: strong spirit really means figuring out a way to take care of the task sooner than tomorrow.

The point is, ALWAYS answer your sempai, and always do it promptly. Anything less is rude, and a violation of the code.

What if hours have passed since an (electronic) message was sent, and you're only now just receiving it? Well, the Budo karate student, coming to understand that his/her sempai might be reaching out to him/her by that method, would check his/her e-mail more often, and of course there's nothing wrong with "sorry, Sensei, I didn't check my e-mail until just now!" but if that's the response that comes too often and the teacher starts to feel that it's a matter of failed responsibility, be careful!

Your teacher might start to think that you are one of the dojo's weaker students.

28. Do Not Disappoint / Inconvenience Your Sempai!

A no-brainer?

You'd think so, but it's pretty remarkable how some new students become comfortable in a constant state of disappointing their teacher/sempai and aren't aware of it being wrong, because they've already defined karate training, in their own minds, as something in which "this person up there at the front of the room is *supposed* to get on my case to make me stronger."

Since it's pretty painful to imagine yourself as an adult in this situation (believe me, some of you get there!), let's imagine the child student, practicing a basic kata called *taikyoku sono ichi*. All of the stances are long stances, but the child is fairly challenged, he/she lacks discipline, and so his/her stances are rarely long enough. The teacher counts, "Ichi!" ("One!"), and all the students perform the first movement. The one child in question does it too, but his/her stance is too short. That student stands our like a sore thumb, so the teacher calls him/her by name and says, "Long stance, please!" The child says "Osu!" and makes his/her stance longer. The teacher counts, "Ni!" ("two!"), and all the students perform the second movement. The teacher sighs, because once again, the same child's stance is too short. So he calls the student by name again and says, "Long stance!" The child complies, but it goes on each time until it becomes clear that the child is confused. It becomes clear that the student has come to define karate training, in his/her own mind, as an activity in which the teacher always calls for strength when it's required, and therefore, "The times that Sensei doesn't tell me to, I don't have to do it."

Consider the following two situations as if they were music.

Case A. "One! (A unified powerful motion, and the sound of dogis popping.) Two! (And again, the same energetic response.) Three! (And the same response again.) Four!" (And again.)

Case B. "One! Long stance, please!" ("Osu!") "Two! No, long stance!" ("Osu!") "Three! I told you, long stance!" ("Osu!") . . . "Eight! If I have to tell you one more time, I'll have to ask you to sit out! Long stance, please! Come on! Get with the program!"

Be careful before you conclude that this doesn't apply to you.

The point is the frequency with which some students, child or adult, frustrate their teacher or sempai, *and can't figure out how*. The student doesn't know what to fix, and falls into a habit of thinking, "This is what karate training is at this dojo. I do it the hard way whenever that guy at the front of the room raises his voice."

Please notice if your teacher is frustrated with you, chronically. That is, not just here and there, but for a period of time.

If you haven't clued in to why, it's better to ask.

If you read this book carefully, it's likely you'll be the opposite kind of student and never find yourself in that situation.

So just remember!

Is your teacher telling you the same things over and over again? It's against the rules (see #3, *Follow the Rules of Etiquette*), but it's also weak. Figure out that you're supposed to make the CHOICE to realize that that one piece of instruction your teacher gave you (over and over again) is the most important thing in this particular situation, and make sure you provide it without him/her having to ask for it again.

Read #69, *The ACB Ease, Not the ABC Lock*.

29. Encourage Your Koohais, Don't Be the Koohai That Needs Encouraging

Reading #40, *Example First, Words Second* would benefit your reading of this section. Reading #24, *Train Yourself to See the WHOLE Dojo, Understand Dojo Priorities* will help you as well.

Encouraging your koohais means, in this case, calling out reminders to your koohais during group exercises to help empower (or remind) them to do the things that your teacher expects them to do (and usually that they're having trouble remembering to do at that particular moment). You know that your teacher expects the class to be in straight lines, for example, and you realize that the lines are not straight, so, since YOU are responsible for your dojo, and you want to always try to fix a problem before your teacher has to, you shout out the reminder, "Straight lines!" Everyone answers "Osu!" and fixes their lines, and your dojo is stronger, and your teacher is grateful.

One student doesn't answer "Osu!" promptly? Then if you can remind him/her, "Say 'Osu!'" before your teacher has to, you're on your toes, and are valiantly working to uphold the dojo's high standard. You are *getting your teacher's back*. (See #41, *Get Your Sempai's Back, Get Your Teacher's!*)

Remember that you become a sempai the moment someone joins the dojo after you did. If you join on Monday, and someone else joins on Tuesday, that person is your koohai. Of course white belts are generally lost enough to leave each other alone for their first couple of months, but understand that it is the job of at least every colored belt student, at the very least, to keep their koohais walking the right path. In other words, YOU are responsible for the strong behavior of your koohais. If they make chronic mistakes, it's YOUR mistake for not fixing it. It's your mistake for not being a stronger role model.

Therefore, every time your koohai moves too slowly, it's disrespectful, and *you* are expected to tell him/her, "Hurry up!" If your koohai fails to bow when he/she enters the dojo, *you* are expected to explain, or scold, or do whatever is necessary to fix that problem so it doesn't happen in the future. Of course a good sempai starts in a kind way, and a T-type student only needs to hear it once, but if the student is an H-type student and keeps dropping the ball, the sempai (yes, that means YOU!) may rightly get frustrated and resort to stronger tactics to try to make your koohai become the T he/she is required to be.

Common encouragement heard in my dojo is, "Guard up!" "High energy!" "Make your voice powerful!" "Don't be the last one!" Really anything that's concise, and can be intoned to sound like a command, and that supports, directly, one of your teacher's priorities. Make 100% sure that if you're going to throw your voice out there into the mix of the energy of your Budo karate dojo, your tone and volume is powerful and inspirational. At the same time, make sure that you're not speaking over one of your sempais — for example, when your teacher is giving an instruction.

Now, on to part two.

It's important for you to look at this from the other direction.

In the same way that you must always encourage your koohais, you must also be sure to make yourself into the type of koohai that doesn't need encouraging.

You can test if you are:

Next time you're training, listen for one of your sempais to call out some *encouragement* to the class. Then ask yourself, "Was I already doing that, or did I have to adjust based on his/her reminder?"

An example. Everyone is practicing kumite. The sempai notices that several of his koohais have dropped their guard, and, since it's not a full-contact kumite situation — in which one might fix that problem by kicking hard to the head — he shouts out a reminder instead: "Guard up!" Several people, the T's, shout "Osu!" in response.

But ask yourself:

Did you have to raise your own fists at all?

If you did, you were one of the koohais that needed encouraging, and you should immediately try to adjust your attitude for the future. Was your answer, on the other hand, "Osu!" but inside you know that you were already there, that you were one of the T's that didn't need to be told?

If so, good for you. That's the test.

Remember that you're failing if the only times you do the hard things is when someone reminds you to do them.

Develop the mentality that it's always the weak students that are being reminded when the sempais encourage their koohais, and make sure YOU are not one of the weak ones that needs to be reminded. Stay on your toes, follow the rules of etiquette, fight to be first in all things. You'll find life in the dojo much easier this way. You'll find it much more rewarding.

Please read #60, *Everything You Do Is FOR EFFECT!* Show *That You Did What Your Teacher Asks, but Be Careful!* to understand a potential contradiction. If you're told to do something you have to SHOW that you did it, and yet, if you're *encouraged* to do something that you should have already been doing, there should really be no adjustment that needs to be shown! It's a bit complex, but the answer there is just to understand that you can SHOW you're following an instruction (or *encouragement*) by doing it even better, or even more strongly, even if you were already doing it when the instruction or correction was issued. Read #60, and I think this will become clear.

Remember that about the worst thing you can do in response to a sempai's encouragement is to make no adjustment when you were one of the ones that needed the encouragement in the first place. H-type students will do this either because they don't hear the instruction, or, worse, if they're pretending to be one of the ones that doesn't need to be told, and therefore, proudly and rudely, refusing to adjust.

This is the student that is fair game for being adjusted harshly.

30. How Do You Pay for Your Karate Lessons?

Your teacher has paid for his/her knowledge with blood, sweat and tears, and with years and years and years. Like the Japanese student who is taught from a very early age to revere teachers far more than our (American) public school system ever could, please keep this always in mind.

Whatever you PAY the dojo in dollars can't possibly be enough.

Think about your dues as what it costs just to enter and hang out in the dojo. What the teacher teaches you is different. You don't pay for it with dollars, because you couldn't possibly afford it. It's also not free.

You have to pay for the teaching, on the other hand, with blood, sweat and tears of your own. You pay for it with your *attitude*.

Read this book. Ask questions when you have them. It's right here for you. Contained within these pages is a roadmap for having the proper attitude with which you can, in fact, *pay* your teacher for what he/she is teaching you.

Students with the improper attitude can adopt the proper attitude. It's never too late. Students who don't *want* the proper attitude, however, are stealing, and should go away.

It is rude to come to a Budo karate school and resist the teacher's teaching. It happens in the American system, but please! Not in my dojo!

Remember, I don't care about your kicks and your punches; I only care about your Budo karate attitude (as described in this book) because then, if that's correct, your kicks and your punches will actually mean something.

See #54, *"I'm Gonna Buy Me Some Karate."*

31. Treat New Students Delicately? No! Slow Motion is Akin to the Assassination of Learning for the New Student

There will certainly be some variation from dojo to dojo in terms of what exercises are a regular part of classes in which beginners are present. At my dojo, we tend to work a lot in long parallel rows, facing each other, each person with a partner, practicing kumite techniques, and then rotating every couple of minutes so each person gets a new partner. It is of this situation that I speak here, and in so doing reveal one of my own personal pet peeves (exactly because it's so destructive to the dojo's average).

It is one that has a very strong correlation to #14, *React Inversely to Hardship 1*, and to #5, *The Toes-Not-Heels Dojo*.

Simply stated, don't move in slow motion, or gently, or break complex motions down into their individual parts, or stop to explain to your partner with a whisper, when you're working with a new student (especially a first-day student!), or one who is smaller, younger, or weaker than you.

Slow motion on your part is akin to assassination of learning for a new student. It is your ENERGY and your SPIRIT that will propel your first-day koohais into imitating the movement that they see. Yes, the teacher may demonstrate a movement in slow motion or stop to explain it before the exercise begins. But once you're working with your novice partner, if YOU do the same, you will confuse your partner and alter their thinking so that they will try to work out the movement's components individually, rather than just imitating the movement as a whole.

Who are our species' fastest learners?

Children, of course! Babies, in fact.

Those blank sensory slates drink in knowledge from their new environment (life!) from the instant they take their first breath. As adults, once we've spent half a lifetime learning how to rationalize everything, our learning process is actually far slowed down. Is it easier for you to learn a language from a textbook, or for a child to do it, growing up immersed in that language?

Of course it's the latter, and learning physical motions is the same. If you do a movement with spirit and energy when working with a partner, your partner will often just do it right back without even thinking about it, and they will do it mostly right.

However, if you break it down, explain it, or slow it down to a crawl, it will take them out of that automatic drinking-in-knowledge learning mode, and allow them space for confusion.

Why is it one of my pet peeves?

Because if a new student is exposed to this kind of learning in his/her first class, it can set them back by months!—because their brain will align itself behind "Oh, so THIS is how I'm supposed to learn karate movements." Sadly, this is one bad habit that forms almost immediately.

So if you're a new student, be warned, your partner won't hurt you, but if he/she comes at you fast, he/she is doing exactly what he/she is supposed to be doing. If, on the other hand, your partner comes at you slow and starts whispering explanation, you have a right to complain to your teacher. That partner of yours is an H-type student, and he/she is failing in his/her job as a role model.

How is this related to #14, *React Inversely to Hardship*, and to #5, *The Toes-Not-Heels Dojo*?

Exactly because the H's in the room are sinkholes of energy. Instead of lending energy to the dojo, the H's draw energy out. So, imagine that you as a sempai are standing next to a brand-new student (an H because all brand new students are H's before they realize their proper pace). For you, the sempai, standing next to the H is a hardship. So, how are you to respond? Do you slow yourself down to match the H, or do you *turn on the animal*, and rev yourself up to draw that new student out of their shell by example?

It may be counterintuitive in Western culture, but you ought to have gotten it by now.

That's it, you have to turn on the animal!

(See # 15, *React Inversely to Hardship 2: Turn on the Animal!*)

Finally, I would only add: Be very, very careful here!

It IS apparently right at the core of our Western personality to approach the weak in a weak way. Yet in the dojo, it has to be the opposite. If you approach the weak in a weak way, everyone gets weaker.

Please! No SLOW MOTION for the sake of your novice partners in the Budo karate dojo!

32. Easier Training When Sensei's Not Looking?

If it is, you are succumbing to an H-type training mentality. See #4, *On Your Toes, Please, Not Your Heels!* If it is, you are failing to *fight to be first* (see #1). If it is, you are in fact slipping outside your training in Budo karate, and moving into the realm of the pretend, mass-market karate we see in every strip mall in America.

Of course it can be more difficult to train hard *when Sensei's not looking*, especially if the sempais present are also weak along these lines. It IS a more challenging environment, because your teacher knows how to rev up a class and hold the line better than your sempais do in some cases. As we've already seen, your teacher is conscience bound to maintain a standard, and your sempai, teaching the class, may not have acquired that moral directive yet.

But wait!

What was that?

Did we just say that it's a more challenging environment?

That should have rung a bell!

"Oh, yeah," you might say, having read the earlier sections of this book, "Osu! It's a more *challenged* environment, so we're supposed to have an INVERSE reaction to hardship! It is harder sometimes to get revved up when sensei's not watching, so we're *supposed* to train harder to compensate!"

Of course you are! (See #s 14, 15 and 16 about reacting INVERSELY to hardship.)

More than that, though, your sempais are supposed to develop that same moral obligation to maintain the same standard your teacher struggles to teach them. And so are you. If your teacher is the only one with a moral commitment to maintain a standard, how exhausting for your teacher! How weak this dojo will remain!

But if everyone, every sempai, begins to develop that moral standard, so that he/she doesn't hold a line because he/she's been told to do so, but rather because falling below that line insults his/her sense of dignity as a karateka, and because he/she now KNOWS what that standard means to the dojo, and what it means to karate?

If so, the sempais in the room have finally unlocked the secret to successfully *channeling* their teacher's teaching.

Step back for a moment and consider Budo karate's do-or-die roots in the samurai era. According to the medieval *Hagakure* (*Code of the Samurai*), when a samurai dishonors his/her community—even merely by a display of public drunkenness!—he is required to take his own life through ritual disembowelment. In other words, according to these guys' code of living, they weren't required to commit hara-kiri only because they lost in battle, or failed to support their lord; they were required to commit hara-kiri just for simply behaving badly!

Of course we don't live that way now—we don't promote disembowelment for failure in the Budo karate dojo!—but the sempai in the Budo karate dojo would do well to adopt some of that do-or-die spirit towards their commitment to Budo karate. They would do well to develop their sense of duty to the point where they might feel it in their gut, not unlike a knife blade, when the standard of the training they're responsible for falls below the standard set by their teacher.

And just to be sure . . .

Which sempai in the training is thus responsible? Only the instructor? Far from it.

Everyone is jointly responsible.

If the standard's fallen, turn up the steam! If it's fallen for the student next to you who should know better, get angry!

It IS the correct response.

33. When Will THAT Dojo Get Stronger?

Make sure you understand # 5, *The Toes-Not-Heels Dojo*.
You will be familiar with these two cases:

Case A:	T T T T T	Case B:	T H T H T T
	T H T T T		H T H H T T
	T T T T T		T T H T H T

Now, however, consider these two (this time BOTH are H-type dojo scenarios):

Case C:	H T H T H H	Case B:	T H T H T T
(Monday)	T H T T H H	(Wednesday)	H T H H T T
	H H T H T H		T T H T H T

It just so happens that case C and case B are exact opposites, but that's just to make a point.

Now imagine that these 18 students in each case are sitting in *seiza* (Japanese kneeling position with their backs straight and their fists on their hips), both Monday night and Wednesday night, the exact same students in the exact same positions.

The first student (top left in Case C), on Monday, is an H-type student, i.e. he's on his heels in terms of attitude, and is behaving badly. On Wednesday, however, the same student had his snack after school, and got good rest the night before, and now he's a T-type student, i.e. he's on his toes like he's supposed to be. In fact, because I made them opposite in this case, every student has flip-flopped from Monday's class to Wednesday's.

Since they're all sitting in seiza, the T's are all sitting very still and upright; their position is very proper, as it should be. The H's, however, are fidgeting. Like many Western students who are learning that they can actually be comfortable in this position (but who can only figure that out through perseverance), they are leaning forward and swaying side to side in order to relieve the discomfort they feel in their ankles. Since the instruction for seiza is to sit properly, still and upright, no matter what, because dealing with this discomfort is part of becoming strong through karate training, the H's are failing (and lowering the class standard), and the T's are succeeding (these particular nights).

Now, the question I want to pose is, "When will this dojo become strong?"

The answer is "Never! It will NOT become strong."

Surprised?

Without intervention, this dojo will NEVER correct this problem.

Look back to Case A and case B.

This dojo will not start to get strong until classes routinely resemble Case A. Of course, that one lone H might be a different student each night, and some nights there might be more than one. BUT if individual students are H's some nights and T's other nights (as in Case B and C), THEY SHOULD NOT BE COLORED BELTS. They should go back to white, or orange at the most.

You can read in #64, *Succeed Consistently, You Can't Buy A Break by Showing Strength Every Once in a While*, about the importance of consistency, but, in the meantime, please understand that WORSE than a dojo that is only 50% T-type students is a dojo in which a majority of the students flip-flop routinely from strong to weak, from H's to T's, depending on how they feel each particular class session. This type of dojo will NEVER GET STRONG, and my advice to the instructor is to be so hard on this class that some of them even quit, if that's what it takes to whittle the class down until only those who can be consistent remain. Sure, try to get through to them first! Read them this book! But—and here's the rub:

Budo karate has NOTHING to do with strong performance only when you feel strong, and it has EVERYTHING to do with learning to act strong even when you feel weak. It is your duty to learn how to train as described in this book, even as a white belt, and then stick to it. It is the prerequisite for entering the dojo to begin training, not something you should wait to get along the way.

Sure, everyone can be allowed a grace period!

But if the grace period you want extends to black belt level and beyond? If months are becoming years and you still lack consistency?

You're not learning a vital lesson, and you need to go back and study this book again! Demand of yourself, today and every day, that you stand on your own two feet. Have a little dignity! Without it, you're fooling yourself. It's not Budo karate for you otherwise, and you're in the way.

34. There's Really Only One *How*

In one particular series of classes recently in my new dojo, in which many of the students were new students, I sought to make them understand the nature of the unified, powerful fulfillment of a group instruction, in which getting them to understand "unified" was the central theme of the lesson.

I'll quote here from #1, *Fight to Be First*.

> *Consider:*
> *Your teacher asks you to line up for class. Everyone fights not to be last, by racing to be the first one to get to their places. Who wins? Well, probably no one. Almost everyone gets to their places in about the same time. This is a UNIFIED powerful action. Good for you! You're practicing Budo karate. The important thing is not being first, it's that everyone uniformly fights to be.*

In order to get this point across, (a bit frustrated that I had to do so, because they were not taking the leap of faith I was asking them for), I made them a chart of *how's* and *what's* (See #2, *It's the How, Silly, Not the What*), in which the *what's* were simple commands they could perform powerfully as a group (e.g. "line up!"), and the *how's* were how to fulfill those commands in a powerful, unified way (e.g. quickly, powerfully, fighting to be first, etc.).

In fact, it was through a list of about 20 of these *what's*, with corresponding *how's* written in a second column, that I finally got this group to understand. (See Appendix #3 for a sample of a what/how chart you might use.) Once they figured out that they could do those particular things in a powerful, unified way, once they figured out how powerful that made them feel to be able to execute such tasks as a team, they began to lend that understanding to other tasks that were not on that list.

It was then that I was finally able to make the point that I had tried to make from the beginning:

There is only one *how* for everything you do in the dojo. Here is how I defined it that day:

The What: Everything you do in the dojo.

The How: Do it with courtesy, with spirit, with determination, with intensity, with alertness, and with a moral obligation to do it as your teacher would have you do it.

In fact, if you can do that, it's the only rule you'll ever need! If you can do that, you don't need this book. Throw it away! That's all this entire book is, a lesson in how to do the things you do in the dojo with courtesy, spirit, determination, intensity, alertness, and with a moral obligation to do them as your teacher would have you do them.

The problem, of course, is that the average Western student doesn't know HOW to do things with spirit and determination. They don't know what that means in the Budo karate sense.

One way to look at this entire book is that it is an explanation of HOW to fulfill that one *how* for everything you do in the dojo as it was fulfilled in Mas Oyama's world headquarters dojo when he was alive.

If you grasp that one concept, though, it's certainly true that you won't have to study a whole bunch of rules.

Let me say that again, and I'm aware that I say it other times in this book:

It is NOT necessary for you to learn every single one of these rules to have the correct attitude in the Budo karate dojo. Once you understand the concept—and that's one single concept!—once you adopt the correct training personality—and that's one common personality!—your task becomes easy!

It's then, too, that your dojo becomes as strong as it can be. It's then that Mas Oyama would be proud to see what you've done.

35. Weak *Osu* Has No Meaning, Unheard *Osu* Might As Well Not Have Been One at All, Not Even Trying *Osu* Means You Might As Well be Home

"Osu!" (long o, silent u) means "I will fight forward in the face of hardship." However, it is not a word you would find in a Japanese dictionary. It's a combination of words used in the Budo karate dojo to express that concept in a single syllable.

It is a *power word*, a word that embodies the spirit of never quitting to fight to be the strongest, and the best, and the most correct. It is a raw expression of spirit to win. It is a raw expression of one's desire to master karate.

"Osu!", therefore, has no meaning if it is not spoken with an intonation that expresses that meaning.

A tiny, timid, or weak "osu" thus has no meaning. Just by saying it that way, you have betrayed the Budo karate code. Fighting to be the strongest "OSU!", on the other hand, embodies the strength at the heart of the word.

Please remember as you begin your karate training that even if you feel awkward shouting a word you didn't know before yesterday, if you say it sheepishly, you are embarrassing yourself in the eyes of the people who know what it means. Please, even from day one, roar "OSU!" and you'll be on the right track.

What if your "osu" is a response to your teacher or sempai's command and he/she didn't hear your response?

You may in fact have said it, but did it have any meaning?

Correct! It had none at all if your teacher or sempai didn't hear it.

It's your job to make sure your "Osu!" is heard. I'm reminded of that paradoxical question: What sound does a falling tree make if there's no one in the forest there to hear?

Here's a funny story.

Back in the day, one of my well-intentioned residential students and I were training every morning on the college track. I was running one morning, he was doing push-ups and sit-ups and squats. As per our rule of etiquette in which you have to stand up and bow and say "Osu!" whenever you enter a space where your sempai is, or when your sempai enters the space you're occupying, this student should have stood up from his exercises to face me, and bow, and say "Osu!" each time I ran past him on that quarter-mile track (i.e. once about every 2 minutes). He knew me well enough, and I had already explained to him that I didn't want him interrupting his exercises for me (that's MY prerogative as his sempai, not his, to decide, i.e. to curtail a rule of etiquette) by jumping up and bowing each time I ran by. I told him that it was enough that he just said "Osu!" to let me know he wasn't ignoring the rules of etiquette he was in those days fighting to perfect.

So the next time I ran by, after the time in which I explained his special-case responsibility, he was doing sit-ups and he didn't say "Osu!" as I ran past. Nothing.

"Hmmm," I thought, "that's not like him," but I kept running. Two minutes later I passed him again, he was still doing sit-ups and again he didn't say "Osu!" This time I was mad, and I stopped to ask him what his malfunction was.

It turns out that he had indeed been saying "Osu!" while he was doing his sit-ups, but that I hadn't heard him because each time, curled up into a ball at the top of a sit-up, he would gasp "osu. . ." with his eyes closed and, basically, to his own crotch, because his chin was between his knees each time.

We laughed when we figured out his failure, and he immediately corrected it.

The story's moral?

When answering your sempai, you have to make sure that you "deliver" your response sufficiently that your sempai hears it, or you might as well not have said it at all.

You might be in a loud room full of students training, but if you want to make sure your teacher hears you, you might have to be aware of where your teacher is and you might have to *telegraph* your voice to make sure you're heard. If your teacher just reminded you to have a powerful voice, especially then, you might have to use an even more powerful voice if your teacher has then walked to the opposite end of the dojo. Bottom line:

Make yourself heard! You are saying "Osu!" TO somebody, not just throwing it out into empty space.

Finally, before moving on, I should mention the case where the student doesn't say "Osu!" at all, the oh-so-common case where the new student uses "osu" sometimes, but not all the time.

Please stay home if you can't be courteous according the rules established for the dojo.

I hope that this book will help with this point, but EVERY student I've ever had has tested the waters, in the beginning, to try to find out which is more important, the "Osu!" or the performance of the task that was required of them. Please don't have any doubt: The courtesy is most important. When in Rome, do as the Romans do.

But don't despair!

It's very common for beginners to forget "Osu!", particularly when the sempai asks them to perform some task that requires concentration. They are dutifully trying to please the sempai by concentrating hard on the task at hand, but, misunderstanding the dojo priorities, they start at the back end (concentrating on the task), rather than the front end (saying "Osu!").

Please understand that ALWAYS answering with "Osu!" is a factor of the class average. If the sempais miss them, so will the new students. Please understand that answering with "Osu!" is not only an important part of the dojo routine; it is the MOST important one.

See #112, *Pronunciation, Enunciation* for a discussion of how you can embarrass yourself mispronouncing "Osu!"

36. How and When to Bow in the Budo Karate Dojo: The "Two, Three, One"

This is language to help the beginning student understand how to bow properly in the Japanese way: Two, three, one.

Consider a total of three relevant body parts: your head and your two fists. It might help, for the sake of this exercise, to think of them like stones, or some other blunt, lifeless objects.

1. As the title to this part suggests, first move TWO of them, alone: your fists. Cross your arms under your chin to where each of your fists is near your opposite ear. You have NOT moved your head or spine yet, you have just raised and crossed your arms.

2. Second, move THREE parts forward and down, your head and both fists. Uncross your arms, thrust them out in front of you at hip level (not unlike low blocks, but knuckles in a vertical line and facing forward when you're done, elbows slightly bent), AND bend your body forward to 30% at the waist, at the same time, so that your head, the third part, moves forward and down simultaneously. Make sure you don't curve your spine (i.e. it bends only at the lowest point of your lower back) or your neck (forward or backwards), or bend at the waist to lower than 30%. You might look at the floor, but technically, respect is shown — in the samurai fashion — by lowering your eyes below the line of sight to your sempai's eyes, while not lowering your gaze to where you couldn't see, from under your brows, the belt area (and hence the sword hilt, were there one) of the person(s) you're bowing to. It's critical that you hold this position for a long half second. If you don't feel this *work* as a twinge in your lower back muscles (as a result of the stopping and holding while keeping your spine straight), you likely have not bowed correctly.

3. Third, ONE part, your head alone. Leave your fists where they are, and stand back up to vertical (with your lower back muscles). Your fists will still be in front of you, facing forward at hip level, your arms slightly bent at the elbows, but you are once again standing upright. This is fudo dachi (your basic, ready stance).

Another Point or Two:
First, one can ONLY bow correctly if one's parallel feet are also pointing in the direction one is bowing. I.e. you can't bow correctly without fully facing the person you are bowing to.

Second, you can't bow while you're walking. You have to stop, bring your feet to parallel facing the direction you're bowing, bow, and then resume walking.

Third, you can't bow while you're on the floor, stretching. Stand up, face the direction you're bowing, and bow, before sitting back down.

So, when *are* you supposed to bow?

Not only every time you greet your sempai, but *every time you enter a space where your sempai is, or every time your sempai enters your space, no exceptions.* I'll help you with a couple of examples:

Your sempai enters the room where you are, you (stand up, and) bow.

You enter the room where your sempai is, you stop and bow.

Your sempai approaches you from the other side of a large room: when he/she approaches (even if just walking by), you (stand up and) face him/her, and bow.

You walk across a large room to where your sempai is (even if you're just waking past him/her), you stop and bow.

You excuse yourself from your sempai's presence for just a second and then come back: You bow when leaving, and you bow when returning.

The novice student might ask, when do I *not* bow?

The answer: Never.

Please bow *every time you enter a space where your sempai is, or every time your sempai enters your space.* Consider #1, *Fight to Be First.* Now ask yourself: *Are* you fighting to be the most respectful if you pick and choose and *sometimes* decide NOT to show a gesture of respect?

Now, of course your sempai might be annoyed (or embarrassed) by your bowing under certain circumstances, and he/she might tell you to not bow in that certain circumstance. That's okay, but can you, as the koohai, ever decide on your own the time when you're supposed to make an exception?

No.

The basic rule should be that your sempai should never tell you not to bow (even under special circumstances) until you show yourself to be strongly committed to the rule. Once you show that you've got it, however, the sempai is likely to tell you to chill out a little bit, particularly if you're in public or coming and going many times.

But be careful!

If you "chill out a little bit" because you've earned it, you need to be careful you're not influencing your koohais to do the same before they've earned it. You're also responsible for them! If they see you not bowing, they will be confused unless it's clear why you're not.

This discussion continues in #51, *When Do I Gain Enough Seniority That I Don't Have to Follow One of These Principles Anymore?*

You'll read that the critical turning point is when it becomes clear to your sempai that you feel more uncomfortable NOT performing the gestures of respect than you do performing them. If you skip one, one time, because you're too tired to do it, for example, you've shown that all of it is a bother for you that you'd rather not be doing in the first place, you've shown your sempai your true stripes, and your sempai is likely to watch you bow, and whether or not you do, for the next 100 or so times you're supposed to. It's about then that he/she will start to forget that you didn't bow to him/her that one time, so many weeks before.

This is serious business, folks, and YOU should instigate a move upwards in frequency in your dojo, even if your sempais seem less interested in this rule than I suggest I am by writing this passage. It's not me, of course! Imagine that every time you bow (or fail to bow), you're bowing (or failing to bow) to Mas Oyama himself. He would see you bow (or fail to bow) to your sempais and feel it himself, just as acutely as if he had been the one you were bowing (or supposed to be bowing) to.

Consider also that, as an instructor, teaching the student to bow — to ME! — is one of the hardest challenges I face. I tell the student, "You have to bow when you greet your teacher," and the average unprepared American student is at risk of thinking, "Hmmm, this guy wants me to subjugate myself to him so he can feel big."

But, oh, if they only knew!

In my case, I was the only American uchi deshi (residential student) of Mas Oyama to train under him for an extended period of time. I have no choice but to try to propagate the correct dojo traditions. I am conscience bound to do so. I bow to all *my* sempais, after all! When my students bow to me, I don't think, "I'm so great," I think, "Look! I'm finally succeeding to teach karate correctly in America. Mas Oyama would be proud to see it!" When my students, on the other hand, fail to bow to me, I don't think, "This jerk didn't show me the proper due," I think, "Oh my gosh, I'm still failing. Mas Oyama would be so disappointed."

So, please.

It's not about me. It's about Budo karate. You came to the dojo to learn Budo karate?

Then here's how it's done.

37. Think Three Times Before You Speak: If That's Hard for You, Shut Up!

One of the most valuable lessons my first teacher (Mas Oyama's nephew) taught me as a young teenager (and not only because I was a teenager, but also because I was an American) was to "shut up!"

"Use your eyes," he would say, "use your ears. Learn to think three times before you speak! Don't ask stupid questions."

And then, inevitably, I would ask some stupid question anyway, and he would say, "Shut up! I told you, think three times, and then don't ask if you can use your eyes and your ears, and know the answer on your own!"

After learning that lesson—and it took me three years!—I would only say that it is ALSO your duty to make sure that you ask questions when you have them. You just have to apply this mentality to make sure your questions are important, and that you're asking them under the correct circumstances.

As it says in the title of this section, if it turns out you're failing to curtail your tendency to blurt out whatever's on your mind all the time, just *shut up* for a while (a couple of weeks, maybe even?), use your eyes and your ears, and see what you can get without blurting out questions on a whim. Blurting things out on a whim is an American trait. We are a young people (a young country) and we tend to be impatient, and we want things NOW. Yet to other, older cultures, like those of Japan and Korea, in which the people use their senses to *read* people far more than we do here in America, Americans tend to be fairly annoying for just blurting out what's on their mind.

Remember that in order to learn Budo karate, we have to learn something about Eastern culture. Most of karate we will do less well unless we do it through the culture that created it.

One quick story:

I once had a couple of teenagers with developmental difficulties as students. Day after day, the second I would walk into the dojo, they would run up to me and compete to ask me some question or tell me something about their day. Of course that's somewhat endearing, and you should always want to be closer to your teacher. The closer you are (the more affinity between you), the more you will learn. But remember the way to do this is *through* the rules of etiquette, and that includes thinking three times before you speak. Your teacher would rather see you bow properly, get to the business of training, and/or preparing for class, and then ask the questions later if they don't get answered on their own during the class period.

38. Be Strong to Become Strong

A huge degree of *strength* comes from a decision (or natural tendency) to behave strong. In a sense, the person who *behaves strong* does in fact become immediately stronger.

This is different, of course, from pretending to be strong, or fooling oneself, putting on airs, or being cocky. One can only become stronger, physically, through a regimen of hard physical training, rest, and good food to eat.

However, there is also a HUGE psychological element to strength, and definitely to one's capacity for getting physically stronger, and a single decision as to how one behaves can have a HUGE impact.

For example, the H-type student (see #5, *The Toes-Not-Heels Dojo*), could conceivably read this book, have a resultant eureka moment, realize that the difference between an H and a T is just a decision to behave like one, and then, all of a sudden, in an instant that student would become 100% stronger, and thus able to develop *physically* 100% more efficiently.

There's also confidence, and opening the doors to it by deciding to behave confidently, and how much power it lends to your actions and executions *in fact*. Consider the student punching a pine board to practice board breaking. The fearful one pulls his/her punch and as likely as not fails, whereas the confident one punches without inhibition and succeeds (provided the stunt was also *physically* possible given the material and the motion). In this case, the punch was *actually*, physically more powerful, just because of a frame of mind.

Now, consider that board break as training.

Consider the two punches. One student punches a makiwara board or sand bag with the confident punch 1000 times per day for 365 days; the other student strikes the same piece of equipment the same number of times with the physically reduced, fearful punch. Which one makes greater gains?

Clearly, the one whose *behavior* is stronger not only punched stronger, but also *became* stronger during the one-year period.

Maybe fear vs. confidence is harder to change than just making a single decision, but there are hundreds of ways you can decide to behave stronger that will have a similar effect. How about deciding to sit up straight when sitting in seiza, and standing still when standing in fudo dachi? The H-type student who does will immediately get stronger, both in terms of immediate performance and in terms of an ability to get stronger.

Study this book. It's like a recipe for strong behavior. A lot of the ways the beginner behaves weakly are a surprise to them, because a lot of what's presented here is counterintuitive due to the cultural difference.

Learn the principles presented here, and you'll understand exactly how to define strong behavior in the dojo.

If you understand it, it should be relatively easy to implement.

If you do, you will have made yourself stronger simply by deciding to behave that way.

Not only will you perform stronger immediately with the current set of physical attributes that you have, but you'll also develop those physical attributes faster from now on.

Do you want to spend three years and be exceptional, or the same amount of time and only be mediocre?

Of course you'd prefer the former, so it's very important:

Be strong, therefore, to become strong.

39. Hang the Dog, Leave Him at Home, Drive Him Out of the Dojo!

I'm a little bit conflicted about including some of this content, because I'm not sure to what extent my encountering this problem has to do with the disadvantaged demographic I work with through the nonprofit that I run. In #14, *React Inversely to Hardship 1*, I have already broached the subject.

It is important for EVERY student, however, to read this section carefully, because even if, as you start reading, you think this doesn't apply to you — "That's not MY demographic," you might say — I'm going to take the discussion to a point where it will apply to you as well. The content here applies to all students, but I'll use those with one particular disadvantage in order to make my point more accessible.

Please read carefully.

Let's define *hangdog* first. It's a term that one of my students brought up and that we adopted into our dojo vocabulary:

> Hangdog: *To assume the demeanor of a beaten dog. To show with one's posture and facial expression anguish or defeat, and then, in some cases, when that first attempt fails to invoke the sympathy reaction that person seems to expect, an angry or overly proud secondary response, usually in the form of an involuntary facial expression of anger, or false pride.*

In a different type of disadvantaged student, this might also manifest itself in his/her eyes as they gloss over with what could become, at any moment, tears. In a third type, the student might *blank out* and stop responding to subsequent instructions, revealing that he/she is having so much difficulty processing being singled out for the first failure that he/she no longer seems to understand English.

Either way, this is a student who is accustomed to a reaction of demoralization. Either that student has been beaten down outside the dojo, probably in his or her youth, or that person has grown up in a household or community that's been beaten down, so that the student has absorbed the lesson from elders and peers that that's an appropriate response to being made to face their personal limitations. In the case of my inner-city dojo, I even fear that some have learned that response *in the dojo*, absorbing it from other students surrounding them who also have that reaction.

Of course it's hard not to be filled with grief to behold, particularly, an individual who actually has been beaten down, but that student, as well, has to learn to overcome, because it's exactly that kind of reaction to facing challenges that will keep them from achieving. In other words, their symptom becomes a greater cause of failure than whatever the cause was that led them to the symptom in the first place.

The dojo has to be the one place, for the sake of that truly disadvantaged student, that mounts a unified, powerful charge to maintain an environment in which there is no refuge for a hangdog response to A correction. This is even more important for the larger group, those who learned that kind of reaction not because they've personally been beaten down, but because they've grown up around enough people who have so that they believe a hangdog response to be an acceptable type of response to have.

And here's where this section starts to apply to even the non-disadvantaged student.

Everyone faces criticism in the dojo—and sometimes that criticism is sharp—but it's critical that you, as a student of Budo karate, respond to that criticism in the correct way.

"Your stance isn't deep enough," your teacher might say, and you have two possible ways to respond. "Osu! Sensei, I'll fix it!" you might say, and you immediately lower your stance, and are filled with excitement since you realize you have a teacher who cares enough to notice, and knows how to make you stronger, and is willing to challenge you to push your limits in the quest for better strength and health. On the other hand, you might respond "Osu! Sensei, I'll fix it!" because you know you have to, but on the inside you're sad that you *got criticized* again, or mad at the person who wasn't sympathetic enough and made you feel that way.

The important point to make here is that ALL criticism issued in the dojo is issued *to make you better* and *to make the dojo stronger*. All of it, therefore, is a gift. There's no confusion about this in the Japanese dojo. But in the American one—where every individual is so accustomed to doing things in an individual way—there seems to be some confusion.

So, you are the T-type student, the Alpha adult, and you think you don't respond this way?

Excellent! If that's the case, help your teacher out!

Make a concerted effort to respond to all criticism—even when it's sharp!—in such a powerful, positive, and humble way that it drives the *hangdog* out of the dojo!

In one recent class, I corrected an Alpha-type adult student (the opposite of the disadvantaged youth) because he was concentrating so hard on himself that he didn't realize he was out of sync with the other students (they were all punching with their left hands, let's say, and he was punching with his right). He was strong enough to be supporting his dojo by looking beyond himself, but instead he was helping only himself, by looking only at his own technique. In doing so, in fact, he had become a part of the dojo's H population during a time when all students were struggling to learn a new, complex motion.

"Careful, you're embarrassing yourself!" I told him. It was a harsher critique than he was accustomed to (as a proud Alpha-type adult), and his involuntary, spur-of-the-moment response was a flashed look of indignation towards me, his teacher.

It was involuntary, but, clearly, it was the exact opposite of the humble reaction expected in the Budo karate dojo.

To continue the story, lo and behold, a second student, his sempai, who'd been around a lot longer (but still not very long yet), saw him have that reaction — and mirrored it a moment later when I criticized her for being off count when *she* should have been prioritizing the dojo rather than herself. She'd never responded that way until she saw him do it. I don't think either student was aware. Both cases were minor, and have not been repeated because both are very good students, but it does go to show you that even the strongest of the strong are not immune to having this kind of reaction. Clearly, though, even the strongest students have to fight to prevent this from becoming part of their dojo culture, exactly because it clearly is part of our Western culture. Just like we fight to be first in all things, we also have to fight to be first in humility, even in the face of sharp criticism. If senior students chronically start flashing around looks of indignation, mightn't it adversely affect the new students by inducing them to acquire such a response themselves?

"Thank you, Sensei, may I have another?" the Japanese student says when whacked. "How dare this guy whack me!" thinks the American student who doesn't practice seeing the other side of the coin.

Be careful though! Be always humble! Your teacher has been at this for 30 years longer than you. He/she knows a thing or two you don't know. Trust that he/she's got a good reason to be as sharp with you as he/she was. Swallow your pride, and appreciate the correction. In the case of the above two students, why did the correction need to be sharp?

Exactly because those students were *sharply* focused so hard on figuring something out internally that it took a sharp critique to jar their heads out of the sand.

Maybe on another level, for that matter, the lesson WAS the sharp correction. You were showing your inability to deal with pressure, because you weren't aware of the students around you, so your teacher showed you what real pressure was. Yet your flashed look of indignation revealed more personal shortcomings than just that, didn't it, because, in the end, both students know that their teacher is on their side, right?

Excellent! Now everyone knows what you have to work on!

Easier said than done?

No, I think it IS easy, provided the student is prepared, and reading this section should be sufficient preparation for most students.

Just remember that aggressive, teary, or blank responses to sharp criticism in the dojo are inappropriate, but that sharp criticism IS sometimes appropriate, and it's not yours to decide when.

Imagine this easy scenario.

You're the Alpha adult, usually the strongest of the T-type students.

I tell you that your stance is weak, and you agree, you're humble, you're grateful, but the statement catches you off guard because you thought your stance was fine. Instead of saying "Osu! Sensei, I'll fix it," you're silent as you look down at your own stance to try to figure out what's wrong with it.

Yes, your intention was correct, yes, your heart was in the correct place, but your reaction was not. By your silence, you taught the *hangdog* in the room, the one who really is disadvantaged, that even you can have a muted reaction to criticism.

How about this scenario?

I tell you that your stance is weak, and you say "Osu! Sensei, I'll fix it!" and you do fix it, but two minutes later you've allowed your thinking to stray and you're back to the same poor stance again. Your teacher, who tends to see EVERYTHING, sees the at-risk student watching you and realizing that your stance is weak again, so I tell you again and you correct it again. What have you taught the at-risk student?

You've got it. You've taught him/her that even you, the pro-social Alpha, can resist the authority figure who is your teacher. You were absent-minded, not belligerent, but to the at-risk student, you appeared belligerent, a reaction that that student understands all too well.

So how do you drive out the *hangdog*, and how do you drive it out of yourself?

First of all, keep yourself powerful, and, above all, 100% humble and 100% compliant in the face of your teacher's or sempai's corrections.

Second, provide no refuge. Make sure the *hangdog*-type student knows you disapprove. Make sure your reaction is not a sympathetic one. Are you going to coddle him or her? Don't do it! In an isolated case it might be the charitable thing to do, but in the broader sense of helping not only that student but also many more in the future, make sure you don't provide that kind of refuge.

Sure, *encourage* that student after class by helping him/her to gain perspective. But make the dojo a *hangdog*-free zone. The dojo may lose a *hangdog*-type student or two in the process of becoming an institution that operates in such a way that the *hangdog* of the future can learn, by absorbing it from those around them, that they don't have to respond that way.

By your steadfastness, the *hangdog* student of the future can learn to overcome.

It's an excellent opportunity for you to get stronger!

Learn *tough love*.

Drive the *hangdog* out of the individual by showing how opposite you can be, not how sympathetic.

40. Example First, Words Second

I've cited in a previous section how it's your job to *encourage* your koohais (see #29, *Encourage Your Koohais, Don't Be the Koohai That Needs Encouraging*).

When one of your koohais is in the wrong place at the wrong time, you are responsible. When he/she is supposed to answer "Osu!" and doesn't, you are required to flag it. When he/she kicks with his/her right leg, but is supposed to be kicking with the left, it's your job to fix it. The colored-belt student who is blind to his/her koohais should in fact not have a colored belt. To be blind to one's koohais is to suggest, "I only care about me," which is ironic, because to "only care about me," in a Budo karate dojo, is to make the dojo weaker, and a weaker dojo can only make a weaker individual.

That said, consider that students learn very little from what you tell them, compared to how much they learn, how quickly, from what they see you doing, particularly if you're their sempai. It's therefore HOW you behave that's the far more important concern for you as a role model. The expression "actions, not words" most certainly applies here.

If you're a T-type student (See #5, *The Toes-Not-Heels Dojo*), as every sempai should be, and you're training in proximity to an H-type student, train harder yourself, respond *inversely* to the energy *sinkhole* next to you, and you'll have a bigger effect than you would by merely snapping at them to train harder.

Finally, and it's kind of a no-brainer, consider whether your koohais are likely to discipline themselves to do something you tell them to do when you don't do it yourself.

Of course they won't!

How many times does a sempai have to tell his/her koohai, "Answer with 'Osu!'" to make up for one single time that the koohai sees that same sempai fail to do just that? Five? Ten?

One hundred?

If your teacher is trying to get a group of beginners to answer "Osu!" and they see you, their sempai, miss even one opportunity to do so, does it not teach them all immediately that answering with "Osu!" is, in fact, optional?

It's so easy to learn, "Oh, I don't have to say 'Osu!' all of the time, I just have to say 'Osu!' MOST of the time!"

All this, perhaps, is just an alternate perspective on concepts already presented. If you're *fighting to be first* in all things at all times, you won't ever be the weak role model, right?

Please do note, however, how destructive it can be to YOUR training environment when you fail to be the correct kind of role model.

41. Get Your Sempai's Back, Get Your Teacher's!

If you walked out of a club and saw someone jump one of your friends, would you charge in to help your friend?

Of course you would!

Even if it was just by separating the two angry fighters, or calling the police, or whatever the situation required, you would be inclined to help your friend, would you not?

What if it was a family member that was getting jumped?

In the same way, you should start to think of your dojo-mates as this kind of family or friend, and you should fight to stand up for them.

This is perhaps obvious.

What I'm going to say next might not be.

In the dojo, your teacher and your sempais are fighting, always, to raise the standard to where the dojo, collectively, becomes stronger. They are fighting to make the students stronger fighters, but they're also fighting to make each individual stronger physically, mentally, and spiritually so hopefully no one will ever have to (actually) fight, and so that you and your dojo will be your community's most successful members.

What kind of help, after all, are you more likely to garner from your friends at the dojo? Defense in a fight, sure, but isn't it more likely that your friends from the dojo might help you in other ways, like helping you to get a job, helping you to load your moving truck on a Saturday, all the kinds of things friends and family do for one another? Would you rather have the help of the friend who is physically, mentally, and spiritually stronger, or the one who's not? How about in a real crisis when it really matters?

Of course, the more able everyone is, the more your friends will be able to support you and vice versa.

So far, all this is pretty obvious.

The part that doesn't always seem to be so obvious in the Western dojo, however, is a koohai's getting his/her sempais' back in terms of the hard lessons that they're trying to teach, class by class, in order to raise the standard and make you and your classmates stronger.

As unbelievable as it might seem reading this, I've seen it happen that somehow the Western personality inclines the karate student, in some unfortunate cases, to get his/her classmate's back — or so he/she believes — by supporting that classmate in failures, in terms of giving moral support for "it being okay to fail sometimes," rather than supporting that student's ability to succeed!

Open your mind, and clue in to what your teacher is trying to teach in any one given training session. See #44, *Parallel Lessons: The Surface and the Esoteric, Identify the Task at Hand, Fulfill It, Support Its Delivery in the Eyes of Your Koohais*. If your teacher is any good, he/she's probably teaching far more than just kicks and punches. Your teacher is probably teaching something about character, or attitude, or manner, or some other attribute that's also present in the activity right beside all the kicks and the punches. I can assure you that all of MY lessons, these days, are about the content of this book: I struggle to teach the correct Budo karate attitude, knowing that my students' kicks and punches will become far stronger as a result.

Clue in to what your teacher's actual lesson is, and make sure you've got your teacher's back.

Perhaps your teacher is teaching blocks for roundhouse kicks, but he's also, behind that, trying to get students to behave more confidently, or, in another case, to pay better attention. If you, present in this class, only care about the blocks against the roundhouse kick, but are either not doing them confidently, or your mind is wandering and you are perceived as not paying powerful attention, in terms of setting a strong example for your koohais, you've not got your teacher's back, have you?

See how this works?

Bring your training up a notch. Open your mind to it being something a bit more serious than the dance class at the community center. Consider that this group you're training with is a group that would fight for you if you'd fight for it.

Then consider the situation in which you should fight.

Of course you'd fight to protect them physically if they were ever in danger. But are you also fighting for them in the dojo night after night in order to support your teacher's lesson?

If you're the Budo karateka, you are!

See #19, *You Ask Yourself, "Am I Important? Does My Teacher Value Me?"* and remember that the extent to which someone will fight for you depends also on the extent to which you're standing up for them. If your personality is such that you'd rather stand up for that bum who doesn't want to make a stronger set of life choices, i.e. if you want to support that student's decisions that keep him/her a bum, all power to you!

You'll wind up with bums for friends, and all your karate training will have been for naught!

If, on the other hand, you discipline yourself to stand up for those who are pursuing a higher ideal by remaining true to that ideal yourself, you'll wind up with friends who are the most successful folks in your community. You'll be friends with the folks who are making a difference, those who are working tirelessly to reduce your community's percentage of those who have such a poor self-image.

42. Respond to ALL Challenges

You'll have a leg up here in terms of understanding this principle if you review first #25, *Challenge vs. Command*. Your teacher or sempai often tells you what to do as he/she guides your workout, but he/she often prefers to *challenge you* to do something better, or stronger, or more often.

#25 points out the importance of *clueing in* to those challenges, and acting on them as if they're commands. The Budo karate student does, the fantasy karate student does not. The T-type student does, the H-type does not. Of course we don't always win! We don't succeed at all challenges, and that's okay. It's the student who tunes them out, however, and thinks, "That didn't apply to me," who's in the wrong dojo.

You have to hear the challenges.

You have to let them appeal to your sense of dignity. Feel them in your gut, and act on them to the best of your ability. It's counterintuitive, perhaps, but if you respond to your teacher's or sempai's challenges, your training becomes easier. And you certainly get far stronger.

However, in the Budo karate system, you should also challenge *each other*, and you should clue in to THOSE challenges as well.

Having trained in Mas Oyama's dojo in Japan, it's amazing to me to see, in my own American dojo, a ferociously motivated student training right next to an unmotivated one. The T-type student kicks so hard his/her dogi pops, that student is soaked with sweat, and screaming his/her head off when it's time to kiai, and that student never misses an instruction or fails to respond to a challenge. And yet the H-type student, standing so close that he/she is getting sprayed with sweat, crawls along at a snail's pace, as if there's no connection between the two.

And therein, perhaps, lies the cultural difference. In the American dojo, often there's *not* a connection.

In Japan, you can't train next to someone like that without getting revved up yourself. The shame would be too great. The Japanese student would be so embarrassed to be seen not working hard next to someone who was that he/she would be unable to deny a fire rising up within, and he/she would fight to match the student alongside.

And this was men, women, and children, folks! It was the young and the old, the athletic and the nonathletic!

It doesn't have so much to do with physical ability; it has everything to do with attitude!

Yes, I trained in Mas Oyama's world headquarters dojo, and there were some champions there, but most of the student body were moms and businessmen and schoolkids, just like they are in my dojo in America, and yet they all, always, responded to challenges, not just those of their teacher, but also challenges of this type, the unspoken ones issued by their classmates.

If someone next to you kiais louder than you, you have to fight to match it and surpass it. If someone next to you has a deeper stance, you have to fight to make yours deeper. If someone next to you never misses an instruction, you must feel ashamed to miss an instruction, and fight harder to make sure you never miss another.

If the student next to you kicks 40 times per minute, are you really content to only kick 20? You might not be able to suddenly do 40, but fighting to be at the front of the curve, you'll probably up your average to 30 by increasing your commitment to the task.

If you're not fighting to be at the front, something's missing.

In my new dojo, I love to see students clueing into this in terms of responding with "Osu! Sensei, I'll fix it!" when I correct them as a class. In Mas Oyama's dojo, we used "Osu! Shitsurei-shimashita! (Osu! I was very rude to make that mistake!)," but I've decided not to teach my students this Japanese phrase. They use, "Osu! I'll fix it!" instead.

I'll give you an example.

Students are practicing kata but the grid is weak (the lines in which they're training), and they should know better, and so I tell them so.

"Fix the lines, please," I'll say, and this is something they should have taken care of by themselves, so, "Osu! Sensei, I'll fix it!" the T-type students respond. But then, the cool thing in this particular class of adult students is that then, inevitably, a second chorus of students, those that are more at the H end of the spectrum, echo, "Osu! Sensei, I'll fix it!" In other words, some percentage of the class didn't respond powerfully immediately, but they heard their classmates' power as a challenge that they could not deny, and then they respond.

And it's always better late than never.

So, what about the student in that class that STILL kept his/her mouth shut?

You got it. That one's still missing the Budo karate boat. The student who simply tunes out the student body's inherent challenges should adjust his/her attitude.

If that's you, please do from this day forward.

43. Imitate Someone Strong, Not the Other Way Around

For the T-type student (see #5, *The Toes-Not-Heels Dojo*), this is a no-brainer.

You should always compare yourself to the strongest in the room and aspire to be like them, not like the ones in the room who are weaker, more timid, or slower. In fact, in the Budo karate system, you should aspire to be BETTER than the strongest person in the room (See #1, *Fight to Be First*) to the extent that, if there's not a strong person in the room, you have to fight to be stronger than the strongest person you know, but who is not present.

We've used this chart, time after time.

            T H T H T T
            H T H H T T
            T T H T H T

In this class, who are the H's supposed to aspire to be like? Of course, they should aspire to be like the T's. If they don't, it's not Budo karate. (To be sure, as stated earlier, this is a difficult training environment, since it's a 50% T and 50% H class. It's easy for the H's to be confused and copy the other H's. It is their nature, after all. Rolling stones gather no moss, but H's apparently like sprouting moss. We've already established that this is a challenged class, and that it's therefore all the more important for the T's to *turn on the animal* in an effort to clear away some of the moss, and win an H or two over to the correct side of the divide. See #15, *React Inversely to Hardship 2: Turn on the Animal!*)

Consider this class, in which the high numbers are the best of the T's and the low numbers are the worst of the H's:

            9 1 7 3 8 8
            2 8 1 5 9 7
            9 8 3 8 1 8

I intentionally left out most 4's, 5's and 6's, because that's usually what the H/T divide looks like. Students are usually not right in the middle, they're either on the ball, or they're dead on their feet. But what about that one 5 right in the middle of the class? That is a fence rider. Which way is that student going to go? Is he going to be inspired by the 7's, 8's, and 9's, or lured down the wrong path by the 1's, 2's, and 3's?

Hopefully, the reader will start to see how important it is to remain on the correct side of the fence. Concentrate on yourself first. Fight to be first. Be the T-type student. Fight to win over the 5's and the 6's, and over time the 1's, 2's, and 3's will be so lonely in their "H-ness" that they'll start to get with the program. Remember, there should be no H's in the dojo. Be strict, be ferocious. Kill the moss.

But remember!

It all starts with YOU. Keep yourself strong first. After that, make sure you take away weaker students' chances for refuge.

44. Parallel Lessons: The Surface and the Esoteric, Identify the Task at Hand, Fulfill It, Support Its Delivery in the Eyes of Your Koohais

Be sure that you've read #8, *Drink Some, Spit Some? You'll Fail*, in which I introduce the surface lesson and *the esoteric*. Read also, perhaps, the "I Don't Care About Your Kicks and Punches!" section of the introduction.

Imagine your teacher rolls a ball, at a steady pace, from one end of the dojo towards the other. The black belt in the room steps in and gives it a gentle nudge along the same course when it starts to slow down, and then the brown belt steps in and follows suit. The ball had started to slow, but the brown belt gave it a third additional gentle nudge to help keep its gentle momentum constant. And next comes the green belt, and so on, until students at all levels have participated in the same unified task, and the ball reaches the other end of the room just as the teacher intended.

Now imagine a second case where the teacher initiates the same task, but the students ignore it and don't help, and the ball rolls off course and then to a stop. OR, conversely, the ball starts to slow, and the black belt student comes along and shoves it, but he/she shoves it too hard, or at the wrong angle, so it veers off course. The next student, thinking that veering along that new course is correct, comes along and shoves it further off in that direction, and it speeds up. The teacher then issues a verbal correction, and so yet another student comes along and overreacts and kicks the ball so hard in the other direction it flies across the room and bounces off the wall.

Now imagine that rolling ball is a lesson the teacher had hoped to convey. In Case A, all the students in the room *clue in* to the teacher's intent, and are therefore able to support the lesson through their choices of how to do what when. In Case B, however, the students remain clueless to the lesson, and the teacher is disappointed throughout because he/she gets no help. The teacher is having to carry all the sempais just like he is having to carry all the white belts. There is no hierarchy in the dojo. The teacher might as well have started from scratch with a group of first-timers.

Of course, the teacher, too, in this case bears some responsibility. If he/she has promoted students in the role of sempai who have so little clue about what their responsibility is, the teacher probably should have prepared them better before giving them belts.

To make the dojo operate like the Budo karate dojo should, it's important to understand, first, that you must *clue in* to your teacher's intent in the given lesson, and, second, that it's every student's job to act accordingly to support the delivery of that lesson. Perhaps the best way to ensure you're successful here is to 1. develop the priority, simply by reading here, to stay aware of what your teacher wants to see, and 2. understand that there's often a parallel lesson that's *esoteric*, i.e. one that's the teacher's greater intent that lies behind the more obvious one of the activity at hand.

For example, imagine that you're participating in a kata workout.

Your teacher is teaching a mid-level kata like Pinan 4, and several of your koohais are learning it for the first time. Ah, but look again! If you've been concentrating on your teacher's words, if you're listening for the *how*, not the *what* (see #2, *It's the* How, *Silly, Not the* What), you've caught on to the fact that the teacher is actually teaching something far more important to everyone's future than simply Pinan 4. He/she is teaching the class *how better to learn kata* in the future. That is: your teacher is providing shortcuts in the form of advice on how to cut through the mundane of the *what*, thus taking you straight through to the *how* of learning kata as your teacher has learned, through years of experience, works best.

In another situation, imagine you're doing pushups. Of course the exercise at hand is pushups, but if you listen, you might hear that your teacher is rather teaching you how to approach the challenge of doing more pushups than you think you can with strong spirit. Perhaps he/she's relating how that kind of *more than you think you can do* approach will help you beyond the dojo, in your workplace, at school, and more. In both situations, there's a surface exercise and a deeper lesson.

How can you support the deeper lesson if you've reduced yourself to only hearing, or caring about, the surface one?

The important point to understand here is that it is your duty, as a Budo karateka, to *channel*, not deflect or resist, your teacher's teaching—and not just the part of it you like or are comfortable with. (Some students resist what scares them. Some students come in thinking they're going to get just kicks and punches, and then find themselves resistant when they find out Budo karate is more serious than just that.) If you don't *clue in* to what your teacher is teaching and behave in a way that helps deliver it, your teacher has a right to be disappointed, particularly if you are a student with rank. By remaining blind to the *something more*, you have shown that you don't have your teacher's back. See #41, *Get Your Sempai's Back, Get Your Teacher's!*

Here are three obvious ways you might clue in to your teacher's intent without having to have it all spelled out:

1. The Bare Suggestion, the "Eyes-Only" Instruction

Sometimes when teaching a class, I give a particularly *with-it* student an instruction with just a glance. I'm counting, for example, we're performing many reps of a continuous exercise, I'm about to reach ten, and I glance at the student who I want to resume the count, and — since he/she is a strong student — that student understands, and he/she starts over at one without breaking the rhythm.

Other students I've had, however, some with low confidence or creativity, get all *up in arms* when I suggest that they ought to know what I want them to do, even when I don't expressly tell them. This has to do largely with habit, I think. Some students figure out how to learn karate, or so they think, in just their first several weeks, and then just keep right on along struggling to learn in exactly that same way. The problem is that white belts learn karate in a much different way than a black belt should. The teacher DOES have to spell it all out for the white belt, while the black belt ought to be able to communicate with his/her teacher on a deeper level, sometimes without even so much as the glance described above.

Since this is (or can be) largely habit-based, think, given the *Toes-Not-Heels Dojo* description of #5, how important it is that new students witness their sempais communicating with their teacher at times in ways that aren't *all spelled out*. If it's the norm for your dojo for the student to tune in to "eyes only" instructions, the newest student, even, will learn to see them without having to struggle.

But that's "eyes only" instructions.

How ELSE might you read your teacher's intent?

2. Reading Your Teacher Based on a Long History Shared

If not verbally, if not visually, what other sources of guidance might you rely on?

That low-confidence student (who had poor role models him/herself) is up in arms again!

But if you've been in class with your teacher many times before—and the higher your rank the more times you will have been—it should start to become clear to you what your teacher's intent is, because of what you've seen your teacher's intent to be in the past in a similar set of circumstances.

And, yes, you are supposed to be able to read your teacher's intent based on this type of knowledge as well.

Imagine your teacher is teaching basic defenses against kumite techniques, and he/she calls you to the front of the class to help demonstrate. Your teacher doesn't address YOU, "Please kick me with front kick," but, rather, he/she addresses the class, explaining, "So . . . when your opponent kicks you with front kick . . ." In this case your teacher didn't tell you what to do, but you could infer from his/her describing a situation to the class that his intent was for you to kick him/her with a front kick so that your teacher could demonstrate the successful block. Right?

That part is pretty easy, because even though the verbal instruction wasn't direct, there was still a verbal clue.

However, it's amazing to me, when I bring students—sometimes senior students!—up to demonstrate with me at times, how clueless they can remain about my intent if they lack confidence. What is our purpose in front of the class? To fight? Of course not! It's to show the class how to block a front kick, right? So, in order to have a successful demonstration, I have to be able to demonstrate a successful block. Is that the time, therefore, for the student to try to land the blow at all costs? Of course not: the student should throw a correct kick, but also a kick that I *can* block so that the students see success. Is it time to kick me as hard as they can? Of course not! How rude! Or if the block is designed to *spin* the attacker (i.e. to deflect his/her attack aside and around), is it helpful to the demonstration for the student to resist being spun? What about the opposite case, when I'm showing the class how to *take down* an opponent and I would like to show somewhat of a realistic situation, but the student, overcompensating, throws him/herself to the floor like rag doll, without my having had to apply any pressure?

In this easy case, the student who is assisting in the instruction has to understand what the intent of the lesson is in order to know how to be a valuable partner, and if that student has been around to see that lesson taught over and over again, should the teacher really have to teach the demonstration partner how to demonstrate every time?

Of course not.

So, there are verbal instructions, instructions that come in the form of gestures or nods, and even optical "eyes only" instructions to reveal to you your teacher's intent. Now, we see that there are also patterns and prior experience. If you've seen your teacher teach something before, you should be able to identify what he/she is teaching when he/she starts teaching it again.

Easy, right?

3. *The Intuitive Read*

But we're not done yet.

You should also learn to read your teacher. You should lean to know your teacher so well that your intuition tells you what your teacher wants before he/she even has to tell you.

"Yikes!" that aforementioned student with limited confidence or creativity exclaims.

And I'm about to stop, and refer you to several other sections, after merely cautioning you to look for ways to read your teacher that aren't so obvious. Do imagine this scenario, though:

Pack hunters. Wolves or lions do it all the time while hunting. They *read* each other's intent and never pivot right when the pack needs them to pivot left.

Well, I'm here to tell you that humans can read each other, too, and your developing ability to read your teacher in the Budo karate dojo is a critical part of your training to get to where you can utilize all of your senses when it comes time to have to fight for your life.

* * *

Align your heart with your teacher's (not just your head), and you'll form a connection with your teacher that will allow you to communicate in ways that are far more subtle than having to have it laid out for you all the time in words.

Look for it, and you'll find it. If you're in the Budo karate dojo, you ARE required to try. Denying it, and telling yourself, "I just want to learn how to fight," disqualifies you from participation. Please visit the martial arts school down the street.

Please see #20, *The Deepening of Human Relationships.*

Please see #70, *Your Teacher Can Read YOUR Mind, Learn to Read your Teacher's.*

Please also see #71, *Telepathy? Hyper-Empathy?* And #72, *"Channel" Your Teacher's Teaching.*

Please also see #96, *Grasp Your Teacher's Priority, Understand your Teacher's Intent, See the Dojo through your Teacher's Eyes.*

45. Karate IS Your Teacher's Karate

"It's my way or the highway," your teacher tells you, and your teacher is correct.

For all intents and purposes, karate IS what your teacher tells you it is. There might be something more to it that you can get someday once you've moved on to another city, or another dojo, but as long as you're training in this dojo, Karate IS what your teacher tells you it is. If you look outside of that closed environment before first giving your heart and soul until you learn what dedication is, you cause damage to your own learning curve, and therefore to your dojo, by questioning and looking outside.

Perhaps you travel to fight in a tournament, and while you're there you see something new, a technique that worked, for example. You incorporate it into your training when practicing kumite. That's fine, because kumite is a time for improvisation. But, on the other hand, what if your teacher has told you to stand up and bow to your sempais when they enter your space, or when you enter theirs, but when you get to the tournament, you see other karate students not doing what your teacher has told you to do? Some of them are strong, and one of them even won the tournament.

What are you to do—idolize and imitate in all ways the *tough guy* who won the tournament?

Of course not. Do what your teacher told you. That's your karate.

Those other students are doing what their teacher told them. That's their karate.

The Budo karate spirit is to get your sempai's back in all cases, and to stand up for your dojo in all ways. If you're really distracted by such a thing and made to doubt, the reason why YOU didn't win the tournament was your doubt, not the fact that your teacher does some things differently.

What about a situation where you join the dojo having trained in another dojo first? Your prior teacher told you to hit all training partners hard, all the time, yet your new teacher is teaching that there are situations to hit hard in, and other situations to take it easy in. Yet, you LIKE hitting hard, and it seemed to work in your other dojo, so even though your new teacher is telling you how to participate as part of the team in your new dojo, you're stubbornly doing as you used to do.

Fairly rude, isn't it?

More than that, it's counter to the Budo karate code. You've disrespected your new sempais.

What if, on the other hand, you attend an international seminar, or a seminar between dojos, and your teacher's teachers or sempais are present? What are you to do if you learn something there?

The answer is quite easy.

If your teacher embraces it and tries to learn it and introduces it once you go back home to your dojo, then you should embrace it too. If your teacher does *not* embrace the new material, however, you still have to follow your own teacher first. Remember the surface lesson vs. the esoteric? It's the previous section. Read it again, and remember that there are many cases in the dojo in which your teacher has a reason for teaching the things that he/she teaches that he/she is not always able to make clear to you on a day-by-day basis.

The Budo karate way?

Follow your teacher first and always.

Read the previous section, #44, *Parallel Lessons: The Surface and the Esoteric, Identify the Task at Hand, Fulfill It, Support Its Delivery in the Eyes of your Koohais.*

What if, yet another situation, your teacher is trying to teach you some element of the Budo karate attitude present in this book, and it's hard for you? You're struggling, and your teacher is frustrated with your performance. One day you talk to your friend in another state who's learning karate from another teacher. That teacher believes that that aspect of Budo karate training shouldn't be pushed in the American dojo.

Ah ha! That's all the support you needed! "Maybe karate isn't what my teacher is telling me that it is!" you say.

Ah, but you'd be wrong.

You can't succeed that way. In YOUR dojo you can only succeed through your teacher's way. If you pick and choose, you'll fail.

What if your teacher tells you you have to wear colorful hats to class from now on? (Of course I don't know what teacher would, but to make a point, please imagine such a silly scenario.) You think that's stupid, so you mostly refuse, and only sometimes do what your teacher asked you to do.

I think you're probably starting to catch on. Yes, you've got it: you're failing. You can't succeed. Your days are numbered, and you're only in the way of the unity your teacher is seeking.

So what are you going to do about it?

You got it! You can either quit the dojo, or you can wear the hat.

Perhaps, for the beginner, the sooner he/she understands this fact, the better chance of success he/she will have once that student hits his/her first bump in the road, and finds him/herself questioning some lesson the teacher put forth.

In the Japanese Budo karate dojo, no one ever questions, at least never overtly.

In the Japanese dojo, the student is going to persevere and wear the hat for days and days and days before deciding, finally, that, since that student still can't understand why it's important, he/she is going to stop coming to that dojo, but with his/her head hung low for having failed.

In this case, amazingly, the student believes him/herself to have let his/her dojo down, not that his teacher was stupid for asking the students to wear colorful hats. The Japanese student thinks, "I failed to understand, and I couldn't overcome my pride and get with the program."

The American system is quite different, isn't it?

In the American system the student is already training at the dojo down the street, and saying rude things about the first teacher. Yet this is a symptom of why American karate is so much less than Japanese Budo karate.

Let me say it loud and clear!

To learn Budo karate, some of the lessons your teacher will ask you to face will baffle you, and some of them might even hurt to learn. One or two might really make you suffer.

Overcome that, though, and on the other side, you'll find a great truth.

"Oh, I see now!" you'll say the day you realize why it was important, and in that instant you'll get ten times stronger.

The Americanized student denies him/herself the chance of ever having that moment of surprise and wonder, because the American student tends to pick and choose. The American student tends to quit when the going gets rough, and go try and buy what he/she thinks he/she wants at the dojo down the street where *those* students are getting quick-fix karate lessons.

Read #8, *Drink Some, Spit Some? You'll Fail.*

46. How Hard Do I Hit?

For the director of an American dojo, I'm fairly proud of the fact that ALL of my students learn to hit hard (full contact, even!) during kumite without sustaining injury and without having their morale broken. In other words, all of my students, men, women, and children, learn kumite safely, in steps, in such a way that it becomes an activity that they enjoy, and that they can do safely.

Based on my experience training in Mas Oyama's dojo in Japan, there are three basic principles that I employ to set the level of contact so that all students learn to be comfortable with contact.

First, we make "soft targets" illegal during sparring. Soft targets include the face (for punches), the throat, the groin, the kneecaps, etc. Most of the legal targets in Kyokushin competition are either re-enforceable parts of the body (like torso and thighs, where fighters can build muscle to the point where they can take an amazing amount of punishment without suffering damage), or, in some cases, vulnerable parts (such as the head) where it *is* legal to kick because it becomes so rare that kicks land there. We're very careful to teach students how to protect this difficult target and don't let them let loose to fight hard until they can do it well.

Second, in my dojo, we employ levels of contact. There are four: light, light-heavy, heavy, and full contact. 1. In *light* kumite, students are required to touch their opponent with their strikes at speed, but there should be no sound of impact, i.e. they're not hitting the air, but they're striking (not in slow motion but) so softly that they're hitting little more than the surface of their opponent's clothing. 2. In *light-heavy* kumite, all strikes should produce a pitter-patter sound of impact, but should have no weight delivery. There is impact for the first time, but it's so gentle that aside from making a small thump, it never "moves" the body of the person struck, i.e. there is no shock to the opponent's body. 3. In *heavy* kumite, we start to use real power, in that the pitter-patter of tiny little strikes becomes heavier thuds of impact, and blows are allowed/expected to move your opponent's body. Here you have shock waves that rattle the skeleton. HOWEVER, in heavy kumite—and here's the key difference between it and full contact—both fighters are still working *with* each other, NOT to injure each other. You might deliver a very hard blow to the reinforced muscle of the chest, abdomen, or thigh, but you do it with a partner who's tough enough to take it, and if you know how to push through to break the rib, you don't.

If your opponent miscalculates and leaves his head wide open, and you could kick it if you wanted, you don't. It's counterintuitive for beginning students because the blows of heavy kumite become so powerful, but in heavy kumite the goal is to work *with* your partner in harmony to achieve a level of impact that does NOT injure. 4. In *full-contact* kumite, of course, then we remove that final restriction. In my dojo this is mostly the kumite of the belt test or the tournament, but in full-contact kumite the goal does become to injure sufficiently to break the opponent's will to fight. This occurs, however, at a level where the students have become so comfortable with blocks and heavy kumite that it's a gentle transition and nobody tends to get hurt or demoralized.

Third, in the dojo we have a strict rule for handling impact between students who are not matched in terms of body mass, ability, experience, or strength. Imagine the child sparring with the adult, for example, the black belt with the white belt, the (large) man with the (petite) woman, or the athletic with the nonathletic. In these pairs, there's no need to temper light or light-heavy kumite, but heavy and full-contact kumite change dramatically. In most cases the bigger/stronger student tempers his/her blows so as not to cause unnecessary injury or demoralization, and — here's the counterintuitive part! — the smaller/weaker student takes advantage of the situation to strike *harder*, if not as hard as they can.

NOTE! If you're the bigger/stronger/senior student, and you temper your blows in heavy kumite when working with the smaller/weaker/junior student, and if that student is a beginner who is unfamiliar with this concept, he/she is likely to follow your example and temper his/her blows even when he/she is not supposed to. If in this case, you allow them to, you will, in the case of my dojo, have failed to support what your teacher is trying to teach; you will have shown yourself to be a weak role model who does not have your teacher's back. In this case, please remember to insist, verbally, that your partner hit you harder. You're big, so you're safe, but if, when you temper your blows, your koohai doesn't hit hard, you're both practicing play karate instead of the real thing.

NOTE!! If you ARE the smaller/weaker/junior student, make sure your partner knows this principle before you let loose. If he/she is your sempai, he/she should answer your full-contact blows with ones that are slightly lighter. In the rare case, however, the new or H-type student will not be familiar with this set of expectations, and you might put yourself at risk by hitting too hard.

Remember that all of this talk of tempering blows has to do with levels of contact below full contact, practiced with the intent of making all students comfortable with hard kumite. There is, of course, no tempering of blows in the full-contact fight. (For more on safety and injuries, see #56, *Most* Injuries *in Karate Are Really Just Karate's Normal Aches and Pains*, and #62, *Budo Karate is for Every Body*.)

47. Unified Action Makes Karate Budo

I have deliberately chosen, here, to restate a point earlier made in order to drive it home. It is that important. Quoted from #1, *Fight to Be First*:

> *Consider:*
> *Your teacher asks you to line up for class. Everyone fights not to be last, by racing to be the first one to get to their places. Who wins? Well, probably no one. Almost everyone gets to their places in about the same time. This is a UNIFIED powerful action. Good for you! You're practicing Budo karate. The important thing is not being first—it's that everyone uniformly fights to be. What if 1/3 of the students take their time getting in line? What if another 1/3 don't know where to go and wait, always, for someone to tell them? This is a MIXED reaction: Some are strong, but most are weak. This class will fail. Sorry, it is not Budo karate.*

This is pretty clear, I think, but I will add the following now that the reader has made it about halfway through this book, and more of the concepts present are familiar ones:

The physical aspect of this is pretty easy once you apply yourself. Don't be last, don't be quietest, don't be weakest, don't be slowest. The mental aspect is a bit harder only because it might not be immediately obvious what your teacher is trying to get across.

Don't let yourself be the one who misses an instruction. Don't let yourself be one who misses a rule of etiquette. Don't let yourself be the one who focuses on the *what* at the expense of the *how*. Don't let yourself be the one that doesn't *clue in* to the esoteric, the more important lesson behind the lesson. Don't let yourself be the one that doesn't have your teacher's back. Don't let yourself be the one who acts disappointed / demoralized in the face of criticism. Don't be the one who tunes out the challenges issued either by your teachers, or by the intense students training near you.

Now, apply all of this, and every other principle explained in this book, to the concept quoted above in italics. If you fight not to be the one who drops the ball, and so does everyone else, you've got a dojo that is unified in its desire to have strong Budo karate attitude as well. Yes, you have to have a strong UNIFIED effort, but not only to be loud, or strong, or fast. You also have to develop a powerful unified effort behind everything else.

You have to fight to embody the spirit described in this book.

I fight for it in my dojo, but all too often I find myself alone in that fight.

Yet, I've never seen it before in America—not, I think, because Americans can't do it. But rather because they have difficulty grasping the cultural aspect of Budo karate spirit. That's why I've written this book. (Of course all of my students show me glimpses from time to time, but there's nothing Budo about *sometimes*. Budo has to be all the time!)

I've seen glimpses in OTHER countries, but any country that's not Japan must fight to be the best, also, and face the fact that there's always room for improvement. Even in Japan, I have seen groups training who are less than what existed in Mas Oyama's dojo. Mas Oyama himself observed this. He regularly decried how America was the worst place to try to introduce Budo; he cited OTHER dojos in Japan that were becoming Americanized, and told us how *Japanese* instructors he sent to America themselves changed to accommodate a new lesser American standard. Before anyone becomes offended that I'm criticizing American Kyokushin, however, please consider that according to the principles cited in this book, it is our DUTY to assume that our karate is less than it could be. If we think, instead, that it's all it was meant to be, we won't be able to improve it. To assume that we're doing it right is to take out the fight to be first.

Mas Oyama, who spent most of his latter years having given up on teaching Budo in America, would approve, I think.

I write this book-length definition of *how* to pursue Budo karate, and I can feel my teacher smile.

48. Don't Let Yourself Be the One Who . . .

This is perhaps another way of stating what this book suggests is the number-one core value of the Budo karate system. It can't be stated enough. See #1, *Fight to Be First.*

How does one ensure that he/she is not last?

Answer: He/she fights to be first.

Yet, fighting to be first might be a difficult concept for someone who, athletically for example, has never been first. How does one fight for something one's never had?

So, here's an alternative perspective, for those having difficulty.

Make it a matter of pride. *Don't let yourself be the one who* is last.

Don't let yourself be the one who is slowest.

Don't let yourself be the one who is quietest (when a powerful verbal response or strong kiai is required).

Don't let yourself be the one who learns something the slowest.

Don't let yourself be the one who didn't hear the instruction.

Don't let yourself be the one who didn't follow the instruction.

Don't let yourself be the one who is focusing on the *what* rather than the *how*.

Don't let yourself be the one who doesn't follow the rules of etiquette perfectly.

Don't let yourself be the one who doesn't respond to challenges.

Don't let yourself be the H in a room full of T's, or even in a room full of H's!

Don't let yourself be the one who isn't close to your teacher.

Don't let yourself be the one who comes *back* into training with the same level of confusion with which you left the last class regarding a complex series of motions.

Don't let yourself be the one who doesn't *own* the complex exercises you've been shown.

You can re-state every single principle in this book by saying, "I won't let myself be the one who . . ."

Remember that *the trick* to maintaining a minimum level of performance in the Budo karate dojo is to develop a sense of shame vs. honor that mimics the Japanese one: "It is an indignity for me to be the one who . . ." and "I feel honorable, and I know in my bones that I am, when I'm sure that I am the one who successfully . . ."

49. It's Your Dojo, Not My Dojo: If That Was in Your Living Room, Would You Walk Right Past It?

If your dog or cat pooped in the middle of your living room carpet, would you leave it there? Would you sit there watching TV and playing video games waiting for it to dry up and stop stinking?

Of course you wouldn't.

You'd clean it up, and spray some air freshener, right?

Please consider failures in the Budo karate code, the principles outlined in this book, to be like something equally foul dumped in the middle of YOUR dojo, and make sure you clean it up.

I do.

At least I fight to do so every day of my life.

If I see a student who is not fighting to be first, and they are a beginner, and if the role models present are poor, I understand that student's challenge, and do my best to compassionately clean up the mess.

However, if I see a senior student *who should know better,* because they've been training with me long enough to know, and they're still failing to fight to be first because they've got a *strong today—weak tomorrow* attitude, I do in fact see that attitude in the middle of my dojo floor as a stain that needs to be removed. My respect for that person diminishes if it becomes clear that he/she does not want to learn.

Please do not underestimate this point, and make sure you're not one of those with an attitude that's in the way.

Of course sometimes I'm still patient with folks who have been around long enough to know better. Other times I'm harder. But what everyone should understand is that what will never change is my expectation that students get with the program. If it really does become clear (and sometimes it does) that that student really doesn't want to change, I really do start to see that student as an impediment to progress, and if that's you, you'll likely start to know it.

Remember that I am conscience bound to achieve and maintain a certain minimum standard. If you understand and embody this book, you're golden, so don't worry! How important are you to your dojo? That depends on you. (See #19, *You Ask Yourself, "Am I Important? Does My Teacher Value Me?"*)

If you are not fighting to get with the program, you are in the way, and you should go away. If you are fighting, on the other hand (you might not be perfect, but at least you're fighting to be!), then you are a pleasure to have in the dojo (even if you're not perfect). Your goal and mine are unified, and we're both fighting to clean up the messes.

In that sense, be sure to clean up any messes that you see! It's YOUR dojo, too.

If you see a line that's not straight, or a koohai that doesn't answer "Osu!" or someone who's not paying attention, it is your job as sempai to fix it. If you don't also notice someone who should know better who's not fighting to be better, and you don't also see that behavior – or even that person if his/her resistance is that disrespectful! – as a foul stain in the middle of YOUR dojo, your spirit is not as well aligned with your teacher's as it should be.

Stains should make you angry. They should make you hold your nose and work to make your training environment pure. Of course, be patient with students who don't know better! I probably err on the side of being too patient, and it probably gets me in trouble.

But if they DO know better, your koohais, and they're still not trying?

Yes, you too should hold your nose, and do whatever it takes to clean up the mess.

50. Grow Your Dojo, or Get Out of the Way

The student who doesn't grasp, even from his/her first day, that this is YOUR dojo, is by definition a weaker student until that student figures it out.

If there was a mess in the middle of your living room floor, would you pick it up? What if there was one in the middle of your dojo? The student who walks right by is confused. Of course it's your dojo. That means YOUR mess, so pick it up!

In the same way, it is your job to grow your dojo.

Your dojo is stronger if it has more strong students in it. It's your dojo, so of course YOU have to make a constant, unified effort to bring in new students. Invite your friends, tell your colleagues. Target one particular friend or family member who you think might be interested. Put up some fliers.

Of course you can't *make* anyone join, but if you make no effort at all, you're missing a key point to demonstrate your dedication to your dojo upon which you will build your own strength and your own growth curve. Fighting for your dojo is one of the ways you get stronger, so without the development of this priority, too, your attempt at Budo karate is incomplete.

Consider these two dojos once again:

Case A:	T T T T T	Case B:	T H T H T T
	T H T T T T		H T H H T T
	T T T T T T		T T H T H T

Apply this point, fighting to grow your dojo, to these two scenarios. If you're a part of the class represented in Case B, most of the students in the room are unhappy because the teacher is likely going to extreme lengths to get all of the H's to fall into line and behave like the T's they're supposed to be. Are the H's, therefore, fighting to grow their dojo?

Obviously not!

They're in the way.

Imagine the prospective new student who stopped in to watch a class and decide whether or not to join. Is he/she really going to want to join that dojo, even if the teacher isn't struggling at that moment?

Probably not, right?

So here, too, if you're not fighting to be the T-type student, you're also not fighting to grow your dojo.

Look over your head. Whose lights are those?

They're in your dojo, so they're YOUR lights. How do you pay for them to come on? With your membership fees? Well, only in a weaker perspective. You should take the strong route: Pay for them by bringing in more students so YOUR dojo's manager, whoever it is that's doing that service for you, is better empowered to pay for those lights to come on.

Take a moment and ask yourself, "What if we didn't even have a dojo?"

What if your dojo had suffered hard financial times, and all your "dojo" had was an empty athletic field, and all your trainings were outside? Would you quit? What about when it rained? What about the wintertime? Would you train less?

That depends, really, on whether or not you are the Budo karateka.

The Budo karateka would train MORE and HARDER in the challenged environment, thus *growing the dojo* until it got back on more solid ground and was back indoors again.

For that matter, what if your dojo didn't have a teacher that day, or that week, because he/she was out of town, or under the weather, or whatever?

Would you not come to training?

Of course you'd come . . . if you were a Budo-ka. You'd volunteer to teach. You'd ask your teacher for a key, and volunteer to open up the dojo at class time to keep an eye on the kids, and help in the best way you know how.

Are you going to *buy you some karate*, or are you going to sacrifice so that you become a strong karateka? (See # 54, "I'm Gonna Buy Me Some Karate.")

Has it occurred to you that it is easier to *grow your dojo* if you're in it, training hard, more frequently? Of course it is! New prospective students want to join a dojo where there are lots of high-energy people exuding positive energy. If you can't *grow your dojo* by bringing in more students, understand that, for this reason too, it's your duty to be in the dojo more often yourself. Your simply being there (and being a T-type student) helps grow the dojo.

51. When Do I Gain Enough Seniority That I Don't Have to Follow One of These Principles Anymore?

Take bowing to your teacher, for example.

There will actually be a time when your teacher might get annoyed by your demonstrations of deference. "Okay, okay, that's enough! Don't bow to me any more tonight!" your teacher might say. "Don't say 'Osu!' quite so much!"

The key point there, however, is that it's your sempai who's telling you to do less, not you deciding that you've earned it.

Herein lies a huge difference between the Japanese personality and the American one. The Japanese *feel* that the demonstrations of deference are correct, and therefore *feel awkward* when not doing them. The American student tends to feel the opposite: it's awkward to bow or say "Osu!" so he/she tends to miss one every once in a while. The problem, of course, is that the teacher trying to establish a stronger dojo tradition can never reach a point where he/she can say "Take it easy!", because of the student's occasional omissions.

Imagine that you always bow and say "Osu!"—you never miss an opportunity. But then, one day, you come into the dojo having just lost your job and with a head cold, and you don't bow and say "Osu!" when you meet your teacher. The point is that the Japanese student would have bowed especially then, because the demonstration of deference is the *easier* state for the Japanese student. Not doing it would be hard for the Japanese student.

To succeed in the Western dojo, better even than *making yourself do it* every time would be to *come to feel* that it's the only way, because it's giving to someone who's giving to you, someone whose ingrained notion of what's polite is different from your cultural standard. It's supporting Budo karate as an ultimate force for positive change in your life, rather than a hobby or, worse, a chore. If you do it with your head, it's too much to do it right all the time. If you do it with your heart, however, it becomes too much *not to do it* right.

And, of course, by taking this step you are also making yourself ten times stronger. Giving yourself over makes your pursuit pure. Instead of applying yourself partway, you're applying yourself all the way. Your strength, and your ability to get stronger, will double.

Remember that the sempai/koohai system should bring you CLOSER to your teacher . . . but that's up to the performance of the koohai (see #11, The *Sempai/Koohai System Brings You* Closer *to Your Teacher*). If the koohai is so correct that it's apparent that the koohai feels uncomfortable not being that way, that's the time that the sempai really starts to feel the respect of the koohai, and therefore really starts to admire the koohai in return. That's when you bridge the gap and start to be friend, confidant, and partner with your teacher, rather than where you may have started—the burden that has to be carried along, coaxed daily into taking the required leap of faith.

All students in the Budo karate dojo should fight to have the closest relationship possible with their teacher. They do this by being so correct that they switch over from being someone who has to be taught the attitudes contained in this book and become, instead, one of the people who helps with the teaching, both by example and through more direct guidance of their koohais.

Again, the same applies.

If you become closer to your teacher, you become twice as strong, and your ability to become stronger through the training quadruples.

52. Know the *How,* Know Your Teacher's Words For It, SHOW That You Know It

Please make sure you've read #2, *It's the* How, *Silly, Not the* What.

If you pay close attention you'll note that your teacher repeats certain phrases to describe certain *hows*. That is, generally, when your teacher is working on repairing the same issue, he/she uses the same words for it.

For example, if your teacher is dealing with a group of students who aren't keeping their guard up high enough to be safe in kumite, he/she might remind everyone, "Keep your guard up!" Everyone answers, "Osu!" and the majority raise their fists. But the next minute, or the next hour, or the next day, you want to offer the same encouragement, and you shout out, "Keep your fists up!" or "Protect your head!" or "Keep your guards up!"

Well, all of those are better than nothing, but the point I would like to make is that the continuity of the message is better if you also adopt *even your teacher's words* for the concept that needs to be expressed. Budo karate relies on knowledge being *channeled* from sempai to koohai, onward to that koohai's koohai, to the next level down, etc. In a successful dojo of T's, this channel is smooth and continuous. (See #44, *Parallel Lessons: The Surface and the Esoteric, Identify the Task at Hand, Fulfill It, Support Its Delivery in the Eyes of Your Koohais.*)

If you pick up and use the same vocabulary, you both make this transmission smoother, AND show stronger support for your teacher. Use the same words, and your koohai thinks, "My sempai wants to emulate our teacher! Maybe I should want to, too!" If you use different words, however, your koohai might think, "My sempai thinks he can do it better than my teacher if he does it differently!" Here the continuity is a little less strong.

America is a wonderful place, but it's also a country of individuals who run in groups when it comes to taking paths of least resistance, and who unknowingly fight to defend their right to do so under the guise of "I have a right to be me!" This is a primary cultural disadvantage to trying to teach (and learn) Budo karate. Let go a little. Take a leap of faith. Try to channel the strong parts of what's going on in the dojo. Make sure you blast out the weak parts. Make sure you're properly identifying what's strong and what's weak. Sometimes it's counterintuitive.

In any group, there will be some folks doing things in a weak way. Your natural tendency may be to follow along. But in the Budo karate dojo you have to make 100% sure that you take the opposite path. Identify the strong trends in the dojo, and follow them!

In this case, emulating your teacher is the stronger path.

That final part of this section's title, "Show that you know it," demands a moment of mention.

It's *action, not words*, right?

First off, no one will listen to your using even your teacher's words if you don't also DO what you're telling other people to do.

But more than that:

Consider that it also STRENGTHENS the continuity of the flow from your teacher to your classmates if you SHOW that you know the concept being urged, and if you even emphasize it, so that your koohai can see that you're paying attention.

Your teacher asks the class to perform an exercise your teacher calls "deep squats!" (I use this term in my dojo for full-range "jumping squats," but without the jumping.) Another time, however, when it's you that's leading the class, you say "Deep knee bends!" and then everyone is confused, because you can't even channel your teacher's terminology successfully. But, yet another time, your teacher asks for "deep squats" and you jump right into position, fighting to be the first to get there, and you emphasize by your immediate, powerful response that you were clued in exactly to what the next exercise was to be: you've SHOWN that you understood the terminology immediately. So far from *confusing* the transmission of the exercise at hand, you have in fact *strengthened* it.

In the Budo karate system, you must fight to be the best at *channeling* your teacher's intent. Clue in, and show that you know it. When called upon to do so, use even consistent vocabulary to evoke the desired response in your koohais.

See #60, *Everything You Do Is FOR EFFECT!* Show *That You Did What Your Teacher Asks, but Be Careful!* and #72, *"Channel" Your Teacher's Teaching*.

53. How Often in a Week Do You "Do Karate"? That's All? Okay, So No Excuse! Do It Right All the Time That You Do It!

Here is an answer to the folks who *know not what they do* as they battle with the leap of faith that training in the Budo karate dojo requires of them.

Practicing Budo karate requires a certain kind of behavior. One behaves strong to become strong. One *fights to be first*. Start at #1 in this book and you can, point by point, understand the Budo karate personality. Some lucky few will have it already, but, in my experience, since we are on a different continent where this type of behavior is culturally *foreign,* many

Western students of karate will have to take a leap of faith in order to be 100% consistent and make their karate Budo.

"Whew, that's a lot of work!" says the American karate student who does struggle, but who also fundamentally resists taking that leap, and that student is right: If you resist the leap, if you don't go all the way, it is a lot of work. It is exhausting both for you, and for your teacher, and for your classmates who have to deal with your fluctuating levels of commitment.

But here is my answer!

First, take the leap and your training will become easy by comparison.

But, second, if you're one of those—and there are enough of you that you shouldn't be ashamed!—who really have to fight to let go, and who finds the fight to do so to be overwhelming, take a second and console yourself.

How many hours per week do you *do* karate?

If you attend two two-hour classes per week, you "do" karate for almost four hours. It's six if you do three classes, eight if you do four, etc. Either way, it's a very limited amount of time, considering there are 168 hours in a week!

So, yes, you have to fight to behave like you've taken that leap, and, yes, that fight might be exhausting for you. So, psych yourself up for those four, six, or eight hours per week that you have to fight that fight. If you do, BOOM, Budo karate starts to become yours because you're consistent. If you fail to do so, if you OPT not to get psyched up for that fight, and if you therefore are strong, weak, strong, weak, you're in the way, you're the H, you're the one who's not fighting in the midst of true *fighters*, so you're the one not practicing Budo.

That perspective should relieve some of your concern. You don't have to be 100% 24 hours per day. You just have to be 100% during the couple of hours per day that you do karate.

But wait! Before I let you move on, there's one more key point to make.

When DO you do karate, exactly?

Yes, as mentioned above, you do karate when you're in class, but I need to broaden those limits by just a few minutes each week. You also do karate *every time you interact with one of your koohais or one of your sempais, whether inside the dojo or not.*

Consider: you encounter one of your sempais by chance at the mall, or at a restaurant. The total duration of your encounter might only be a few seconds, or it might be longer if you decide to stay around and chat, but the point is that if you are interacting with your sempai (or your koohai), you have to do so, then too, within the framework of behavior established as correct for the dojo.

Do you shout "Osu!" and bow like a crazy person in the middle of a shopping mall, thus making a scene in front of a lot of people who don't know you or karate?

Of course not.

A muted demonstration of deference is required here. "A little bit" of a bow, for example, a smaller "Osu!" that doesn't embarrass everyone. But what if you did nothing? What if you made no attempt? What if you felt inclined to wave and say, "Oh, hi, Sempai!" instead?

You got it. You blew it.

To maintain your fight, you have to fight ALL OF THE TIME that you *do* karate, and that includes anytime you interact with someone from the dojo.

What about telephone calls? What about e-mails?

Now you're catching on. Any interaction between sempai and koohai means you're *doing* karate, so you have to do it powerfully.

Dare to go the final mile?

There are actually two more dimensions to this, each one smaller, but neither less important.

First, what if your sempai has asked you to perform a task (See #10, *Complete Tasks That You've Been Assigned Promptly and Powerfully*), but it's not one that you do immediately — i.e. it's homework.

Maintaining a Budo karate level of responsibility to do that homework also falls into the limited number of hours per week that you *do* karate, so you have to fight then as well.

Second, and lastly, since Mas Oyama would only give his nod of approval to this section after I add this final point:

Of course you also *should* maintain an attitude 24-7 that you *are* a karateka, not just *doing* karate. In this case you have to modify ALL your behavior up a notch. This doesn't mean walking to your workplace in your karate uniform, it just means keeping your behavior in check. Remind yourself that you are representing your dojo every minute of your life, not just during those few hours that you're engaged. Remember the part of karate that's about deepening human relationships (see #20, *The Deepening of Human Relationships*)? Of course, your karate is really with you all the time, right?

You should endeavor to make it so.

It certainly is for those who manage to fight a bit *less* hard than you, because they've successfully taken the advised leap of faith.

But if that leap is hard for you, console yourself by considering the number of hours per week that you *do* karate. Psych yourself up to fight consistently during those hours. Make that your habit, don't let up, and before you know it, that leap will come. You will morph from someone who *does* karate, and you will become a Budo karateka.

54. "I'm Gonna Buy Me Some Karate!"

Really?

If that's what you want to do, please go shopping somewhere else.

Karate is not for sale. Your dues aren't enough to buy something that only comes through years and years of dedication and spirit.

If you think just by being in the dojo you deserve to have karate, please adjust your attitude.

You're been in the dojo for six months, so you deserve the next belt?

Look again! Maybe you've been *in the way* for the past six months. Maybe you've been the H.

But don't panic!

Just take charge.

Take a leap of faith, and fight to be best at adopting the principles described in this book. Don't be the passive one that waits for karate to fall on you from Heaven. It won't ever.

You have to reach up to Heaven and try and grab it!

Reach!

Fight!

That's it! Now you don't have to buy what you can't buy anyway. Now you're becoming a Budo karateka!

55. Your Teacher Has Been There, Your Teacher Has to Know 10 Things to Teach You One

I am currently embarking on my 30th year since I began my karate training.

Perhaps it would be different if it were my 10th, but, even then, it would be very likely that I—and *your* karate teacher as well!—have experienced before any difficulty that you're experiencing now, and have experienced it in 100 different ways, and experienced 100 things worse.

Your ankles hurt when sitting in seiza?

Yes, but your teacher's did too when he/she was first beginning karate—and not only that, your teacher has experienced that challenge 1000 times since then with 1000 different beginning students who each tend to sit awkwardly and resist the discomfort in exactly the same way as you, before finally, those that are going to succeed at karate figure out how to relax in the face of that discomfort and join the ranks who know what you haven't yet learned.

It is amazing to me when, in the American dojo, students of whom I ask a leap of faith look at me like I made it all up yesterday. If your teacher tells you to "sit up straight" every time you're sitting in seiza "even if it's uncomfortable," why continue to test, time after time, if your teacher meant it or not?

The Japanese student of Mas Oyama's era would not. Just do it. Take the leap of faith.

Try to understand that the things your teacher is asking of you are things that your teacher has done and seen done 1000s of times. The ways that your teacher is asking you to do them, your teacher's seen it done that way 1000s of times. It is an aspect of American personality that the student thinks, "I'm something different! Yeah, those other 1000 might have responded that way, but I must be the first that's like me that my teacher's ever encountered!"

But it's not true. Your teacher and all of your sempais have been there before you.

In one way or another, your teacher has ALWAYS been there. Whether your teacher's got 5 years on you or 30, your teacher has been there, and you would succeed so much faster, and become so much stronger, if you could take the necessary leap and trust that that is the case.

Remember that most of this book is not about something you have to learn; it's about something that you just do, one decision to approach your training in the correct way. Open your mind. Take the leap of faith.

My student with a jammed finger who can't close his/her fist tightly might look at me like I'm nuts when I say, "Oh, don't worry about it. Force it tight, and forget about it. Just keep training." They think I'm nuts, and they want to ice it and elevate it, and go to an orthopedic surgeon, and yet I've had EVERY joint in both of my hands jammed half a dozen times and several of the bones broken, and I know. I've been there 100 times over, and in 100 different ways. I have no arthritis or problems in my hands. Just train, forget about it, and your hands will get tougher.

I will be the first to say "I don't know" if I really don't, but if I'm giving you advice based on my experience, take the Japanese route. Take the Budo karate route. Take a leap of faith. Trust your teacher.

Kancho Royama made a similar point in a lecture in recent years in Japan.

He reminded us that, as instructors, we must often have an understanding of ten other things in order to teach the one point we want to teach well. Personally, I often find myself stymied in class because I want to teach one or two of those other related concepts, but can't because of the students who still have to learn the basic lesson that *the class* has to get past before that second or third lesson would make any sense.

The moral here is that if you take the leap of faith and grasp the lesson at hand, there's often a more exciting one to follow. *Channel* what your teacher is presenting, fight to be the first to really get it, fight to promote a unified front in that effort. If everyone does, you'll find that everyone gets it, everyone's at the front of the curve, and your teacher is likely moving on to something else, something more exciting.

56. Your Teacher Sees You in High Definition

One aspect that's often a little frightening to my students—and shocking when it dawns on them!—is that once I've had them in the dojo for awhile I can see them, inside and out, in high definition.

One way to define karate is that it's the art of undoing weakness and mastering strength. I can assure you that once I've had you for a little while, pushing you in class to your various mental, physical, and spiritual limits, I can see—in high definition!—what your weaknesses are.

As you can imagine, this is pretty scary for some students when they figure it out, because we—as a culture—don't want to let other people see our defects. We often prefer to hold on to them under the guise of "I have a right to be me!" Yet my students somehow always seem to reveal themselves, and I always seem to see them. Some run when they realize they're thus exposed, but the Budo karate student wouldn't ever.

One way to look at Budo karate training is that it's the art of locating and rooting out our weaknesses.

And how does one do that?

Well, first one has to discover exactly what one's weaknesses are, and Budo karate training has a way of revealing them. Does every student, when training, have the same set of goals to get black belt, and second degree black belt, and so on?

Only on the surface. Only in the Americanized understanding.

Yes, there is a list of skills you have to master, and those skills—the ones on the list—are the same for every student. Students have to learn certain kicks, certain kata, certain partner exercises, and more.

But then there's always a lesson behind the lesson, and each individual student exposes to his/her teacher exactly what that particular student needs to learn to become a well-rounded black belt, and second degree black belt, and onward.

Hence, YOUR to-learn list might differ from that of the student next to you. This understanding between teacher and student tends to HONOR the Japanese student, while, at the same time, it tends to threaten the American one.

Do you want Budo karate, or the Americanized version?

If you want Budo, then understand and allow that your Budo karate teacher is looking in your performance for this kind of limitation as well, and he/she will be working with you, teaching you, training you, to overcome even that kind of weakness that exists on a more *esoteric* level. If you're my student and you reveal to me a certain weakness—and if it's there, I'm confident I'll eventually see it—I can assure you that I'm going to provide for you opportunities to face it. I promise you, in other words, that I'm going to take you there. Your training in my dojo *will* take you to that place you need to go in order to overcome.

Might that make you angry?

I think that it has in the past with students who didn't grasp the fact that that was part of the training.

So in order to overcome that potential pitfall?

Make peace with it—appreciate it!—and your success will surprise you. Resist it, on the other hand, and you might find yourself in the way. You're the H. Remember, you have to channel your teacher's teaching. It IS your teacher's way, or it's the highway.

57. Most Injuries in Karate Are Really Just Karate's Normal Aches and Pains

Karate will hurt you in all kinds of ways.

Hopefully most of those ways are small and manageable, and healing from them WILL indeed make you stronger.

Beginners often have trouble with "injuries" when they lean too heavily in the direction of what their inexperience tells them is *an injury*, when what they more often face is actually an ache or pain that's a common part of being a karate beginner. One problem occurs when beginners either take time off from training unnecessarily, or train in an overly cautious, weak way, not realizing that the physical damage they sustained is of a nature that's far better to ignore and push through.

I have to be careful, here, to point out that I'm talking (in the example immediately below) about the case in which the students are young, athletic adults who really LIKE to fight, and who want to learn to fight by fighting.

Every dojo has them: the gung-ho crowd.

Among this group, broken fingers and toes are common. (The parent reading this book cringes!) But, yes, frankly, I've broken many of mine, fingers and toes (ribs and noses are next in frequency), but the point I'd like to make here is . . . well, actually there are three:

First, this type of *injury* is common for the gung-ho beginning young adult who wants to rush into hard contact kumite. Whether or not you get *hurt* depends you. Of course accidents happen, but notice that the above description was targeted towards the *gung-ho young adult*. It's generally the *gung-ho* part (i.e. the *impatient* part) that gets the student hurt. If you're more patient, you'll be less likely to sustain this kind of injury. I will withhold judgment on which type of student is better. Both are fine. It takes all kinds to make a dojo.

Second, the frequency with which this type of injury occurs decreases with time. As we get hurt, we learn not to get hurt that way the next time. So, be encouraged: if you're hurt, or even hurt for the second time in as many months, keep doing what you're doing, and just around the corner you'll find yourself not getting hurt anymore.

Third, you'll note that the aforementioned gung-ho type is more likely to KEEP training in the face of an injury. One student jams a thumb because he/she didn't have a tight fist, and that student yelps and instinctively asks to be excused from the training, comes back in a splint, and then takes three more weeks off. Another student, a second type, jams his or her thumb in the same way, winces, growls, finds a different way to make a tighter fist, and keeps right on training, and never misses a beat.

Which one is correct?

Well—I have to be careful here!—it does fit within the Budo karate *fight to be first* spirit to likewise fight to be more like the latter case above, and less like the former. The general rule is that you should always fight to push through no matter what hardship you face, and not allow even what you consider to be *injuries* to keep you out of training.

But be careful! Fast on the heels of that rule is this one:

When in doubt, ask your teacher.

Your teacher has been there before. Your teacher has hurt and been hurt in the same way you are 100 times and in 100 different variations. Once again, we get into the realm of having to take a leap of faith.

Sometimes your teacher may tell you something that's counterintuitive, particularly in the West. Once when I was fighting 100 rounds of NOT full-contact kumite with two students (on a rotation, so we each rested every third minute), I made a poor choice and dislocated my smallest two toes on my right foot by accidentally kicking my opponent in the shin. There was a CRACK, we looked down, and those two toes were sticking out sideways, perpendicular to my largest three. What could I do? I knew from my overseas training experience that there was nothing to do. I knew that it was going to hurt, but that I could keep right on training and take care of it later if it turned out that there was anything to actually take care of once the swelling went down. So I bent down, pulled those two toes back into position, and kicked my opponent again with my shin. I didn't miss a beat in that training, and then just took it easy when walking (but not when training!) for the next couple of weeks. Soon it was forgotten, and those two students learned that the rules, as they understood them, didn't always apply in the Budo karate dojo.

Ask your teacher.

Trust that he/she knows what he/she's talking about.

In a rare case your teacher might say, "Go directly to the ER, hurry up!" but otherwise, at least ask before you go.

Dare to take the leap of faith, if one is requested of you.

I admire the spirit of a student who comes to class on crutches to

WATCH two classes per week, so he/she is there *in spirit*, if not completely in body. (Presumably he/she is on crutches, because of a accident playing basketball at school.)

Please continue this discussion by reading #58, immediately below.

58. It's YOUR Responsibility Not to Get Hurt

Fight full contact to where you're trying to break your opponent! Push your body harder every day! Always fight to be first!

Yet, it's your responsibility not to get hurt?

Isn't that counterintuitive?

No, it's Budo karate SPIRIT!

In Japan, that was the understanding. Yes, push your limits every day! Yet it's your responsibility not to get hurt, because if you get hurt, you have to interrupt or curtail your training.

Yet in Japan there was, in most cases, not really any *stopping training* when we suffered damage that most, here in the West, would consider *injuries*.

We trained anyway. We trained with battered knees, swollen joints, and broken bones.

If that's your attitude — that you have to keep training anyway — of course you're going to be super responsible in your efforts to not get hurt while also pushing your limits.

It's just a different mentality.

Yet it's one that we can adopt here in the West, too.

Give it a shot?

I dare you! Charge to the front of the curve!

59. Train Twice Per Week?

I require that my students do, but I want them to understand what's behind that.

It is a minimum for safety, and for a learning curve that allows them to just barely keep up. My classes are often two hours long. We cover a lot of material. I caution my students that training two times per week (eight times per month) for three months should be a minimum requirement for promotion at our quarterly belt tests.

There is also certainly a safety concern.

Unlike other martial arts imitations in the West, Budo karate training will make you a karateka, not just teach you a skill called *karate*. To learn Budo karate, your body (as well as your heart and mind) has to change. In the Kyokushin karate dojo we tend to fight much harder than the other styles, yet we have many fewer injuries.

How can this be?

It's because there are exercises we practice on a daily basis that fortify the body at its weak points and thus prevent injury. We don't have knee injuries in my dojo (of the type that arise from tendon and ligament strains). I never saw them in Japan. Yet Tae Kwon Do schools are rife with them. Why? Because our regular training fortifies the joints so that they're safe.

But what if you're not training regularly?

Of course, if your training is sporadic, you'll be more likely to get hurt. If you can really only train two times per week, therefore, it's far better to spread them out. Train Monday and Thursday, for example. It's far better than Monday and Tuesday.

Now, Mas Oyama, of course, made it his goal to train more hours per day than he slept. How many days per week is that?

You got it! That's many hours every day!

Training twice per week is also a number that I've chosen to try to build a dojo in America where most of my students tend to be, also, bogged down with work, and school, and family, etc. I have always endeavored to train every day. When I was a teenager, I was on sports teams at school (wrestling, cross country, and track), and yet every night, after dinner, I went to the dojo. Every night!

I insisted on a minimum of a 3.5 grade point average, and yet I often had 4.0.

So, yes, please train a minimum of twice per week in my dojo. But can you come every day?

No?

Okay.

Shoot for four?

In my first dojo, when I was a teenager, learning my earliest — and thus most formative — karate lessons, we trained four times per week, Monday,

Wednesday, Friday, and Sunday, and since most of us didn't miss classes, our teacher rarely had to repeat lessons.

Remember #1, *Fight to Be First*? In this spirit, you should also fight to train as often as possible.

One last thought?

When everyone fights to be first, who actually is?

Exactly! No one!

It just ensures that everyone is charging to the front of the curve. In the same way, you should always strive to train MORE than you did last week. Yes, if you always strive to train more, won't you eventually be training, like Mas Oyama, more hours per day than you sleep?

Hopefully, but that's not the point. The point is, never be content with the amount of training that you are doing, and you'll always be as far forward on the curve as you possibly can be.

60. Everything You Do Is FOR EFFECT: Show That You Did What Your Teacher Asked, but Be Careful!

When your teacher asks something of you, answering with "Osu!" is only half of what you have to do. You also have to do the thing your teacher asked of you.

More than that, though, you have to do it overtly enough that your koohais can see that you did it.

Imagine students punching in kiba dachi (a low broad stance that tends to make students' thighs burn with effort). They do ten punches, and the teacher points out that their stances aren't deep enough. "Deeper stances!" the teacher challenges.

Everyone answers "Osu!" but no one changes anything because it hurts. These are not Budo karateka.

However, if everyone (not just half of them, but everyone) shouts, "Osu!" AND, like the floor falling out, everyone drops down two inches lower to where their muscles REALLY burn, then this starts to resemble the Budo karate dojo.

But wait!

Is that really enough if, EVERY TIME those students practice that same exercise, their teacher has to remind them, "Deeper stances, please!"?

Of course it isn't.

Enter the potential for a group of Western students to develop a negative habit. What if they only show the greatest strength for those moments when specifically challenged to do so by their teacher?

This would be a failed attempt at Budo karate, too. In this case, kiba dachi is the *what*, "deep" is the *how*—but that has to be your *how* for all time, not just when reminded.

Budo karate students, in the above situation, do three things:

1. They answer "Osu!"
2. They make the adjustment in an overt way that everyone can see.
3. Like a bell ringing in their head, the next time the teacher tells them it's time to do that same exercise (the *what*), they REMEMBER the challenge of the previous time they did it (the *how*) and start out in that deep stance without having to be told.

After all, in the Budo karate system, we endeavor to not make our teachers and sempais have to repeat themselves, right? Think of it this way:

Your teacher has 1000 things to teach you. If he has to teach you the first 10 over and over and over again, he/she will never get to the more advanced things. Do what your teacher challenges you to do, do it overtly—and make sure that's the new way you ALWAYS do that same exercise.

This is the Budo karate spirit.

Everything for EFFECT! That is, *the effect your correction has on your dojo's average.* If you start out really low in kiba dachi, you'll make the other students look bad, and they will fight harder. If you do have to make a correction when told, make sure you do it *overtly*, so your koohais can see how eager you are to comply with your teacher's requests. And the next time?

You got it!

Do it without having to be corrected!

61. Learn to Reassess Yourself, and Take the Opposite Path: Stop, Drop, and Roll

This is an extreme case, but I, myself, have done it, so I know that it's not an unreasonable suggestion.

The realization occurred when I was 17 and a freshman in college. I was enrolled in a class called *Religions of China and Japan,* and we had just learned that the Confucian scholar Mencius taught that all of our *first* impulses as humans are impulses to do good, and that the times that we do the opposite, it's because of conditioning that we've received or habits that we've adopted. He used the case of a child drowning in a well. Even the meanest of us will have an impulse to rescue that child, he argued, but some people, particularly if they're really twisted by experience, will decide on the spur of the moment to take the opposite course.

"That's not my problem," they'll say. "It's not my child. After all, I've seen so many other people decide against what I might do, too, if it were a perfect world. But who am I to try to be perfect?"

It was during that week of study that I became aware in myself of a double impulse regarding nearly every decision that I made. I walked past a soda can that someone had discarded on the lawn, I had an impulse to pick it up, but, before I did, I decided that it wasn't my problem.

"Wow!" I thought when it occurred to me, and I turned around and picked up the can.

That same week, with an armload of textbooks, I pressed the elevator button to ride up to the second floor for class. "Wow!" I thought when I realized that I'd had an impulse to jog up the stairs because I knew it would make me stronger, but that I'd decided, instead, to hit the elevator button and wait for a ride. Suddenly it became exciting for me to run up the stairs!

I was taking charge in a way that I never had before.

In the dojo, you might try doing this with every decision that you make, particularly if you've having trouble making the appropriate *culture shift* from *how you are* to the Budo karateka.

It's hard to make the stronger choice, right?

Well, it probably is if you're used to making the weaker one most of the time.

But here's how you can take charge:

Become aware at the moment of each decision—or better!—each decision you are *about to make*, and reassess. Even if you feel like there wasn't an impulse to take the harder road—but I'll bet there was!—why not imagine that there had been one, and leap to take that road instead? Revel in it! Get excited by your newfound ability to do so, and suddenly your life in the dojo will become easy by comparison to how it was before.

If this is really that foreign to you, why not make a game of it?

You were about to *not* be the one who answered with a powerful "Osu!"? You were about to let it slide and remain silent? Why not *celebrate* the opposite path and issue a powerful "Osu!" even if it was a split-second late? Why not get excited about how cool it was that you were able to overcome and take the high road?

You were standing there in a weak stance in the middle of your kata because your legs were burning, and it occurred to you? Why not get excited about the fact that *you are now aware*, and lower your own stance?

Your habit was to respond in a weak way to a correction, but—lo and behold!—on the spur of the moment you realized it was weak to be less than humble, and you switched your behavior to "Osu! Sempai, I'll fix it!", coupled with a powerful correction and a powerful decision not to make that same mistake again.

Wow, you're taking control!

You're learning to celebrate the harder path, and, in doing so, you've actually found that it's really the easier one in the dojo!

Good for you! You're becoming the Budo karateka!

All of this is hard for you to imagine?

Consider for a moment "stop, drop, and roll." This is what even grade school kids are taught to do if they're in an accident and their clothes are on fire. The terror-born instinct may well be to flee, as if the accident victim can escape the flames, but he/she cannot escape if his/her clothes are burning. We're taught instead to STOP, drop to the ground, and roll our bodies across it to try to extinguish the flames.

In short, we're taught to *reassess* on the spur of the moment and take an opposite course from the knee-jerk one.

Why not apply the same to your strong vs. weak decisions in the dojo?

Your instinct is to take an easier path?

Your instinct is to resist the lesson?

Then STOP before you burn! Take the opposite road. If your goal is Budo karate, you will not be disappointed.

62. Budo Karate is For Every Body

Men, women, children, young, old, learning disadvantaged, blind, you name it, everyone can do Budo karate. It doesn't matter if you're athletically talented and in great shape or 100 pounds overweight: everyone can join.

One great mistake that some prospective beginners make is to believe that they have to get into shape before beginning training. This is silly, of course!

It's your training that'll get you into shape, after all!

This may be counterintuitive when you consider the full-contact nature of the training.

But look at the history.

Even in Japan, Kyokushin karate was originally just for the young male who was willing to risk life and limb to become the strongest fighter in the world. Mas Oyama, even, did not believe that it was an appropriate activity for women, except in a "gentle" way to "promote beauty and grace." Well, unfortunately for that old-fashioned notion, some young women in Europe and Canada had different ideas, and they showed the world that women athletes can do just what the men do. Now, of course, a Kyokushin karate tournament wouldn't be a Kyokushin tournament without female divisions.

Children came next, and whereas at first kids were treated as delicate, it quickly became apparent that kids were actually far safer, because they're not powerful or bulky enough to hurt each other too much—and that if they engaged in *real* karate from that early age, they were also far safer as adults, because defending against full-contact blows was so much a part of their nature that injuries almost went away altogether.

Most Kyokushin karate people (adult competitors) who know serious injuries experience them when they find themselves unexpectedly breaking people in a fight in the real world against attackers who are NOT trained in Kyokushin. Injuries in the dojo occur when students are impatient, or when teachers don't establish proper controls. Please see #46, *How Hard Do I Hit?* And #56, *Most* Injuries *in Karate Are Really Just Karate's Normal Aches and Pains.*

63. Disappointed? Yes, But If You Show it, You Blew It Again

Here's a hard cultural adjustment for some here in the West.

If your teacher corrects you, and you feel disappointed because you had to be corrected, how are you to respond?

Well, the Budo karate system is simply to say "Osu!", stay bright-eyed and bushy-tailed, and jump to the task of making the correction at hand. This is also the NORMAL, mature, human response to constructive criticism issued by an authority figure, even when that criticism is harsh.

After all, that's what you came to the dojo for, right?

And, after all, it was YOU whose performance was substandard, was it not?

Children will hang their head and sulk . . . or cry, or get mad. Adults will not unless they've missed some developmental step along the way.

Whether it's a child, however, who still needs to learn, or an adult who never did, consider this type of reaction in the light of the *Toes-Not-Heels Dojo*. You've read enough of this book to know what I mean by a *sinkhole* in the grid of the T-type dojo? Sulking, or hanging your head, responding with a weak "Osu," or getting mad in response to criticism is about the best way imaginable to create a sinkhole in the energy of the dojo. There is no place for it in Budo karate. Please see #39, *Hang the Dog, Leave Him at Home, Drive Him Out!*

Perhaps it's in the nature of the fact that I work, through my nonprofit, with at-risk demographics that I get to see a good number of students who display their disappointment in a way that is so unproductive.

So let's explore that for a second, because all students should understand.

Consider the H-type student who, out of pride, or thanks to a low degree of personal confidence, resists, for all intents and purposes, a correction recommended by his/her teacher. "You have to kiai louder," your teacher might have told that student, but, lo and behold, the next kiai isn't any louder. Your teacher repeats him/herself and then again, and the next day again, and the next week again, and sometimes from the very first correction, and other times after however many corrections it takes for that particular student to reach his/her threshold, that student starts showing disappointment or resentment like a child would. Perhaps he/she will hang his/her head, sulk, get mad, or cry.

What's the answer? What are we to do?

Clearly this is conduct unbecoming of the Budo karateka, it's behavior that never should have stepped in through the front door.

The hard answer IS fairly hard.

The student has no choice but to come to understand that the power to make the difference and not feel disappointed in the first place was in that student's own hands all along. After all, if the student cited in the example above merely *turned on the animal* (see #15, *React Inversely to Hardship*

2: Turn On the Animal!) and kiai'ed like a madman (or woman), that same student would have been congratulated for showing strong spirit!

If YOU, however, have suffered from this type of difficulty in the past, and if you ALSO have the ability to push your way through this book — if you're reading now — please do consider:

The power is YOURS alone to avoid this type of situation.

Remember that Budo karate is not a strength that you acquire, it's a decision that you make.

If you are resisting your teacher's lessons, you have a weak teacher indeed if he/she stops trying to teach you in response to your failures, or your decisions not to learn. Often the answer is as simple as just *turning on the animal*. But is there something wrong with your teacher for finally getting mad, if that's what it takes, to try to get through to you and make you one of the T's in the dojo?

There is not!

There would be something wrong with your teacher for NOT trying every possible avenue to get you to see the light regarding your own shortcomings, particularly if your willful resistance was lowering the standard of the dojo. That's why you came to the dojo in the first place! That's how one gets strong: by realizing their weaknesses and blasting them out through the blood, sweat, and tears of training.

Oh, but that's not why YOU came to the dojo, you say? You wanted to learn kicks and punches, but you didn't want to have to face your personal limitations? You came to the dojo for recreation, not to get stronger through Budo karate training?

If that's the case, and if that continues to be the case, I am sorry, but you're in the way. Budo karate has little to do with simple recreation.

Remember that in the end, in the Budo karate dojo it's the Budo karate way or the highway. If you resist for too long, you'll just be one of the ones that isn't around anymore . . . and the fact that you're not is because of you.

How important are you to the dojo?

Every *child* is important, because, as adults, it's our job to give each and every one of them a chance. But once you're an adult, how important are you?

That depends on you.

List the top five broadly successful individuals you know. Can you imagine them dealing with adversity by crumbling in the face of it, or by getting angry, and attacking whatever valuable institution helped them to identify their own shortcomings?

Obviously not.

They've learned how to maintain their dignity — learn from their mistakes! — and push through, even in the face of adversity far greater than that which you and I face.

64. Succeed Consistently, You Can't Buy a Break by Showing Strength Every Once in a While

Make sure that you've read #53, *How Often in a Week Do You "Do" Karate? That's All? Okay, So No Excuse! Do It Right All the Time That You Do It.* There's a good description here of the difference between the student who consistently struggles, nipping at the heels of figuring out the Budo karate personality once and for all, and the student who snaps right into the right groove, and then doesn't have to struggle nearly so much in the future.

If it clicks for you, if YOU take the required leap of faith, there's no more struggle, following the way becomes easy, and then you can concentrate on what's meant to be hard in karate training, i.e. the physical challenges that become spiritual/mental challenges those times that they become so hard.

This section is, perhaps, written more for the student who's still struggling for the self-confidence it takes to take that leap of faith.

I've seen it over and over again that this type of student *permits him/herself* to buy breaks from their hard work. In other words, I see them console themselves, "I'm working so hard in general! *This time* I'm justified in taking it easy!"

Oh, but isn't it exactly that self-granted permission that keeps them distant from the leap of faith that they should have already taken?

The Budo karateka *always* shows strong spirit in the dojo.

Okay, that's easy if it's clicked for you, and you've realized that the dojo is the place where you always have a strong *attitude* towards adversity.

However, if you have to fight all the time to maintain that demonstration of strong spirit because it has not yet clicked for you, it can be quite exhausting indeed.

So, what happens?

It's quite normal for this type of student to award themselves breaks, because they somehow think they deserve them.

In the Budo karate system, you can take all the breaks you want as long as they are outside of the dojo, or rather outside of that which is considered the dojo in the Budo karate system, which is (see #53, again) any interaction you have in the dojo OR with your sempais or koohais outside of the dojo OR when you're fulfilling any challenges or tasks outside of the dojo that you've been assigned by your teacher or sempai. The basic rule is that *everything dojo* has got to be strong and correct or it all becomes a lie, you become a hobbyist, and you are working against your teacher's commitment to propagate Budo karate.

So you absolutely CAN take breaks, just make sure you don't steal them from your dojo. Don't take them either in the dojo itself, or any time you're in the company of your dojomates, or when you have some task to perform that one of your sempais has given you.

Are you going to say "Osu!" with powerful spirit nine times, and then believe that you've earned the right to say "osu" weakly the 10th time?

It doesn't work that way, but it's amazing the frequency with which the struggling student seems to think that it does.

Take a leap of faith.

Take all the work out of the struggle, and then it will no longer be an issue.

For it to be real, your karate has to be consistent. If it's something you have to *put on*, of course it's a struggle, but if, instead, you *become committed* to the Budo karate ideal, there's no longer any question, is there?

65. If Someone Drops the Ball, Make Sure It's Your Koohai: This is the Sempai-Koohai Machine for Strength in the Budo Karate Dojo

Here's a gem!

Japanese sempais don't let their koohais see them dropping the ball. Nothing could shame them more. This shame is SELF-generated, i.e. they FEEL so ashamed if they let their koohais see them dropping a ball that it virtually doesn't happen.

Therefore, if anyone drops the ball in the dojo, it should always be your koohai.

Are you REALLY going to follow instructions less well than your koohai? Are you REALLY going to let your koohai kiai louder? Are you REALLY going to learn the kata less well than your junior? Are you REALLY going to let your junior defeat you?

The Budo karate system is to fight, always, to make sure that any dropped balls are dropped by your juniors, not you.

Ah ha! So what, then, is the responsibility of the koohai?

There's the trick to it all! There's the key to Mas Oyama's genius!

The Japanese koohai feels so ashamed to let the sempais see them *not* battling to surpass them that they virtually never stop fighting to do so.

Once again:

The koohai *always* battles to outdo the sempai, AND the sempai *always* battles to make sure the koohai never does.

The result, of course, is like a steam engine getting ready to explode. Everyone becomes strong! And everyone becomes stronger than they could ever possibly imagine in a non-Budo dojo. The result of this struggle is like a machine for generating not only powerful fighters, but also powerful people.

There was no question in Mas Oyama's dojo.

In the American dojo, on the other hand, it's apparently fairly easy for sempais to show their weaknesses to the koohais. For the American personality, apparently, there's no dignity lost. If we want to have any hope of making Kyokushin what it was meant to be, however, we have to try to imitate the Japanese way.

What would Mas Oyama say?

Karate is not karate, *he did in fact say*, without the sempai-koohai system. Play karate, maybe, but Budo? No way. Without this machine, forget about it.

It's that fundamental.

Please try to surpass your sempais.

Please make sure your koohais can't surpass you.

Is the result a big fight?

The American might think so.

On the contrary, the result is a FAMILY, in which everyone comes closer together. Everyone stays at the front of the curve. It's a brother/sisterhood, not just a club.

Achieve this and you WILL find an ideal that's worth sacrificing for.

66. Volunteers?

The Budo karate spirit: Always volunteer.

You're always fighting to be first, after all, right?

Your teacher asks the class, "Can I have a volunteer?" Everyone's hands go up. Ah ha! Excellent, that's the Budo karate spirit.

The cautious, the fearful, the meek, the hesitant: we don't let them in the dojo. These are the H's. Of course you might FEEL this way, cautious, fearful, hesitant, but in the Budo karate dojo we learn that *showing strength begets actual strength.* Therefore, unlike in the American system, where you actually don't volunteer unless you feel gung-ho, in the Budo karate system you MUST volunteer, in order to get strong.

What about the time when your teacher does not request a volunteer? Even better!

Volunteer anyway! Spill more sweat than what's required of you. Kick higher, kiai louder, learn faster than those around your because you choose to go the extra mile voluntarily.

Why not find something to do that might benefit the dojo and offer to do it? Come up to your sempai or teacher at a time when he/she's not busy, and say, "Sempai, can I clean the locker rooms after training tonight?" or "Sensei, I see that damaged wall needs repairing, can I come in this weekend perhaps, and fix it?" The task of it might be inconvenient, or even difficult, but give it a shot. Take the plunge. Make the offer, and you'll find yourself empowered just by having heard yourself make such a powerful offer.

What about harder things like tournaments ten hours away in other states?

Your teacher asks the class for those who might want to go to represent the dojo.

Should everyone go? Of course not.

So should everyone volunteer?

Well, that depends, and it gets a bit tricky.

The dojo absolutely MUST develop in the hearts and minds of its students an attitude of loyalty and dedication to the dojo—and to the cause!—AND THAT MEANS that every student has to adopt and project an attitude of loyalty and dedication in all the things that they do. Karate students have to develop something a bit more intense than a "support the home team" mentality; Budo karate students have to develop a "support the home team even if I have to bleed" mentality. Consider the *Toes-Not-Heels Dojo* from #5. How can the dojo ever possibly develop into one in which this mentality is normal until a majority of the dojo adopts this mentality?

It can't really, so someone's got to start.

My advice?

First, take all challenges and all requests for volunteers very, very seriously.

Second, volunteer to do the harder things, too. Let your classmates see you volunteer. They will be moved by your strength, and eventually they'll join you.

What about home team spirit?

Like so much in this book, you can DECIDE to have it. It's not something you have to develop; it's something you can just decide. Some, I think, don't have it because they don't realize they're supposed to. It's right there in the American personality to think, "I'm gonna buy me some karate."

You pay, so it must be something you're buying, right?

How sad is this type of mentality if it persists!

Support your dojo. It's YOURS, after all.

How about this example?

About twice a year for the past five or six years we've taken hard weekend trips to support tournaments in the Northeast. They were a big thing to volunteer for, because the trips were often 12- and 14-hour drives, one-way. Yet my adult black belts were routinely volunteering. One often would not.

If you can't, you can't, but what got to be amazing about this particular student is that when I would ask in front of the whole class for volunteers, this student would blurt out "Osu," and then follow up with a string of negatives of why that student probably wouldn't be able to volunteer this time. There I was trying to create a *be willing to bleed to support your dojo* mentality, and that role model in our midst was teaching all the more impressionable koohais and kids that there were things in life that were *just too difficult* that would make it impossible to have that kind of *win at all costs* attitude.

I finally took that student aside, and said, "Please, next time I ask that question, say in front of the class, 'Osu! Sensei, I'll do my best! Osu! I have to check on my work responsibility, but I think I will be able to work it out!'" Here, the role model presents a fighting spirit even if what's in that student's heart is a defeatist one.

So, yes, in fact. Please lie, if that's what it takes for you to present a strong front—i.e. if that demonstration of strength really does feel like a lie to you. (It looks to me more like an optimistic expression of the same reality, one that maintains an open mind to maybe being able to work out the stronger option!) I would have far preferred for this student to tell me later, in private, that he/she tried, but wasn't going to be able to go. And I told that student so.

Lo and behold, a year later that situation came up again, and lo and behold, that same student revealed to the whole dojo that same defeatist attitude. Right in front of the same group of koohais, "Osu! I'm not sure, errr, I have to check onnn . . ." and then the list started once again.

As of the time I'm writing this book, that student is no longer training at my dojo.

I hope he/she will read this book, figure out that attitude is a decision, make the decision to stay at the front of the curve, and come back and resume his/her training, and do it the right way this time.

There is no defeatist attitude in Budo. If that's what life dealt you, the Budo karate dojo is the place to acquire the stronger way. But be careful! Learning attitude has very little to do with waiting to acquire it. You have to acquire it in the one instant that it takes you to make that decision. The advantage of the dojo is that you surround yourself with like-minded individuals who also routinely make that same decision.

Whether that student knew it or not, he/she was working, hard, to make my dojo into one that supports defeatism, rather than one that supports Mas Oyama's Budo karate.

But it's *my way or the highway* in Budo karate.

That student is no longer around. Lots of sweat spilled. Very little gained in the end.

67. "Long Stance, Please. No, Long Stance!" The H-Type Student's Ball and Chain

I'm almost embarrassed even to write it, because by doing so I'm letting other instructors (and students) in other dojos know that it's a struggle I face in my dojo, and—worse!—letting folks in other countries know that it's a challenge Americans face with trying to grasp Budo karate.

But I suppose I have to be tough enough to take whatever criticism may come. Imagine the following situation:

We're practicing an exercise as a group. Long stances are required, but the H-type student present has a weak stance: it's not long, it's not low, the student is not persevering. So the teacher says, "Long stance, please," and the student responds, "Osu!" and makes his/her stance longer, but not long enough. So the teacher repeats, "No, *long* stance, please!"

"Osu!" the student responds and makes another insufficient correction in the right direction. I already described the situation in section #12, *Hear It Twice? It's Life and Death.*

If you're reading this book, clearly, you want to adopt the training ideals of the Budo karate dojo, so please don't make your sempai beg you for a satisfactory correction! If you hear it a second time, do something drastic! Consider how weak you look to take everyone's time making baby corrections and never getting to where you're supposed to be.

In America, I see students who come to the dojo thinking they can *buy* karate, who do this all the time. They're also the students that seem to be often unhappy in training. It's too HARD for them.

Change your life! Cut the chain! It's hard because of YOU!

Just once, make a big overcorrection and your life will start to change. You'll hear your teacher say, "Good job!" instead of repeating himself over and over, convincing you potentially, on some level, that you are in fact less strong that you actually are.

Be sure to read on to #68 immediately below, *Your Teacher ALWAYS Remembers*.

68. Your Teacher ALWAYS Remembers

As hard as it might be to fathom, your teacher always remembers the thing he/she told you last, and probably even the thing he told you once, *way back then*, in the past.

And yet, your teacher has so many students! And your teacher tells each student so many things! How is this possible? If you understand the answer to this question, it will help you to learn karate better and faster.

If you tried to memorize all the things you're supposed to do or that your teacher tells you to do, keeping up with it all would be quite difficult indeed.

However if you simply VALUE the relationship you have with your teacher and VALUE what you're learning, it will instill in you a FEELING of wanting to do the things your teacher tells you to do. Rather than memorizing bunches of things, if you allow that one FEELING to develop, every time an exercise or a situation comes up about which your teacher has told you something before, just seeing that exercise or that situation again will make you recall that thing your teacher last told you.

Your teacher, by definition, values making you successful.

He/she values YOU, at least to the extent that your teacher values your learning process, because your teacher's success rests on whether or not you learn. If you punch, therefore, and your teacher sees, and then advises you on how to punch better or differently, the image of you, and your punch, and the *how to do it better* all ingrains itself in your teacher's mind. The next time your teacher sees you, or at the very least the next time your teacher *sees you punch*, therefore, right there, foremost in your teacher's mind, is that instruction, and a sense of "Hmmm, I wonder if this student will remember what I told him/her last time, and whether he/she will be able to SHOW me his/her consciousness of my advice by making an effort to make the adjustment happen." You can be assured that if you do, your teacher will feel pleased, and if you don't — if you instead show that you've forgotten, or didn't understand the first time, or have disregarded the advice because you didn't value it enough — you can be sure that your teacher will FEEL that, too.

One might approach the matter by considering that for everything you do in the dojo, there is something that your teacher has told you (or the whole class) about how to do it better. It would be wonderful if each and every one of the *things* that you do sparks a memory of *how* your teacher told you to do it. If you can then show a mindfulness of that *how*, your progress — and your relationship with your teacher! — will be the strongest possible.

But that's still an awful lot of things to remember.

What's the best way to master them all?

Allow yourself to develop a FEELING of appreciation, and of wanting to please. Protect it even if your teacher is cross with you sometimes and pushing you in a way you might not understand.

If you FEEL for your teacher's lessons, they will come back to you.

If you don't, and if each time you punch, for example, your teacher is having to tell you the same things again, you will have conveyed the fact that you don't VALUE what your teacher is trying to teach you, and you will have conveyed disrespect.

For most, this should be a no-brainer.

This is America, though, and there are those who resist this kind of surrender.

Give it a chance, though.

Again, it's a SINGLE attitude change you can make — at least insofar as it is a single value you can adopt — and you will be empowered in a way you couldn't previously imagine. It is the Budo karate system. Take the leap of faith. Give yourself over to your teacher, and you will join the ranks of the best students.

With your bare hands, would you rather fashion a statue out of warm clay, or brittle ice?

Of course, the clay is better; it's impossible to work with the ice without a hammer. So you, as a student, have to make yourself like the clay. Make yourself a pleasure to work with, a pleasure for your teacher to shape, and you will become all that you hoped you could be.

69. The ACB Ease, Not the ABC Lock

Here is a critical concept having to do with following your teacher's *how*, not only his/her *what*. (See #2, *It's the* How, *Silly, Not the* What.) Beginners should read very carefully. Upwards to 50% of all new students find themselves for a time in a situation that threatens their very success as a karate student, and yet, it's one that's very easily avoided if you're aware of it, and if you understand the point here presented.

In other words, understand this concept, and you'll never have this kind of problem.

If a complex motion or series of motions is confusing you, your teacher is very likely telling you the exact shortcut you need to alleviate your confusion, but there's a chance you're not hearing it because you're trying too hard to keep up. That is, you're trying so hard to understand that you're not paying any attention to the answer that would make it easy for you. The solution is simple: Buckle down and remind yourself that you're supposed to listen for the *how*, and SHOW that you did in fact hear it. Understand that in this case the *how* has to do with how best to sort out in your head the complex task being asked of you, rather than the more common case, where the *how* refers to how your teacher wants you do to the technique better.

An example will make this concept very clear. Read the quote and listen for the *what* and the *how*. Your teacher demonstrates the technique as he/she explains:

"When your partner kicks, block while cutting [stepping] to 90 degrees, and counterattack with a kage tsuki, and then gedan mawashi geri to the inner thigh, and then straight punch, like this. *Make sure you concentrate on the step! When your opponent kicks, drop your heel back to pivot on your front foot to face your opponent from the side . . . like this . . .*"

I know that was difficult, even to read, for beginners, but I'll sort it out for you.

You know there's a *what*, and there's a *how*. I've italicized the *how*, and left the *what* in regular font. If you haven't gotten this point already, understand that almost every instruction you hear has two parts like this: first *what* your teacher wants you to do, then *how* he/she wants you to do it. The *how* often has as much to do with *how to learn* something, how to better sort it out in your head, as it has to do with how to make the technique more efficient. We've already established that the student who remains deaf to the *how* is the H-type student, while the T-type student is the one who learns how to SHOW that he/she heard and is trying to accomplish the *how*.

In the above example, it's easy to see how the H-type situation can occur.

The beginning student struggles to understand *what* he/she is supposed to do—note the complexity of the instruction in the example!—and is working so hard on *that* that he/she can no longer hear the critical piece of advice that follows. The student is working so hard to process the *what* that he/she can no longer understand basic English by the time the all-critical *how* comes along.

Here's the completely human pitfall that you can DECIDE not to find yourself in by prioritizing the *how* in this case, where the *how* applies to how to sort out your confusion in a given situation.

Consider ABC, where A is the defense (block/evade), B is the triple counterattack, and C is the critical piece of advice, "concentrate on your step . . . like this." The confused beginner is often working so hard on sorting out his block and triple counterattack (the hand motions) that he/she's dropped C, the critical advice, to the lowest priority, and it gets lost completely beneath the then-futile challenge of memorization. That student's incorrect order of focusing on the detail of the instruction given is ABC.

What's the correct order here?

You got it, it's ACB, or even maybe CB, and I'll get to that in a second.

Your teacher just told you how to alleviate your confusion. Your teacher told you to prioritize the stepping—the footwork. Yet you were so intent on understanding what the hand motions were that you ignored that critical piece of advice. The hand motions won't make sense from the wrong position, and they will therefore be near impossible to memorize.[2] Can you see how this beginner innocently undid him/herself?

So what's the answer?

Make sure you prioritize *hearing* the critical piece, *the how*, in cases where you're confused doing a complex motion. The student here who masters the step—it's only one motion, after all!—and is confused on the hand motions is already 90% correct. The student who attempts to do the hand motions without the step is 0% correct even if he/she is doing the correct hand motions, because they'd don't work from the original position.

Should we not admire the ABC student's determination? His/her desire is correct—he/she really wants to understand *something*, right?

Well, yes and no. The stronger attitude, the Budo karate attitude, is to make sure you *listen* to your teacher, even in situations when it's hard to hear, and prioritize what your teacher tells you to prioritize.

So what about the 3rd option, the "CB" I mentioned above?

If A is your cut-to-the-corner defense, the *what*, C is your footwork, and B is your block and counterattack, I'd like you to consider here that the most successful student starts to transcend the *what* altogether.

Remember my discussion in #31, *Treat New Students Delicately? No! Slow Motion is Akin to the Assassination of Learning for the New Student*

---

[2] Note that in this particular case, from a self-defense point of view, the hand motions mean nothing in the absence of the correct step, anyway. The correct step, on the other hand, means a great deal, because you moved out of range to a position of advantage, even if you don't understand the hand motions. In other words, it was the stepping that saved your life; the counterattacks just took out your opponent so your opponent couldn't attack you again. But you would not have that choice if you were already defeated because you failed to step.

about how babies are our fastest learners? This really might be considered a Zen concept, but the student who is able to take the rationalization out of the learning process and just soak it up, not unlike an imitating child would, actually has a big advantage over those who think about it too much.

So why CB?

Well, the important part of the instruction was the footwork, right? So why not start there? Forget about what you're supposed to achieve and just respond automatically to what your teacher just told you was the most important aspect of the exercise.

Did I lose you?

Figure this one out, *transcend*, and you will have elevated yourself onto a steep learning curve indeed!

70. Your Teacher Can Read YOUR Mind, Learn to Read Your Teacher's

Your teacher can read your mind.

Really!

Remember the *what* and the *how* described in #2? Review that section and you'll see that it encourages you to train your ear to be hypersensitive to the instructions your teacher gives you. Sometimes there won't be a *how*, but most of the time there's a *what* and a *how*.

Your teacher can — and does! — read your mind all the time, at least to the extent that your teacher KNOWS what you're concentrating on when you execute a technique, or, at the very least, KNOWS whether or not you're focusing on the thing he/she has asked you to focus on.

Imagine you're stepping forward in a long stance and punching as in the second count of the kata Taikyoku sono Ichi. Your teacher has just given the class a lecture on the ways beginners (and sometimes non-beginners!) tend to *cheat* in this difficult long step, such as bobbing their pulling fist back and forth, or swinging their pulling hand elbows out to the side in order to build momentum for the difficult long step. (The problem with that, of course, is that it makes a would-be single motion into a double motion, and we often don't survive those in self-defense situations.)

So, one student steps forward on the count and makes no effort to control his/her pulling hand. Another student, however, is red-faced with effort, trying even more than is probably necessary in order to isolate that pulling hand, elbow, and arm.

Does the teacher know which one was concentrating on what he/she just told the class to concentrate on?

What do you think?

Which one is the Budo karateka, and which one still thinks karate is going to fall on him/her from Heaven? Which one is the T-type student, and which one the H?

You can be pretty sure that your teacher is watching to see whether or not you do what he/she JUST advised you to do.

It's always that way.

It's amazing, therefore, to see the number of students who don't realize that fact — in the case of the above example, the number of students who let their pulling hand bob, even seconds after they were just told not to do exactly that.

So! Why not turn this around?

Why not take this for granted, and realize that you can read your teacher's mind, too!

If your teacher says, "Punch harder, please!" you can be assured that he/she's thinking . . . you tell me . . . What *is* your teacher thinking the next time you punch?

Did you figure it out?

Good! Exactly right! Your teacher was thinking, "Let's see how hard these students are going to punch!"

If your teacher says, "Keep your stances low!" you can be assured that your teacher is then watching to see . . . you got it! Yes, he/she's watching to see how low your stance is.

Wow! Isn't that cool!

You've just become psychic!

If your teacher asked everyone in your last class to please make sure their eyes are fixed on their targets when punching, or even if your teacher asked everyone to do so three classes ago, or three months ago, you can be pretty sure that when you do punches in any future class, your teacher will be watching to see if you're going to keep your eyes on your target, and not only that, but also the other limited number of things he/she has advised you to remember when performing punches.

It's amazing to see in the American dojo, therefore, when students come in and punch in class after class, sometimes with zero demonstration that they're aware of what their teacher is likely looking for.

"But I'm doing what you ask!" I see in the eyes of the exasperated student.

But did you catch the mistake?

You got it! I wasn't asking for a *what* at all. I was asking for a *how*!

If this is the case, though, and if you can indeed read your teacher's mind so much of the time, why not use that to try to please your teacher ALL THE TIME? Listen to your teacher's words and you can anticipate what he/she wants to see, all the time!

If you know that—and all of you should now that you've read this book—you can start to show your teacher that you're aware of what he/she is thinking, and your teacher will be like, "Wow! What a strong student! Why don't we move on to something more at his/her level! Something a bit more interesting!"

Your teacher suddenly wants to reward you for grasping the lesson so well!

71. Telepathy? Hyper-Empathy?

"How could I possibly have known that?" I see that question sometimes in the faces of my students when I tell them that I had expected them to respond a certain way, and they failed to do so.

We have a saying in karate that, as a teacher, it's far better to spend a lifetime creating one single student who truly understands than it is to create ten thousand who have missed the point. Although I do not have the experience, yet, of making that one single student who really, truly gets it, I do believe myself to be well positioned for creating a lot more than just one before I'm through. And that's exactly because *I DO have the experience*, maybe, of *being* that one single student to my first teacher, Mas Oyama's nephew Seong Soo Choi.

Now . . . in the Budo karate system I'm not really supposed to say that.

If I said that within my first teacher's earshot, he would angrily tell me that I was out of line. How vain, after all! Nevertheless, for the sake of this book, I will presume to say that I know that I have had a level of connection with a teacher that no other of his students ever had. It felt almost telepathic how well I knew his expectations—and I'll say more about that momentarily — but the point is that when I encourage my own students to read me better, to know what my expectations were earlier, to open their hearts and minds — and eyes! — wider, to perceive me and my lessons better, I do KNOW something about what I'm talking about. I have been there. I know intimately exactly where I'm encouraging my own students to go. Revisit that final point made in #69, *The ACB Ease, Not the ABC Lock*. Remember that in Budo karate there's a surface lesson, and an esoteric. Fight to get the esoteric, and mastering the surface lesson becomes automatic.

But if I'm not supposed say, "I was that student who got it," why put myself at risk by mentioning it?

Because, while I do know that I had a closer connection with my first teacher than any of his other students, what I DO NOT KNOW is whether more of his students might have *also* had such a close connection, had they known that such a connection was both so desirable to have, AND out there to be had.

If they had stumbled upon that channel like I did, would they have had it, too?

Did they not stumble upon it simply because it's such a foreign concept, and they had no one there to alert them to its existence?

In my case, I was so desperate to learn (desperate to remake myself as an unhappy teenager) that, once I identified my teacher as the person that could help me get there, I let down my guard entirely, I took the greatest leap of faith imaginable. I had no inhibitions against drinking every drop from every glass of knowledge he handed me, even when what he was handing me seemed at first to be something that didn't make much sense.

It turns out that INHIBITIONS against thus letting down one's guard might be what makes karate inherently difficult for Americans, and probably even for Westerners in general.

Yet, remember that your karate and, more specifically, your relationship with your teacher, is meant to be your Petri dish for practicing, safely, *the human relationship* at a level of gravity that you might not have an opportunity to do elsewhere (see #20, *The Deepening of Human Relationships*). Of course I have to hesitate to say so, because there is ALSO the case where your teacher, in *your* dojo, might be somehow unethical or incorrect, but if you're relatively sure that he/she is not, I strongly recommend letting down your guard, and stepping out from your safety zone to see if, with this one person in your world, you can't take human interaction, human communication perhaps, to a higher level.

Of course your teacher is human. Your teacher makes mistakes and faces human challenges like everyone else. But if your teacher has spent many years engaging in communication on a higher level (at those times when he/she finds someone with whom he/she can thus communicate), and if your teacher has spent many years seeking and (when he/she is lucky enough) *engaging* in relationships that are held to a higher standard, why not dive in and see if you can be one of the ones to benefit from that rare type of experience?

I can guarantee you that students and teachers in the East often develop channels of communication, and, more importantly, of knowledge exchange, that most of us in the West can't fathom.

Please read #72, *"Channel" Your Teacher's Teaching*. In it, I continue this exact discussion.

72. "Channel" Your Teacher's Teaching

Can you imagine what it means to *channel* your teacher's teaching?

If you've read straight through to this point, I'm sure you're starting to have some idea.

It means helping to facilitate what your teacher teaches to flow not only unimpeded into you, but also through you, and into your koohais after you. It is the type of relationship that every teacher wants to have with a student, and I would like to suggest, here, that you don't have to be anything special to be the one who receives the absolute best of what your teacher has to offer. You just have to open your heart a bit, open your eyes and ears a bit wider, and take the leap of faith.

I'll tell one quick story that might help you understand.

There were times when I was a teenager when I would know what my first teacher was about to do or say, and other students would look at me like I was some kind of freak for my apparent ability to do so.

The easiest example to recount occurred during a lecture he was giving during training in which he was telling a story that he told sometimes about his uncle, Mas Oyama. Each time he got to a certain point in the story he would use his shinai (split-bamboo training sword) to demonstrate a motion to help illustrate his story. One day, having seen the story told two or three times—just as the other students had!—when my teacher got to that part of the story, I broke ranks by leaving the lineup where we were all standing at attention, and took up his shinai where it was leaning against the wall behind him, but out of his reach, and handed it to him at the exact moment when he needed it to tell that part of his story. He complimented me by not even looking up at me to say thank you, but rather by taking the sword from me as if it was HIS telepathic will that had sent me to get it for him in the first place.

Other students' jaws dropped.

"How could Nathan have possibly known!?" they wondered. "How did Nathan dare to break ranks at that moment without being told to do so?"

Clearly, I was getting something that they weren't, and I can only imagine that it had to do with letting myself go and taking that leap of faith. Perhaps, in our culture, it's a scary thing to do because some of the people we encounter are not trustworthy. People are so accustomed to knowing people who only have their own best interests in mind that they don't trust other people, even when they meet someone with whom their best interests are aligned.

Try this on for size:

After eight years with my first teacher, there were some things about him that I did NOT want to follow. Like his uncle, Mas Oyama, he was human, and humans make mistakes. I wouldn't have followed Mas Oyama, either, if he'd ever once asked me to do something unethical—or at least I wouldn't probably in that one particular thing. Yet, since neither man did, and even though there were some things about each man that I didn't want to emulate in my future, by letting down my guard 100%, by taking the leap of faith, and *surrendering to the totality of their lessons* I know that I got far more of the positive that they had to offer than some others around me who were more on guard.

Remember, if you're MY student, that you and I are on the same side. I might be cross with you sometimes—and my disadvantaged students will sometimes sadly conclude that my being cross with them indicates that I'm NOT on their side—but that doesn't change the fact that my goal is to make you great at karate, and your life happier and fuller as a result. Every teacher's goal is to make great students. Why not, therefore, trust me a little bit?

Why not take that leap of faith?

One final image might help you:

Do you know what it means to *make a wave* with your arm (like a break dancer would)? For those who don't, start to move your arm like a bird would flap its wing, but instead of keeping it rigid, allow it to *ripple* like a bullwhip or an ocean wave.

Now, have you ever held someone else's hand and *started a wave* that you let run down the length of your arm and transfer's into the arm of your friend?

Try it 3 times with a friend.

The first time, instruct your friend to relax and help you to make a perfect, continuous wave. The second time, instruct your friend to refuse to be moved at all. And the third, time instruct your friend to make an opposite wave that not only stops yours, but also tries to take you violently in another direction.

In the Budo karate dojo of Japan, the student is always compliant and *supple* in terms of following his/her teacher. The student, therefore, allows him/herself to be moved without resistance. In order to do so, the student also has to read well what his/her teacher's intent was, and let it flow through him/her like that successful *arm wave* would.

The American student, being highly individualistic and prone to thinking about *me first*, is more likely to not interpret the intent properly, refuse to be moved by it, or decide that *my way* is a better way, thus forcing a different message to be transmitted (i.e. to one's koohai) than the one that was delivered.

Endeavor to make yourself like the first case.

Channel your teacher's teaching. Let your teacher's gentle wave *flow* into you, and beyond you to your koohais. If there are choppy waters in the dojo, it's you or your classmates that brought them there. Channel your teacher's lessons, and all dojo waves should be gentle, soothing ones.

See #9, *BE the Ocean!*

73. Karate Teachers Have to Teach Your Parents, Too?

Sometimes, yes, indeed they do, when the student is a child.

As a teacher, it's important to understand that there's a limited amount

I can achieve, because the parent in the home always has a stronger influence in the child's life. Of course, most parents get it, and are my best allies. Some, however, sometimes need a gentle nudge to know how best to help me help their child get stronger.

This was actually a point that Kyokushin-kan's Kancho Hatsuo Royama made during a lecture, but one with which I was already well versed.

Of course when teaching kids your only student is the child, but, at the same time, sometimes you have to treat the parent-child *as a unit* in order to drive the lesson home.

Parents, though?

If you're reading this book in order to help your child better understand his or her karate classes?

Please just recognize that there are times when I will depend on you to help me get a point across. Understand also that if *you* miss the point, you might be making life difficult for your child by pushing him/her in a different direction. If you read this book, even if you don't practice karate, you'll have a clear idea of what I'm trying to achieve, and why team spirit and a strong class average are so important to the development of your child.

74. You Carry the Dojo, Dummy! If the Dojo's Carrying You, You're in the Wrong Dojo

You're supposed to carry the dojo!

If the dojo's carrying you, you're failing! You've missed the point. You don't *get* the workout you're provided; you *provide* the workout.

Read this book one more time.

It's YOUR dojo, not mine!

YOU are responsible for carrying it, cleaning up its messes, and making it stronger!

The passive student that waits for strength and proficiency at karate to fall on them from above will have to wait a very, very long time.

So please! Quit waiting! Make your dojo the strongest one, make your dojo the purest one, and your own karate will be the best it can be!

It's not your teacher's job to give you strength and energy. It's YOUR job to bring it—and develop it over time!

75. Which Path Do You Really Want to Take?

What's the shortest distance between two points? A straight line, right?

Draw two points on a piece of paper, six inches apart. Imagine one point is your day one, and the other is someday when you have become fairly proficient at karate. To complete your ideal timeline, connect the two points with a straight line, with an arrowhead pointing in the direction of progress. Now connect the same two points with a squiggly line. Which path would you rather take, the direct one that takes ten years, or the indirect one that takes twenty? (See the upper of the two diagrams provided.)

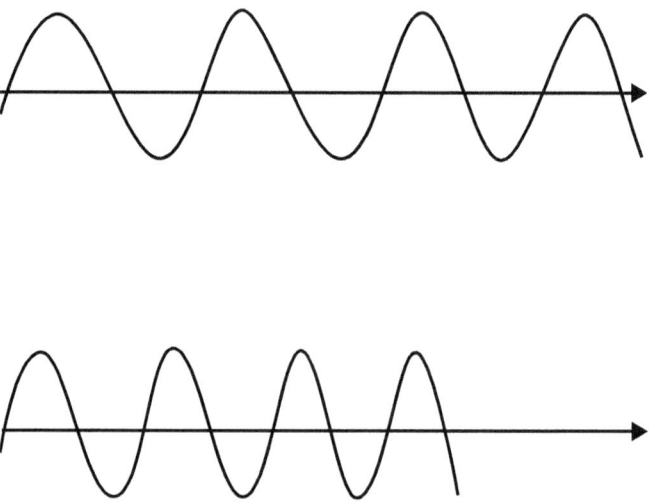

First, please understand that it's your job to keep your progress as straight as possible. When you veer off course, it's your teacher's job to nudge you back into line. Please, therefore, recognize when your teacher is nudging you, and allow yourself to be nudged.

Clearly, we'd all rather get to proficiency sooner, but I need to adjust my model before I make my point. Draw two more points, and connect them with another straight line. Now redraw the squiggly line, but stop the squiggly line short of the destination. (See the lower of the two diagrams.)

Your teacher's job is to guide you along the best possible course to becoming a great Budo karateka. (AND of course it's your job to make it easy for your teacher to guide you!) One might think, as in the first drawing, that if you don't follow your teacher's advice, it will take you much longer to get there, perhaps 20 years instead of 10. But that's not quite it. That's why we made our diagram a second time.

I'd like to suggest that if you don't follow your teacher's advice, you will NEVER get there. You will NEVER achieve what you set out achieve.

Why?

Because following, and knowing how to follow, is a prerequisite for greatness within the Budo karate system.

What's your goal? To be a tough fighter? To be physically healthier? To learn self-defense?

Sure, if you've limited what you hope to achieve through your training to such narrow goals as these, you can battle through ten years, resisting 50% of your teacher's advice, and you might get as strong as the guy who diligently followed his teacher's advice for the first five of those years. You'd have to have started five years earlier than the other guy to make the same progress if you're not trusting your teacher. But a great Budo karateka?

No.

Remember, Mas Oyama said that karate is not Budo without the sempai-koohai system, and getting an A+ in the kicks and punches and an F in the human interaction of the sempai-koohai system is the same as getting an overall F in Budo karate. Who in life cares about a tough guy, anyway?

The bottom line?

Struggle to follow your teacher's advice.

You can't get there without him/her. See #44, *Karate IS Your Teacher's Karate*. Remember *my way or the highway*? It is, in Budo karate. A, you won't get as far, as fast. B, you won't get to the destination *at all*. If your teacher is one you can't follow for whatever reason, if you lack the oomph to try and follow even when the going gets rough, find another dojo.

The Americanized dojo will give you enough of an imitation—and enough camaraderie from others who are like-minded—that you'll be able to convince yourself that your karate is all that karate was ever meant to be. In the West there are plenty out there that will assure you that YOUR karate is complete. They need to, after all, in order to convince themselves that theirs is, too. This is the Western business model for the martial arts school.

76. Be Powerful, Be Confident the First Time, Too!

Remember how you're supposed to take responsibility for owning the complex exercises you've only been shown? (See #7, *OWN the Complex Series of Motions You've Been Shown.*)

It's a common symptom of the beginning student who is stuck on the wrong path, one on which they still think the heart of karate *learning* has something to do with memorization, that the first time in any one class session they're asked to perform a complex exercise they've learned before, they do it in a *tentative* way, a softer, fearful way. That student's demeanor suggests he/she is *questioning* whether or not he/she is doing it right.

And this might go on forever, if he/she doesn't one day move his/her training onto the next level.

This student may not realize that he/she is actually the H in the room, especially because by the second or third time through (the second or third time *in one class session*), he/she may have gained confidence and is now performing the exercise as well as, if not even better than, the rest.

But *better than the rest* doesn't matter, does it, if the important thing is getting it to be powerful the first time?

How many chances to do you get in a self-defense situation? Someone is stabbing you with a knife and you have to block and counter or you will lose your life. Do you get a practice run? Do you get two or three chances to warm up?

No. You get one chance only, so you should steer clear of this type of training that essentially conditions you to fail without practice runs.

It is, perhaps, a habit carried over from when you were a white belt.

White belts are very often tentative in their first motions of complex series of motions because it's all so new, and that's to be expected. Remember, though, that in my introduction I told you that I would warn you away from certain pitfalls? Here's one. Make sure that as soon as you have your first colored belt, you are prioritizing performing the exercises that you know powerfully and confidently from the very first move, and class after class.

You have to in order to break the habit of doing your exercises as if it's your first time doing them.

Here's a prime example of how a habit can lower a dojo standard. Is it your dojo's habit to do a kata for the first time on a given day in a weak way, as if you need to do it once or twice to warm up? I've seen brown belt students who know already a dozen kata beginning each one of their kata this way, clearly revealing that they've fallen victim to a routine they formed when they were much less experienced.

Please, train your ear to hear your teacher when he/she first announces a new exercise for the evening. Is it Pinan 4? Then when you hear "Hajime!" ("Begin!"), make sure that your first motion is powerful and confident, because you know this kata, after all. If you do so, you'll be helping your teacher to raise the dojo's standard. If, on the other hand, you do that first motion in a tentative way because that's your habit, you're keeping your dojo's level down.

The tentative, questioning motion is that of the H-type student. The confident one is that of the T. Which would you rather be? Remember that being the T is a choice, not a talent. Remember that you're required to make that choice to be part of your Budo karate dojo.

77. Seiza, Lines, Fudo Dachi, Raise Your Hand, Listen to Lecture: The How-To's

Please, there's only one way to do all of these things, and it is one of the fundamental rules of etiquette that you do them all correctly.

Note that unlike bowing and saying "Osu!" which are things that you have to DO, the five I've grouped here are more akin to positions that you HOLD. So as not to keep you in suspense, I'll jump first into raising your hand, and listening to your teacher speaking (such as during a lecture), because karate students in other schools might not consider these a standard part of a dojo's rules of etiquette.

To make training in your dojo resemble training in Mas Oyama's, however, they probably should be.

When your teacher or sempai is addressing the group, it is rude if you don't maintain eye contact. If you're looking down to pick at your toenail *and* paying attention, it's not enough, because by looking away you're making yourself an H in a room that's duty-bound to stay a room full of T's, and you have therefore disrespected not only your teacher, but also your classmates. If you're watching an H-type classmate who's misbehaving (and whom your teacher's trying to ignore), you are supporting their H-type behavior, simply by not showing that you're paying close attention to your teacher.

Of course, you should be careful, because most times when you're performing karate motions, your teacher does not want you to look away from your target in order to make eye contact. There's a bit of a dynamic in that situation to learn, but what we can say for certain is that if your teacher is lecturing, and you're just standing or sitting, you must maintain eye contact.

How do you raise your hand in the dojo?

There's only one way, please. Straight arm, straight up, tight fist. If we learned how to raise our hands from public school, there are all kinds of *in-betweens*: hands opened and closed, halfway up and halfway down, as if to suggest, "I think I know the answer, but I'm not at all confident, and I'm really afraid, after all, to speak up."

And that's the point.

The T-type student has to be confident. Raise your hand like you mean it, or not at all.

Not at all?

Well, if your teacher asks you for a volunteer, we know from #66, *Volunteers?* that all hands should go up. Now we know *how* they're supposed to be raised.

What if your teacher asks you a question?

In the Budo karate system, T's know the answer. H's don't. But remember that there aren't supposed to be any H's in the dojo, so you do have to answer. If you've been paying attention and *channeling* your teacher's teaching, you know the answer. If your teacher asks a question your hand should be the first to go up. Make sure it's straight up. Make sure it's a fist. See #72, *"Channel" Your Teacher's Teaching*.

How about lines?

We do a lot of work in lines and grids in the dojo. When you're standing in a line, it's your job to keep it straight, and to keep people in it spaced evenly. If you're in a grid, you have a line to your right and to your left (which you have to keep straight and evenly spaced) AND you have a line in front of you and behind you (which you ALSO have to keep straight and evenly spaced). Here's a key place in which new students confuse priorities. If you are confused as to what you're supposed to be doing (you're practicing a new kata, for example), and you allow yourself to get out of line (or out of the grid), you have affected the whole group. You've encroached on the space of your classmates. If, on the other hand, you're confused, but at least in your proper place, the fact that you're temporarily the H in the room at least isn't *directly* interfering with other students.

A rule of etiquette?

Yes!

Keep your lines straight, keep your grids evenly spaced. Prioritize the line or the grid over your own technique. Don't be the one who has to be told that you've drifted out of position.

I recommend, when you're lined up in a grid, that every other time you come back to stationary (the end of a kata, for example), you look behind you. Why?

What's behind you?

You got it! Your koohai!

Your koohai might not know as well as you to how to maintain a grid, and yet YOU are responsible for the lines behind you as well. If you're five feet from the student in front of you and five feet from the students on your right and your left, how are you going to know if you're only three feet from the student behind you?

You won't, unless you check over your shoulder every once in a while. Remember that koohais and kids tend to creep forward. Make sure you're not the koohai (or the kid) that does just that.

But isn't it that other guy's fault, the guy standing too close behind you?

Well, yes, he's at fault, but you are also responsible. You're the sempai. Therefore, it's both of your faults.

Seiza and fudo dachi?

I'm not going to teach them here. I'll only tell you what the number-one errors made are, and point out that the errors are breaches in the code of dojo etiquette.

In fudo dachi you must be still and have equal weight on both feet. The easiest way to do this is to squeeze your fists so tight they turn white. This is the correct fudo dachi. Any other is substandard. The one who isn't still, but fidgets? It's rude. You have to be still, you have to have your eyes forward, your fists have to be squeezed tight. Maintain eye contact if your teacher is lecturing.

The number one error made in seiza is not to have one's back straight and vertical. Many, particularly adult, Americans complain about sitting in this position. Yet it's a position that 99% of us can sit in comfortably if we only stick it out long enough to figure out how.

Remember above when I was talking about eye contact while sitting during a lecture? How rude it is to look away?

It's just as rude to fidget and lean sideways or forward in seiza because your ankles are uncomfortable.

Remember that EVERYONE has some discomfort at first sitting in seiza. Remember next that Budo karate is SUPPOSED to be uncomfortable sometimes.

This is the spirit of "Osu!": to persevere through hardship.

If your ankles hurt and you run away from the discomfort, it is not Budo. If your ankles hurt and you battle not to let anyone else know, you got it!

Now that's Budo!

Of course there *is* a second way to sit in the dojo. Every time one sits for the first time, one must sit in seiza. Sometime afterwards, however, your teacher will often tell you, "Relax and sit comfortably." Yet even this has a correct *how* to do it right:

Lean forward to bow from the seiza position with your fists on the floor in front of you, cross your ankles underneath you and sit back into a cross-legged position, back upright and with your wrists on your knees. Note that "sit comfortably" does not mean "sit however you want."

Note that your teacher knows if you are uncomfortable sitting in seiza (if you are), and he/she WANTS to tell you to "relax and sit comfortably" if you are persevering and sitting upright anyway. If you're fidgeting, on the other hand, and disrupting the energy of the class by showing, overtly, how much you're suffering, you make it very difficult for your teacher to reward you by saying, "Relax and sit comfortably."

Your teacher will always tell someone who has a genuine problem—an older person, for example—to sit comfortably from the beginning. But be careful!

That's your teacher's job to decide whether you have that handicap or not, and if you're not old or injured and you *ask for it* by showing how uncomfortable you are, the "relax and sit comfortably" you want to hear will likely never come, and you will have merely embarrassed yourself—and lowered your dojo's standard!—by making the display.

Remember that your teacher has been there. See #55, *Your Teacher Has Been There, Your Teacher Has to Know 10 Things to Teach You One,* and #56, *Your Teacher Sees You in High Definition.*

78. Coddle Your Koohai?

Please don't!

Celebrate their strengths with them by training hard beside them, but please don't coddle your koohais for their shortcomings. You can ADVISE them on how to overcome their limitations, but make sure your interaction with them doesn't give them license to hold on to them.

In a later section I will make the point that your dojo is not a Budo karate dojo unless your teacher is pressing you, sometimes, to confront your physical, mental, and spiritual limitations. That's how we become strong.

Confronting those limitations, however, what do you do with a student that expresses despair? "This is SOOO hard!" he/she might complain.

So encourage that student! Tell him/her to brace up, but make 100% sure that you don't either *tell* that student that it's okay to fail, or *show* him/her with your behavior that failing is acceptable.

"Osu! It IS hard at first," you might say, "but if you keep your head up and keep pushing forward—that's what 'osu!' means after all!—you'll figure it out! You'll get there! Fight on!" Here you've befriended your koohai, you've encouraged your koohai, and, most importantly, you've provided no refuge for failure, or thoughts of failure.

"This is SOOO hard!" your koohai complains, on the other hand, and you, the weaker role model, respond, "I know it is, it kicks my ass, too! Some days I just go through the motions. Sensei's expectations are pretty strict. Some of us won't ever get there, so don't worry."

Huh! Really?

Yes, really! And worse than that, worse than commiserating with the failing student verbally, weak role models will commiserate with them, often unknowingly, through their behavior. Strong, strong, strong, weak, is a terrible pattern for a role model, because it teaches the koohai that behaving strong is so hard that every once in a while the normal response is to quit and not try.

I have seen students commiserating with their classmates in this way ... but only in America, never in Japan.

The verdict is still out for me, but I'm developing a hunch that this phenomenon also has a demographic element. I work with some folks through my nonprofit who have had a hard start to life. It's this group that seems most often to jump to the defense of its members' weaknesses. It's as if one such student supports the other in believing it's too hard, because they're afraid of not having that support themselves the next day, when it's too hard for them.

Think about this implication for the *Toes-Not-Heels Dojo* concept described in #4 and #5. If you're trying to develop a brotherhood of achievers, and yet your majority is a brotherhood that reinforces itself for underachieving, how can you possibly succeed?

The answer?

Provide no refuge for weakness in the dojo! Of course there's weakness there; that's normal. That's why people come to the dojo: to gain strength. But be careful to make sure that your response of sympathy can't be construed as coddling your Koohai.

Develop your understanding to where you can see that this type of dynamic exists. Understand it to be a potential problem. Drive it out of personalities of the students in the dojo. If the student holds too tightly to it, be willing even to drive that student out.

The Budo karate dojo can lift up the disadvantaged. A majority with a fatalistic mentality, however, isn't likely to come up with Budo karate all on its own.

79. BE a Karateka, Don't DO Karate

Only misguided karate has anything to do with religious intent, so please don't be confused as I use religion to make a point regarding a cultural difference between Japan and the West.

In America we tend to say, "I am a Christian," or "I am Jewish," or "I am a Buddhist." In Japan, however, those lines are less clear. Nearly all Japanese follow Shinto traditions, but the Japanese considered it a lucky day when Buddhism arrived from China, because the Buddhist priests had a solution for funerals (laying spirits to rest) that Shinto didn't have. And what a lucky day, again, when Christianity was no longer persecuted by the Japanese, because the Christians handled weddings so nicely! Indeed, it's not uncommon for Japanese to ask the Shinto deities for good luck before their exams, to pray to God at their weddings, and to ask Buddha for help when a loved one dies.

How bizarre! we might think in the West.

Set religion aside for now, however, because your religion is your business — you can be any religion (or none) and succeed at Budo karate — but consider, just as the Japanese can *be* a Buddhist and *be* a Christian at the same time, they also have no trouble *being* karateka (practitioners of karate) at the same time that they're also doctors, or lawyers, or businessmen, or students.

In America, we tend to *be* only one thing, and that tends to be our profession. Anything else we do is something that we *do*. Karate, for most Americans, becomes a hobby, even if they actually devote more time in their week to it, in some cases, than do Japanese karateka.

Yet which is stronger?

I would like to suggest that the student who *IS a karateka* but devotes six hours per week, is stronger than the Westerner who *DOES karate* for twenty.

Why?

It's the mentality. It's the purity of the pursuit.

The karateka has decided that karate is something that he/she IS. The hobbyist just dabbles.

My advice for you, the Western karateka?

Realize that you lose nothing by BEING a karateka.

Don't you want to be the T-type student? Don't you want to make sure that your karate is the strongest that it can be?

Then you have no choice.

You MUST BE a karateka. Simply DO karate, and you'll fail. Simply DO karate in the Budo karate dojo, and most likely you don't fit in. Probably — if you insist on resisting over time, or if this point never dawns on you — this is a good sign that you're in the wrong dojo.

80. Budo Karate Remakes You, Americanized Karate Teaches You a Skill

Consider the marathon runner and the linebacker.

They look different, don't they?

The marathon runner is tiny and wiry, and the linebacker is massive and beefy. Why is this so?

Well, of course it may have been a person of a smaller physical type that opted to become a runner, and a bigger, more muscular guy who opted to play football, but there's also no question that as the marathon runner trains to run marathons he/she starts to look more and more, physically, like a marathon runner, and the same for a football player: the more he trains to play football, the more he starts to take on those physical traits.

The point is that our bodies adapt through training and become *bodies built to do* whatever it is that we ask them, in a sustained way, to do.

Could you or I go work as one of those little guys in the Himalayas who carry twice their body weight up the Himalayan slopes every day?

Well, at first it would be much harder for us, but over time our bodies would adapt, and we'd start to *become the one built to do* just that activity.

Please understand that in Budo karate we seek to *become* karateka, physically as well, and that's significantly different from seeking to *learn* karate. Americanized karate is something that you *do*, Budo karate is something that you *are*.

The difference is in the approach.

If we train, like Mas Oyama in his youth, more hours per day than we sleep, of course we become karateka.

Yet even if we can't train that often, our training is designed to re-make us into *ones made for doing karate*. Frequency of training is, of course, important, but even more important than that, perhaps, is the attitude described in this book. If you fight to be the T-type student (as described in #4 and #5), you are becoming a karateka. If you're the H-type student, resisting the lessons and avoiding the hard training, you're merely *doing* karate as a hobby, and like I've said before, you're in the way of progress.

This is a Budo karate dojo.

Please don't try to make it into something less.

Oh, but don't panic!

Don't fret!

It's actually EASIER to follow the Budo karate way in the environment presented by this, your Budo karate dojo.

It just takes a leap of faith, and then your life becomes easier.

Fight to be first, not because you will be, but because if everyone does in this particular environment, everyone becomes a Budo karateka, AND everyone has an easier go of it for just that reason.

81. To Fight For Correct Training Attitude IS to Defend Your Life After All

Consider how tragic it would be if you spent years practicing karate and still couldn't defend yourself in a real self-defense situation.

This is the dilemma of the Americanized karate-for-profit business climate. Sure you could *learn some skills* and defend yourself against someone who wants to fight with you; in other words, you can *learn some skills* and use them to beat someone up who you might not be able to beat up otherwise. These are the types of successes that Americanized karate students might have, primarily because without the Budo, the student of karate is more likely to put him/herself into unsafe situations in the first place.

Please make sure you are defining *self-defense situation* as a Budo karateka would.

A self-defense situation is not fighting with a jerk with a bad attitude who wants to bloody your nose to impress his girlfriend. *A true self-defense situation is one in which you have to defend your physical safety or the safety of loved ones, when you are significantly disadvantaged either because you are much smaller, much weaker, caught off guard, outnumbered, or facing an armed attacker or multiple attackers.* For the Budo karateka THESE are examples of the true self-defense situation:

Someone with a weapon tries to kill you. Five guys jump you and you don't know whether their intent is to kill you or not. You are female, and a physically more powerful male attacks you. You are attacked by a pit bull.

Note that the key defining factor is the risk to your life AND that you are outmatched.

Kancho Royama tells a story about an instructor he knew who defended himself against 57 attackers who wanted to kill him. It was written up in a Tokyo newspaper in the 1950s. The police released him even though he'd killed three people that night, because by that time he was fighting on the same side as the police, who were also fighting, trying to stop the violence.

These were armed, but untrained attackers. They were gangsters in an area of Tokyo then known for its gangs.

So, please, *BUDO* karate.

That said, what is the importance of in-the-dojo training attitude to a true self-defense situation?

It's that you can't expect yourself to perform, on game day, somehow magically better than you do in training. If you train at 70% day in and day out, do you really think you can fight at 110% on game day? No, you'll fight at 85% if you're lucky.

Instead, you have to do on a daily basis what you'll have to do on tournament day in order to win. Of course, in training, there are all kinds of ways that we simulate certain elements of fighting so that we can prepare ourselves without fighting full contact every day. We simulate elements of fighting in time-practiced ways that our predecessors have shown can be *brought together* on game day to make a strong fight.

Oh, but in that light, ATTITUDE is the most important part!

If you get physically tougher you might be able to win in a schoolyard brawl, but if you want to really be able to save your life when it's truly in danger, you have to pursue mastery of karate. Note I said "pursue." Mastery is not as critical — of course, it would be nice! — as a correct attitude in which you are *pursuing* mastery.

In the Budo karate dojo to do otherwise is to fail, because training for mastery IS the correct Budo karate attitude.

If you train for failure, you will fail. If you train with an attitude that's not serious, you also won't be as serious as you need to be under pressure. If you don't win on a daily basis — against yourself — you can't win on game day against someone else.

Please understand that, in this light, training in the Budo karate dojo with the proper attitude, the one described here in this book, IS THE SAME as training to protect your life should you ever have to.

If you want fun-and-games karate, go down the street . . . but remember that *fun and games* is not going to save your life.

Remember, the Budo karateka is going to be *less* likely to fight in senseless situations in the first place because the Budo karateka really knows what it means to fight. The Budo karateka really knows how to hurt someone, and therefore he/she really knows what it means to be hurt, so the Budo karateka is going to avoid situations in which he/she has to put someone at risk.

But also remember that it's training ATTITUDE that determines whether or not your karate is Budo.

Which do you want to be — something great, or something mediocre?

Do you want to be the guy who can bloody someone's nose and is thought of as a thug, or the guy who can defeat 57 armed attackers — although people might not know that because you're also a valuable member of your community?

82. Leaps of Faith, Pride Resistance vs. Shame Resistance, and the Full-Contact Fight

In a full dozen of this book's sections, I discuss taking a *leap of faith* that you would do well to take when following your teacher's advice. If you haven't read those earlier sections, I recommend #72, *"Channel" Your Teacher's Teaching*, for an introduction.

Why is taking a leap of faith necessary?

Because, unlike Americanized karate, your Budo karate training will force you to face your physical, mental, and spiritual limitations at certain times during your training.

Since we've just been discussing self-defense (see previous section), how is the karateka really supposed to defend him/herself when being attacked for the first time (in the real world) if the karateka has never even experienced a situation in training that in any way resembles it?

In my dojo we don't fight hard all the time, but I would be ashamed to have a dojo if all of my students didn't experience hard fighting at least enough so that they know what it's really about. Trust me, if you've never fought and someone comes up and hits you as hard as they can with the intent of injuring you, your body will pump out all kinds of chemicals into your bloodstream that, if you're completely unfamiliar with them (because you've never practiced hard kumite), you certainly won't be able to handle when someone attacks you. Of course, it's not fair for anyone to claim to be *calm under fire* who has never experienced live fire, but in the dojo, we can at least experience something very close to the live-fire situation by practicing full-contact kumite while only prohibiting the most dangerous of techniques — and the most vulnerable of targets! — in hopes of keeping ourselves out of the hospital during the learning process.

That's exactly what Kyokushin tournament fighting does, after all.

If you are not a fighter-type personality, though, and your teachers ask you to fight, have you not just been asked to take a leap of faith?

There are other situations as well.

If your dojo is not pushing you to test your physical, mental, and spiritual limitations at some point during your training, I would actually recommend that you try a different dojo.

This section is, however, about those who resist taking those leaps of faith. Students usually do so out of either shame or pride.

First-day students have to kiai (shout when executing techniques) and answer powerfully with "Osu!" when given an instruction, just like the rest of the class. Some students feel embarrassed to do so; others feel like it's somehow beneath them because it's so counter to anything they've been asked to do before. Yet there is no question that the student who has the strongest voice in his or her first training is very often the student that has the best chances of success, while the student who is most likely to fail is the one who lacks the ability to overcome either their pride, or their shame, in order to shout loudly.

And guess what!

Having a loud voice is a choice, not an ability. My best advice, therefore, for all beginners is to *choose* to shout very, very loudly when called upon to do so, even in your first training.

Note, though, that by saying so, I'm asking you, the beginning student, to take a leap of faith.

And some of you will surely resist me.

Hopefully, by your reading this section, the number who do will be reduced. Understand what might be involved in your resistance.

Are you embarrassed to use your voice?

Do you think it's beneath you?

Are you afraid?

Either way, use this understanding to get over it. You should actually be embarrassed NOT to shout loudly, because that's what you're supposed to do in the dojo. You should consider it beneath you NOT to make yourself stand out by having a loud voice.

There will be other times when you'll hear your teacher tell you the same things over and over.

But take note!

If your teacher is telling you the same thing again, you're probably resisting.

Ask yourself why.

Are you embarrassed?

Do you feel like it's beneath you?

Are you afraid?

Either way, your thinking is backwards, and you should be embarrassed to make your teacher repeat him/herself a second time. You should consider *that* beneath you, and perhaps just reading this section will help you strengthen your attitude and become a Budo karateka.

83. Concepts Not Rules: Use Your Heart, Not Your Head

"Wow," you might say, "there are 118 sections in this book! How am I possibly to learn them all?" There will be other times in your training as well when you might be overwhelmed by the number of *things* you'll have to know.

But consider that the T-type student doesn't have to remember rules — he/she learns concepts, and the necessary detail emerges whenever he/she needs it — and maybe, if you are still struggling to remember *so many things*, simply reading here that there's another way will help you move to a place where you no longer have to work so hard.

Read all these *rules* to understand them, but learn them with your heart, rather than your head.

Take the rules of etiquette, for example. You have to read more than a dozen of these sections to understand them clearly. How can you possibly remember them all?

If you adopt the *concept*, however, that you should always be humble and powerful and show respect through a foreign set of rules (to which you've been introduced) your job will become much easier. You'll get most of them right, most of the time, without having to do any memorization. Even if you miss one here and there, if you're enacting them because you *feel* them, your teacher and sempais will feel that you're really trying, because they can see that that effort is what you value most.

Consider the other type of student who values kicks and punches first, and perhaps his/her own image in his/her own eyes, or in the eyes of his/her koohais. Clearly this student, who doesn't prioritize the concept — to be humble and pay respect, albeit through a (foreign) framework — has to battle to remember and follow all the rules. Clearly this student is going to have more difficulty, and clearly, those times that this student falls short on some point of etiquette, his/her teacher or sempai is ALSO going to feel that that student doesn't necessarily care.

Once you've read this book, for that matter, consider the whole thing as ONE SINGLE CONCEPT, rather than 118 rules.

What's the best summary of the concept?
Fight to be first at all things that are Budo?
Fight at all times to SHOW your strong Budo karate spirit?
Channel your teacher's teaching by embodying his/her intent?
All of these are good summaries.

Try this one on for size:

"Learn with your heart, not your head. Embody the Budo karate way, now that you know what it is!"

If you do, if you FEEL that you're supposed to be strong for your teacher and strong for your dojo, aren't you going to be more likely to be than if you have to try to remember to be all the time?

Make correct spirit a matter of pride (that is, dignity and self-respect, the *good kind* of pride!). Consider it beneath you to do anything less.

Feel Budo karate!

Channel it!

That's it! If you do, you'll get it in just one fell swoop. You'll have the proper attitude right from the beginning, and you can direct your fight where it belongs.

84. Hold the Lines, and Hold the Lines!
—The Sympathy Failure Conundrum

I have previously discussed the importance of holding the lines (when training in lines) and the grid (when training in multiple lines). See section #24, *Train Yourself to See the WHOLE Dojo, Understand Dojo Priorities*. In a nutshell, your priority should be your dojo, not you. So if your technique is off, it's okay as long as you're standing in your own position; you're not interfering with anyone else. But if your technique is off AND you're knocking someone else's off because you're encroaching on floor space that's supposed to be theirs, you're causing a double distraction.

But that's not the entirety of what I mean in this case by "hold the lines."

Do you know what the expression means in a military sense? Remember that Budo karate is based on bushido, a military system of behavior for governing soldiers, also during times of peace.

In a military sense, "hold the lines" means don't let waves of enemy soldiers punch through your defenses, made up, in many cases, of a line of your own soldiers. If the enemy *punches through*, he's suddenly *behind the lines* where he can exact maximum damage by attacking your troops from behind.

My intention here, in this section, is to encourage you to *hold the lines* in terms of attitude. *Fight to be first* (as in #1), and provide no refuge for anyone who doesn't. In an earlier section of this book, I mentioned that in Japan this was often handled with fists: one who had a bad attitude often got beaten into having a better attitude—or chased away to another dojo!—during kumite. Of course that's not advisable here in the West. Japanese students of Mas Oyama's era tended to accept and appreciate the harsh correction, and to hold *themselves* responsible if they couldn't. How unbelievable this might seem to the average American, here where the standard is to seek legal remedy if even our feelings are hurt!

Happily, however, we can beat the bad attitude out of the dojo, *figuratively*, by rushing to the proximity of bad attitude in our midst with an abundance of powerful, correct energy. Have one person in your midst with lazy technique? Like a magnet, it should *pick up* volunteers around it who *turn on the animal* (see #15, *React Inversely to Hardship 2: Turn On the Animal!*) and make that weakling in your midst feel so bizarrely different from the rest that that student will have no choice but to get with the program. (There are no *physical* weaklings in the dojo, so don't misunderstand! Budo karate is for everybody. I use the derogatory term *weakling*, here, for one who has weak *behavior*, and weak behavior is a choice, but one that's not allowed in the dojo.)

In section #39, *Hang the Dog, Leave Him at Home, Drive Him Out of the Dojo!* I discuss the importance of providing no refuge for your classmate's bad (weak) behavior, and in section #78, *Coddle Your Koohai?,* I discuss how much of a mistake it is to *coddle* our koohais just because they know less than we do. Here I'd like to present *the Sympathy Failure Conundrum.*

If through your response you show sympathy for the student(s) in the dojo who wear their weakness on their sleeve, be it frustration, disappointment, aggressive attitude, despair, hangdog, low morale, or just low determination, you will, in fact, be providing an H-type student refuge, and encouraging him/her to bring that attitude back to class in the future. It doesn't belong in the dojo, and you have to make sure that your classmates who display it understand that you don't want it around.

What if your teacher is correcting your classmate who has chronically been the H-type student—so much so that he/she has lowered today's class average—and, in accordance with that personality type, he/she is acting dismayed, or desperate, angry or hurt? One situation in which this *sympathy failure conundrum* shows its ugly face is when YOU allow that other student's hardship to affect YOUR performance in a downward direction. I'm always amazed when I correct a student for performing below level and that student shows some kind of emotional torment, and then the next student next to him/her, reacting to that torment—or to the fact that MY corrections apparently made the student feel that way!—shows the exact same weak performance the next time through, as if to coddle the classmate that caused the disturbance in the first place, and wrap that student up in a security blanket of "I'm with you! You're not alone!"

I don't think this happens intentionally, but if you read this book, you might intentionally decide not to let it happen to you. If you really want to help your classmate, of course, you have to help your teacher carry him/her over the divide, and that means being part of the stronger majority in all cases, even when your teacher or sempai is highlighting one of your classmate's substandard performances. What kind of support does it offer your teacher if he/she is working hard to correct a behavior, that you then immediately emulate?

You're right. That's the opposite of support. It's the opposite of the Budo karate personality.

Does it seem counterintuitive that you might support your classmate better in some cases by holding your ground and refusing to support him/her?

It can be in Western culture. We are trained, hopefully, to rush to the support of the disadvantaged! But let me here suggest *tough love* as the norm for the dojo. If you're not tough on folks who try and skirt the Budo karate way, you will create an environment in which the disadvantaged in your midst have the lowest possible chance of adopting that stronger way—and thus will likely miss their best chance to lift themselves out of their disadvantage.

Be strict with your actions. Be strict with your words. In Japan, remember, my classmates were strict with their fists.

Don't allow bad attitude to exist in YOUR dojo. Attitude is a decision, after all, not an attribute. We can't change what we are, but we CAN decide to behave differently.

85. The Sinkhole, The Buzz Kill, The Drain, The Moss-Covered Stone

Here we look, one more time, at the *Toes-Not-Heels Dojo*. See #5.

If you're the H-type student in a room full of T's, or if you're one H of several, you are the sinkhole into which the positive energy in the room threatens to drain. You are the buzz kill, the counterproductive, you are in the way.

But don't stress about it! Fix it!

Figure out, each day, what behavior you can adopt from the stronger students in the room, imitate that behavior, and make sure you stick with it. If you're having trouble figuring it out, ask your teacher or sempai.

Budo karate is for everybody. Everyone can do it, men, women, children, young and old.

But here in the West we are at risk, apparently, of becoming karate students who don't WANT to do it. A rolling stone gathers no moss, but some students seem to like being wrapped in moss, and don't WANT to fight to keep rolling, or to learn, even, how to roll.

Well, unfortunately in this particular sense, this is America, land of the free. If you're one that likes the moss, you're probably the cause of a lot of the problems that we face in this country, but because America is a free country, that's your prerogative. I.e. if you want to be a slacker, that's your (legal) right in this free country.

As a Budo karate teacher, personally, I cannot afford to be interested in you too much. I'm going to work on those who are either rolling or want to learn how to roll, but you?

If you don't want to *try* despite my best efforts to show you a better way, please remove yourself. You don't belong in the Budo karate dojo. What you're paying would be better spent on an exercise class. Please don't linger on unnecessarily (unethically!) and lower my dojo's average.

Sounds harsh?

Yes, well, one would hope that the unmotivated student would learn motivation. I hope that for you! Some students come to the dojo to learn it, and some parents send their kids to the dojo hoping they'll learn it. And I, as teacher, and all the T-type students in the dojo, do in fact work every day to teach that student how to be motivated.

But after a certain point, enough is enough.

After a certain point, it becomes clear that certain students don't want it.

It's this unfortunate group alone that defies the *Budo karate is for everyone* principle.

Budo karate is for men, women, and children, it's for the young and old, it's for the (physically) strong and weak. It's NOT, however, for anyone who *doesn't want* the Budo part of the karate. It's not for anyone who *doesn't want* to adopt stronger routines in order to become stronger.

86. Monkey See, Monkey Do

It's a tragic day for an instructor when you realize that one of your students, young or old, has slipped through the cracks and made it all the way up to their first test for their first colored belt being only able to perform complex exercises (such as kata, bunkai, or 3-step kumite) by keeping their attention fixed on someone next to them and copying what that other person does. This is the student who can do the exercise fine in a group, where all students learn each exercise for the first time, but then can't do it when alone. As an instructor, if you watch your students' eyes, you'll see the ones that don't know the answers until they see someone near them provide them.

This often applies to children, but beginning students should be warned!

Your first couple of times through complex exercises like kata, you will get through them by playing copycat. And that's fine; you're supposed to. Yet you would do well to understand that just as soon as you can, you have to drop that dependency and figure out the sequences for yourself.

Consider the difference between the introvert, one who always looks inward, and the extrovert, one who always reaches out into the group. The parallel doesn't exactly fit, but this set of opposites should suffice to suggest the difference between how one *first* approaches a complex exercise, and how one *should* approach it just as soon as one can. Just as soon as possible, stop looking to your surroundings to figure out the answers. Look, instead, inward, and show what you KNOW, and use what's going on in your surroundings to reinforce how well you know it.

Insist on it.

With time—not years, not months, but a *little* time!—you should consider it beneath your dignity to perform your exercise by copying someone else.

See #6, *Take Responsibility for Learning Even Complex Series of Motions in Just One Class, Even When Shown Just Once.*

87. Roll On, Role Model!

Remember that it's your job to be a role model for your koohais just as soon as you have koohais of your own. Even the second-day student might become a sempai if a new student joins the dojo on that day!

Remember that it's your job, inside the dojo and out, to behave in a way that encourages your classmates to *channel* your teacher's teaching.

Consider the image of the rolling stone that gathers no moss.

Some students come into the dojo from the very first day as rolling stones. Others are all covered with moss, and have to learn how to roll. Maybe YOU came in covered with moss, but now you've learned how to spin some of it off.

All the more reason why you have to KEEP rolling!

If your koohais see you starting and stopping, and starting and stopping, they will learn incorrectly that that's what their karate is supposed to look like.

Please remain consistent, and by that I mean consistently charging to the front of the curve.

You might only DO karate for 4 hours per week (if you attend two classes per week and do no self training). If so, make 100% sure that for all of those 4 hours, you're doing the activity—Budo karate!—the way Budo karate is meant to be done.

The *moss* of weak effort, or poor attention paid, is not allowed in the Budo karate dojo.

Students who are too content to grow moss should perhaps take up some other activity.

88. The Higher Your Rank, The More Your Responsibility

Beginning students are always in such a hurry to get their colored belts, but I caution them not to be. As a colored belt, you are responsible not only for yourself, but also for everyone of a lower rank than you.

In my dojo, orange is the first colored belt, and although they shouldn't be, brand-new orange belts are sometimes shocked the first time their teacher corrects them, not because they were out of place, but rather because some white belt in the back row was.

"What! Now I'm to be responsible for those know-nothing white belts?"

You got it.

You are.

The higher your rank, the more you're responsible for more of your koohais . . . and that's not the half of it!

To a white belt with a weak stance, a teacher might say, "please make your stance deeper . . . like this! Yes, that's it. Good job," but to a green belt with the same weak stance, the same teacher might say, "Hey! What the &%#*@ is your problem?! Get with the program or go home!"

"Really?" the beginner might ask.

Really!

Why?

Because the green belt should know better, and is displaying attitude unbecoming of a green belt; because, by example, he's teaching all his koohais in the dojo that when they're green belts too, it's normal for them to have weak stances on those nights that they don't feel up to fighting to be first. It wasn't the stance that was so insulting to the instructor's sense of dignity; it was the *attitude* that allowed the green belt to display it as if it were somehow acceptable!

See? You're starting to get it!

This green belt, from the example, shouldn't be a green belt. This is an H-type student who, maybe without knowing it, is trying his/her best *to lower the standard* of the dojo. It's not necessary to have a perfect stance, but it IS necessary to demonstrate a constant effort to have a perfect one, and that's where this student dropped the ball. He allowed himself to be seen by his koohais not caring.

The attitudes described in this book, you should be following even as white belts, but at least as white belts you have some excuse. You're at a level where your sempais will be patient with you for not yet following.

But if you're still not by the time you're a green belt?

Your teacher's language is going to get harsher with you day by day.

Why?

Please understand your teacher has no choice!

Your teacher is morally bound to maintain a standard, just as you should be. If someone of rank is standing there as an insult to that standard, the teacher will have no choice but to call out the behavior as substandard to make sure that the koohais know it.

Just be sure that you're not that one, and that you're doing all you can do to make sure that you're making your koohais understand the importance of not being, and all will be fine!

The point of all of this, remember, is to adopt an attitude by which the pursuit becomes easier by comparison! Sure karate is hard sometimes, but this book should help you to pursue it in a way that's not unnecessarily so.

89. Beginners, Don't Fret!!

"There's so much to learn!" you might think.

But not really. Adopt the attitude of the Budo karateka (described by this book), and that's only one thing.

Make one choice, rather than memorizing 118 rules.

In that sense, it's more important that you *understand* these concepts than it is for you to *learn* them all.

You can either adopt them as a priority in one single moment of "Oh, I see now!" or you can struggle to memorize them so that one day you'll get them—and you still probably won't!

See #82, *Concepts, Not Rules: Use Your Heart, Not Your Head*.

Another reason you might panic, however, upon reading this book, is because I've done a lot of highlighting here of conflicts that have arisen with students who have missed the boat.

Oh, but that's exactly why I'm writing this book!

Your teacher will be patient with you and help you understand up until the point where it becomes clear that you're not trying.

So just be patient, and continue to try.

By reading this book, it's likely that you'll never face 90% of the failed-student issues I've described.

Don't fret!

For every one student who fails, two students succeed. It's always been that way. In a pursuit where individuals seek to surpass the norm in terms of self-improvement, isn't that exactly as it should be?

By reading this book, aren't you showing that *you* intend to be one of the ones that succeeds?

90. Class Instruction vs. Individual Instruction

Remember that you have to train your ear to hear your teacher's *hows* louder than his *whats*?

See #2, *It's the* How, *Silly, Not the* What.

Remember that your teacher ALWAYS remembers what he/she's told you? See #68, *Your Teacher ALWAYS Remembers*.

Perhaps it would also help you to understand, clearly, the difference between an instruction that's given to the class and instruction that's given to you personally. It'll help you because you are responsible for both; you need to make sure that you *tune in* to, and hear, both.

Understand that when improving technique (or attitude), there's always a biggest correction that needs to be made, and a next-biggest correction, and then a next-biggest one after that. Your teacher can probably see the whole string of them in order, but in order to teach you the smaller ones, he/she has to teach you the biggest ones first. Your teacher might, for example, know, "This student can't improve his punch until he corrects his stance." Thus the teacher focuses on correcting the stance, hoping that the student makes the improvement soon and consistently, so that the teacher can then discuss what's not right about the punch.

So, just train your ear.

If your teacher has singled you out specifically when working with a group, your teacher has given you a great gift. He/she has told you the biggest thing that you, individually, have to fix before moving on to the next biggest thing in order to have better karate.

So, in that case, it's very important that you hear, and prioritize, and show that you heard by making the adjustment that your teacher advised you to make.

Your teacher always remembers?

Careful! In my case, I do.

When I tell an entire class of students to adjust their technique in a certain way, I tend to remember the next time, watching a different class do the same technique, which students were present when I said it the first time. That is, I tend to remember who I'm having to tell the same thing more than once, and when I do, you better believe I'm questioning the strength of your commitment. Likewise, when I give individuals instructions, be sure you understand that the next time you're doing that same exercise, I will be looking at you to see if you've remembered. The Japanese Budo karate student almost always does. The Americanized karate student is at risk of liking the *hear it over and over* approach.

Don't make your teacher/sempai repeat him/herself. To avoid that, train your ear to hear instructions given to your class, and take them to heart, and also instructions given to you individually, and take them to heart, too.

Next time you do that exercise, that previous instruction should ring in your head like a cowbell.

Remember that if you try to *memorize them* all, you'll fail.

If you *prioritize them*, however, if you take them to heart, if you remember them by honoring your teacher, they will be far, far easier to learn.

91. Sensei, I Have to Pee!

Not in my class, not in Mas Oyama's.

Our classes in Japan were two hours long, and every day, and sometimes more than once per day, and in two years I never once saw a student leave a class to go to the bathroom.

Neither have my own students.

In my dojo I accept students from 6 years old up, OR from 5 years old if they can stay focused in a 90-minute class without having to go to the bathroom.

My weaker, delinquent students, the H's struggling to find their place, raise their hands: "Sensei, may I go to the bathroom!"

"NO!" I respond. "I told you when you started you can't leave my class to go to the bathroom. Are you going to throw up?"

"Osu, no."

"Are you going to go in your pants?"

"Osu, no."

"Then don't interrupt the class in the future because of your selfish concerns. The dojo is not about you, you have to be here to support the dojo! And when you interrupt training's flow, you lower your dojo's standard!"

"Osu! Sensei, I'll fix it!"

Note: Of course, as an instructor you DO have to make this rule clear to students regularly, so they'll go to the bathroom before class starts. And you do have to know how to judge if it's really an emergency or not.

One little girl had an accident in one of my classes one time, and I felt very bad for her. But, then again, she never did again, and kids rarely raise their hands to ask anymore.

Please, when you make a rule, hold the line. If you're the student and you've been told a rule, make sure you understand that your teacher IS going to hold the line.

See #84, *Hold the Lines, and Hold the Lines! — The Sympathy Failure Conundrum.*

92. It's YOU, Silly, Not Your Teacher!

It seems that I get to tell you, here in this book, plenty of things that embarrass me from my own teaching history.

I have had the experience of being frustrated with a student for not having the spirit to make a change I've requested, and so I make the request again, and that student resists again, and so on, until about every time I address that student on the same issue, it's in a frustrated tone.

But then it occurs to me . . .

The REALLY embarrassing thing!

"This student," I see it in his eyes, "has actually come to think that this is what karate training is supposed to be! He hasn't figured out that, because I'm frustrated, IT'S HIM that's failing to make an adjustment, so that his teacher wouldn't have to be frustrated any more! He actually thinks that karate training IS where some guy named 'Sensei' up there at the front of the room is supposed to nag him to get him to try harder!"

Does that not seem so preposterous that you can't believe it?

Oh, but it happens sometimes. This is foreign stuff, folks, and for some people it seems to be even more foreign! Budo karate is Japanese karate, and by stepping into the dojo you would do well to feel yourself stepping into a foreign culture, where some of the rules you take for granted no longer apply.

Just in case I didn't make that greatest of all pitfalls clear, let me re-state that trying to teach Budo karate in this American environment, I have had students who have *gotten used* to my frustration, and actually come to the conclusion that "that's what a Budo karate dojo is supposed to feel like!"

And I throw up my hands!

It's YOU, silly!

YOU are the reason I'm talking to you in a frustrated tone! It's not that I don't like you; it's not that I've had a bad day. YOU have to make the &%#*@ adjustment, and then I can talk to you in the friendly tone I prefer.

Seems amazing, I know.

But it happens.

The Japanese student would think of his classmate, "What an idiot! Is he retarded?" But no, it's a cultural difference. The Japanese student would be so ashamed that his teacher was inconvenienced that he/she would make the change immediately. It seems that in the absence of that same concept of shame, the American student, when pressed, can become contented being the source of frustration, and think that, because it's foreign, that's what it's supposed to be.

Please understand:

Your teacher WILL resort to all kinds of means, even to *blowing his/her top* on occasion, to get any student who unnecessarily lowers the dojo standard *see the light* and start behaving strong. But also please understand that *your teacher hates doing so*, he HATES having to talk to you in a frustrated tone. Sure, Mas Oyama did sometimes! Every karate teacher does! Sure, Mas Oyama chewed us out when we let him down! But it was also clear to us that once he had chewed us out, he'd never have to again for the same transgression.

We were immediately altered, and immediately more careful not to let it happen again.

If your teacher is using a frustrated tone with you, CHANGE what you're doing! CHANGE your attitude! MAKE the adjustment! If you can't figure out how, at least clue in to the frustrated tone and ask someone for help. Go to your sempai and ask, "Help me, please, Sempai, to make the change I need to make so I'm not causing Sensei frustration!"

Please.

The student who becomes contented with the frustration is the WORST kind of student to have in the dojo if you're trying to raise the bar and establish a standard in which students carry their own weight, and fight to be first.

See #12, *Hear it Twice? It's Life and Death.*

See #13, *Your Teacher Is Angry? It's Life and Death for* Everyone, *Especially YOU if You Feel Like Someone* Else *was Responsible!*

93. It's Probably YOU, Not the Other Guy

This concept is directly related to the previous one, #92, so please be sure that you've read that section first.

Another point of cultural confusion some students may fall victim to is thinking that it's *the other guy* that needs to fix a problem, when really it's you who does.

If you were a Japanese student of Mas Oyama's dojo, if you are the T-type student, the rule is, however, that you should always take for granted that the problem is something *you* can fix. Always. It's always your responsibility, even if it feels like the person who caused the disturbance is all the way on the other side of the room.

One frequent occurrence that, again, you'll think is nuts until you've experienced it:

There are sixteen students in the room and everyone's lined up for kata in four parallel rows of four. This is a grid, or at least it's supposed to be, with equal distance between all students, side to side and front to back.

But somehow the grid is skewed. The distance between rows, or the distances between columns, is off. The teacher says, "Straighten the lines!"

The entire class, recognizing that it was an instruction for the whole class, answers, "Osu!"

But then nobody moves. Instead, a couple of the beginning students start to fidget, and look at each other like, "Where am I supposed to go? What am I supposed to do?"

This happens because some sempai in the lineup, one who should be in a leadership role, has decided that "Sensei's probably not talking to me; I'm already in the right place, right?"

Wrong!

If the lineup is off, everyone is off, and everyone, from the very top all the way down to the newest student, must take responsibility and assume that they are the ones that are off.

Take a step back and consider:

The sempai is responsible, and the sempai shows leadership first by showing, through action, that the sempai him/herself is correct, and, second, by issuing commands when necessary to tell the koohais what to do.

But what did the sempai do in the case of the example?

Nothing!

He/she didn't take action to check his/her own position, and didn't issue any commands. Since the sempai took for granted that "it must not be me that's off," he/she left the newest students in the room to their own devices, and the result was a weak, H-type reaction that doesn't fit in the Budo karate dojo.

If the teacher says to the group, "Deeper stances!" and everyone says, "Osu!" but the sempais don't adjust their own stances, because they think, mistakenly, that their own stances were already deep enough, you got it. It's not the Budo karate dojo.

The advanced student, here, must ALWAYS take for granted that an instruction given to the group applies to him or her. The beginning student sees the sempai react—at the very least sees the sempai check his or her own stance!—and then and only then do the koohais start to see that their sempais are ALWAYS responsive to their teacher's commands, and start to figure out that everyone is supposed to be, all the time.

If the sempai doesn't lower his stance when the teacher says "Deeper stances!" to everyone in the dojo, the koohai learns, by example, that he/she can choose when to make a correction, and when not. Following one's teacher becomes, in fact, optional.

Basic rule:

It's always you! A group instruction DOES, every time, apply to you.

"Look at that first-day student over there with his dogi pants falling down! What an idiot! Now we're having to stop the class because his pants were falling off."

Wrong!

Every other student in the room bears responsibility because that guy is everyone's koohai, and why didn't someone check, or show him properly how to tie off his dogi pants before the class started?

Are you starting to follow?

That student isn't paying attention. That one over there didn't tie his/her belt properly. That student didn't answer in a spirited tone. All of these! In the Budo karate system, it's not the other guy's fault, it's YOURS! Take responsibility for every aspect of your dojo, not just for yourself.

94. There's Always Someone in the Dojo More Challenged than You

It's been a while since we've looked at one of our diagrams of a *Toes-Not-Heels Dojo* (see #5).

Remember, each dojo has 18 students:

Case A:		Case B:	
	T T T T T T		T H T H T T
	T H T T T T		H T H H T T
	T T T T T T		T T H T H T

Notice that in Case A, there's only one H-type student. Everyone else is fighting to be first at all things. Only that one student is distracted and forgot his Budo karate spirit.

Let's instead, though, consider this time that that one H-type student has a true learning disability. Or, let's consider that he/she is not disadvantaged in that way, but that he/she, instead, has just had a death in the family. But do YOU have a learning disability? Did YOU just have a death in the family? The point is that you should always train with the attitude that there's always someone more disadvantaged than you.

This is maybe a reverse way of saying, "Fight to be first."

Don't allow yourself to be the one who's the H!

Don't do it, because you are always more capable than the least capable student in the room, or at least you should take for granted that you are.

What are you going to do, compete with the weakest student to see who gets to hold that H position?

I would hope that your dignity wouldn't permit you!

Fight for that more disadvantaged guy, yes, but do so by fighting to make sure you're not him!

This is how you'll make sure that the disadvantaged will have the best class structure imaginable for helping him/her overcome that disadvantage. If, on the other hand, you join him/her in playing the role of the disadvantaged, you help him/her to hold onto it.

How foolish that would be, no?

95. Provide No Refuge for Pride in the Dojo

Provide no refuge for weakness.
Provide no refuge for dissent.
Provide no refuge for pride.

No matter what it is that any one student brings into the dojo that runs against the current of your teacher's teaching, make 100% sure that you make it clear that you don't approve. Show through your example that your stronger karate is based on the opposite. If necessary, drive it out of the dojo.

In an earlier section (#84), I talked about the sympathy reaction to *the hangdog* (#39). One student has just been addressed in a strict tone because his attitude is bad—he's having to be told the same thing over and over again—and his reaction is to hang his head and feel sorry for himself. It's not his fault, maybe, because he knows not what he does—he's had a substandard upbringing—but instead of adjusting what needs to be adjusted, he's out looking for sympathy. If he doesn't get it, he's likely to get mad.

So let him.

In fact, make him mad.

Refuse to supply the sympathy. It's nothing but a refuge for his weak attitude.

In the same way, provide no sympathy for pride.

Another student's bad attitude is that he thinks he knows it all. He's been training in another style and he thinks they did it better in his other dojo. And he's showing it. He's running his mouth in the locker room after class.

In Japan, full-contact kumite always fixed this problem. Even if the overly proud student was really strong from his—for example –kickboxing experience, there was always someone stronger to make him more humble by beating him in kumite.

In America, of course, we have to be careful. It's the land of the free and the home of the lawsuit. Except in a subtle way, I can't endorse the Japanese system in this one case.

But it doesn't matter.

Just understand the principle, and show the oddball that you don't approve. Make him feel like he's alone, and a jerk (if he is indeed acting like one). If everyone does that, he'll get the picture.

We love to have new strong students . . . just so long as they're humble, and they try to make friends rather than making waves.

But pride is not always the stuff of the strong student.

Sometimes in my dojo we have students whose parents want them to train more than they want to train themselves. In our nonprofit function we've had some sent to us by juvenile court. Some of them are *too big* to bow and say "Osu!"

Please, provide no refuge for this kind of resistance!

If someone doesn't bow and say "Osu!" and you look at them funny, bemused, and then bow weakly beside them, with a weak voice—thus ostensibly joining them in a decreased dojo average—you have just provided refuge!

They interpret your weak voice as support for theirs!

How do you provide no refuge for weakness? Show strength beside them. How do you provide no refuge for bad attitude? Show good attitude beside them. How do you provide no refuge for dissent? Don't have anything to do with it. In all cases, if all else fails, have some words with the confused student. They can be harsh words, or kind, encouraging words, whichever you think will get through. But if the words are kind, make sure the weaker student doesn't misunderstand. Make sure that he knows you're encouraging him to change his ways, not encouraging him to keep on down the wrong path. Make sure *she* knows you're encouraging her to change her ways, not encouraging her to keep on down the wrong path!

96. Grasp Your Teacher's Priority, Understand Your Teacher's Intent, See the Dojo through Your Teacher's Eyes

Okay, so I'm going to quote a passage I wrote earlier (see #68, *The ACB Ease, Not the ABC Lock*) :

Your teacher tells you, "When your partner kicks, block while cutting [stepping] to 90 degrees, and counterattack with a kage tsuki, and then gedan mawashi geri to the inner thigh, and then straight punch, like this. Make sure you concentrate on the step! When your opponent kicks, drop your heel back to pivot on your front foot to face your opponent from the side . . . like this . . ."

What is your teacher's priority?

If you've read well thus far, and understood, you automatically broke that instruction down into *the what* and *the how*, you know that Budo karate is all about *the how*, and that the student who only hears only *the what* fails, so the priority, clearly, is "make sure you concentrate on the step."

In this way, and others, you can begin to know what your teacher's priority is. Make sure you understand that the more that you do, the better a student you will be, and the better your karate will become.

But the purpose of this section is not to review the how-not-what concept already given you in #2.

Take this a step or two further.

Step one, grasp your teacher's priority. Step two, understand your teacher's intent. Step three, see the dojo, and see yourself, through your teacher's eyes.

In #44, *Parallel Lessons: The Surface and the Esoteric, Identify the Task at Hand, Fulfill it, Support its Delivery in the Eyes of your Koohais* I discuss step two, understanding your teacher's intent. Please make sure you've read that section.

So what about this step three: see yourself through your teacher's eyes?

I once had a senior student — who was nevertheless plagued by a poor attitude — look at me like I was totally crazy when I told him/her to see him/herself, and the dojo, through MY eyes. How frustrating it was to have this adult student, whom I'd promoted all the way up to brown belt, still so plagued by such a sense of *I can't do that* that when I asked him/her to consider another perspective, he/she remained in denial, and looked at ME like I was nuts!

"I only have my eyes, Sensei! I can't see the dojo through YOURS! I've never heard of such a thing."

But of course anyone can. We do this every day. It's called empathy. It's a matter of putting yourself in someone else's shoes, a matter of feeling what someone else is likely feeling. This was clearly a student that was having a bad day.

If someone's hurt next to you, you feel it, right? You feel for that person?

You already know from section #70, *Your Teacher Can Read YOUR Mind, Learn to Read your Teacher's* that you can know what your teacher is thinking every time you begin a new exercise during which your teacher has previously told you something about how to do it better. For example, if you begin a kata, and some previous time you've done that kata your teacher has told you (or the class) something about how he/she wants you to do it, you can be sure that's what your teacher is thinking about.

The point is that if you know what your teacher wants to see (and the better you know your teacher, the more you will), the better you will be able to see yourself, and your dojo, *as your teacher would see* those things. If you know your teacher wants to see long, deep stances during the kata Taikyoku Sono Ichi, for example, and you're looking at a group of students performing that kata but half of them don't have long, deep stances, you will start to feel what your teacher would feel, i.e. "Why are these guys we've told so many times before not making an effort to make their stances deep and long?!"

How about seeing yourself?

Ask yourself, "What would Sensei see in me if he/she saw me right now?"

Well, are you doing what you're supposed to be doing in a strong, correct way?

If you're standing in fudo dachi, are your fists squeezed tightly, facing forward in front of your hips, is your weight balanced equally between your two parallel feet at shoulder width, do you have a relaxed but serious facial expression, are you maintaining eye contact, is your uniform in good shape, and is your belt tied properly, are you chewing gum? Have you forgotten to take off your watch or jewelry?

If you are on the correct side of the divide in all of these questions, you teacher is probably looking at you like you're a strong student and role model. If you're smacking your gum, on the other hand, and fidgeting, and you still have your watch on, your teacher is probably thinking how you've got a lot left to learn.

See how this works?

What if everything about how you're standing is correct, but your teacher asked you in your last class to please remember to do some task or another before your next class, and you failed to do so or even mention it to your teacher before class? Yet, you're standing there confident, and impervious, as if you're the best karate student in the world with your perfect uniform and your perfect stance, and your perfect facial expression?

Can you see even better now?

Look at yourself through your teacher's eyes.

What does he/she see?

Well, in this case, he/she sees that you're standing properly, and you know how to wear your uniform, but also that you're fairly proud and in denial of learning what he/she's actually been trying to teach you.

You teacher, that moment, sees you as someone who still has so much to learn, and if you're a white belt, that's one thing. He/she is likely to refer you to #10 in this book (*Complete Tasks That You've Been Assigned Promptly and Powerfully*) so it will never happen again, but if you're a brown belt already, and you've already been through the trenches with your teacher, and STILL, you're standing there as if nothing's amiss, even though you flat-out denied what your teacher asked you to do when last you met?

Well, I'm sorry, but in this case your teacher is thinking of you as someone who is failing. Did other students, your koohais, watch you deny your teacher's request? Were they aware? In that case, even worse, your teacher is probably seeing you as a threat to his/her dojo. You are the disadvantaged youth, perhaps? You're the one who's resisting the teaching?

Oh, but you're in the way!

If you're that proud, and still not getting it, it's probably because you don't want to get it, and you are, in fact, impeding progress. Better to find another dojo.

Do, though, for a moment, consider the student with such self-esteem issues.

Consider how greatly it can fortify that student if he/she looks at him/herself *though his/her teachers eyes* and KNOWS that his/her teacher would be seeing strength and accomplishment. Think how much of a boost of morale that could be!

But look, also, at the other case. What if you see yourself through your teacher's eyes and expect that your teacher would be seeing someone who is failing?

What then? It would wear down the strongest of us, wouldn't it?

See, therefore, how important this can be?

I know that when I was training in my first teacher's dojo — and certainly in Mas Oyama's! — I almost stopped looking at myself and my surrounding through my own eyes at all. I wanted so badly to satisfy my teachers that I almost always only saw myself and my surroundings through theirs!

By doing so, I was very often where I was supposed to be, even in cases where my classmates were not. My teachers were, accordingly, very appreciative.

If you can start to think this way, you will move far ahead indeed!

97. BE the Karateka! No Pain, No Gain

Remember the marathon runner and the linebacker of #80, *Budo Karate Remakes You, Americanized Karate Teaches You a Skill*?

Compare the wiry, high-energy student and the one who tends to be more chubby and slow.

Somehow it's hard for the American student (and particularly the child student) to conceptualize the fact that the reason WHY they're still chubby is because of how they train. If your chubby body wants to move slowly, if that's what's comfortable for you, and that's therefore what you do every day, then that's exactly WHY you're still chubby. To make yourself a karateka, sorry, *to remake yourself as a karateka*, you have to ask your body to do what's NOT comfortable. Ask your body for a bit more, you'll then move OUTSIDE of your comfort zone, and your body will start to change in ways that might surprise you.

You don't have to be chubby, to follow this exact principle.

Even if you're wiry, if you don't ask your body to hurt a little, it too won't change. You want to make your karate better day by day, right? Of course you do! If you are a Budo karateka that's why you're in the dojo in the first place!

You, too, have to discipline yourself to push forward in your training until it hurts a little. You have to deny yourself the out of being able to quit, lighten up, or slow down whenever life gets you down, or whenever you don't feel like it. There's only one way to do karate, and if you've got different speeds, you're following the American model.

Karate training is *always* hard, it *always* takes you outside of your comfort zone, at least to some degree.

One more time to the case of the chubby student?

Maybe you ARE working your butt off every day, maybe you ARE hurting, maybe you are drenching the dojo floor with sweat.

Is your body changing?

No?

Duh, then. Come on, guys!

Change what you EAT! Stop drinking sodas! Reduce the portion sizes of what you eat day by day. Eat more fiber and less sugar.

The fat karateka is the embarrassed one, and believe me, I'm 42, and sometimes get so bogged down by the business end of my enterprise that my routines are not what they could be. Sometimes I feel out of shape, and believe me, when I do, I AM the embarrassed karateka.

Those times I am not content with my condition, if I were also too accepting of my status quo I would be betraying the Budo karate standard. Rome wasn't built in a day, and sometimes in a whole lifetime we can't build Rome, but if you're ever content *not to try* to build Rome in this type of scenario, your attitude is substandard. It wouldn't fit in the Japanese Budo karate dojo.

Nothing can change for you physically, until you stumble upon the right attitude.

98. If Training Doesn't Force You to Face Your Limitations, It's Not Budo

You will encounter, in your Budo karate training, challenges that are physical, challenges that are mental, and challenges that are spiritual. In fact, you will at times, approach what you believe to be your actual limits. "I can't do any more," you might believe, or "there's no way I can keep on going."

A funny thing happens, though, in the Budo karate dojo.

The teacher takes the student a step beyond, and the student realizes, "Oh, I could do more than I thought I could do!" If this happens often enough, the student starts to question, and later to deny, his/her own sense of what he/she can't do.

The Budo karateka learns that limitations are more based in habit and perception than they are in physical reality. "I'm sure I probably can't do that," for example, is the fastest way to ensure that you WON'T do it, but has much less to do with whether you actually CAN or not.

Karate training, folks, is your opportunity to build character.

You can read a book about how to have better character, and you can try to imitate by making the choices that one of superior character would make. By doing so, by practicing stronger behavior, you might start to alter your actual character in small ways. Please note though: it wasn't the imitation that made you better; it was the practice, and practice involves *overcoming* the natural state of not trying.

The value of karate training in terms of improving character comes both from immersing yourself in a system in which people *value* making stronger decisions, AND from *training* in which you are regularly pushed, and regularly push, beyond you own comfort zone.

I have had students who are so used to buckling in the face of challenges that it's next to impossible to show them that there's anything beyond their status quo. Help yourself out, though, understand that your karate training in the Budo karate dojo WILL take you to where you feel like you can't go any further sometimes. Make peace with the fact that you'll have to go there for our own good, and then maybe you'll have a better chance of overcoming the challenge when you encounter it, rather than buckling in the face of it.

One step better?

Know that your karate class WILL take you there, and then know that it is the INTENT of the training that you growl and grit your teeth and get it done. This is the meaning of "Osu!" after all.

It's by overcoming those challenges that you develop strength and character. If your teacher asks you to "sprout wings and fly," you would fail and so would your teacher. But if you think you can do 30 pushups and your teacher asks you to do 50, you absolutely must charge forward as if you're sure your teacher knows better than you. Remember that you tend to see your perceived or habitual limitations as to what you can and can't do. Your teacher, on the other hand, has spent a lifetime learning to see your *actual* limitations.

Take a leap of faith. Do, and your teacher will take you to places you couldn't before have imagined.

99. Revealing the True Object of Budo Karate: Fight to Be First, But . . .

If everyone *fights to be first*, who's gonna be?
We've already established that several times in this book.
No one!
That attitude just keeps everyone, unanimously, at the front of the curve.
"So what's the point?" you might ask. "Only one guy is actually going to win, right? I know I'm not the strongest guy, so why should I even try?"
Duhh.
Okay, American karate student, try this on for size!
The true goal of karate training is to win against YOURSELF, not to win against others.
"But that's silly! I want to learn self-defense! I want to learn to fight!"
Oh, but the Budo karateka realizes that, in a certain sense, YOU are a much harder adversary than any would-be attacker. If you train to overcome YOUR OWN weaknesses — and if you win! — you will also be well prepared for a self-defense situation.
So, why do you fight to be first in all things in the dojo?
Yes, to stay at the head of the curve, but also, to make sure that you're fighting your own shortcomings. Insist upon it! With your blood and sweat, with your bleeding knuckles, drive your shortcomings out of the dojo! Drive them out of your life!

Make them, simply, gone.

This is the Budo karate spirit.

See #97, *BE the Karateka. No Pain, No Gain.*

As stated, if you train within your comfort zone, nothing happens. There's no growth. There's no strengthening.

Why fight to be first if you know you're not going to be?

Because it is the Budo karate spirit to venture outside your comfort zone in all things. LIVE just beyond! Stay one step ahead of your comfort zone in all things that you do and you will be fighting to obliterate your shortcomings in all the areas of your life.

100. Harder Training is Easier Training?

It's simple, but counterintuitive and therefore difficult, not only for the Westerner, but also for any inexperienced athlete or nonathlete.

Initially, it hurts a little bit more to train harder, but once you do, once it becomes your norm, as well as the norm for the majority, your trainings become much more enjoyable, and you get much stronger by taking part.

Which path do you really want to be on?

Take the two extremes. Imagine, first, the unmotivated student who's not broken a sweat and who has heavy eyelids and weak techniques. On again–off again, throughout the class, that student's teacher and classmates have to employ various techniques to get him/her revved up to the class average at the front of the curve. How uncomfortable is that for everyone, but particularly for that student!

On the other extreme there's the student that trains like a wild animal with fire in his/her eyes, always hungry for more. "Push us more, Sensei! Push us more!"

This student is in the zone; he/she has at least this in common with the Japanese Budo karate students of Mas Oyama's dojo, and his/her training is ten times more enjoyable, and ten times more beneficial, than that of the student who's not motivated.

And yet, every student should be thus motivated in the Budo karate dojo. Every student should fight to adopt the front of the curve as the dojo's norm, and then training is ten times more enjoyable for everyone, and everyone gets ten times stronger.

101. The Condition of Your Uniform

It's not unimportant.

Keep your dogi in good shape. Wear it properly. Make sure your belt is tied correctly.

Please take responsibility not only for your own uniform, but also for those of your classmates. A dirty uniform, a tattered uniform, a wrinkled uniform, a uniform whose collar is turned in, or one in which a T-shirt is worn underneath (for men), is a uniform that is incorrectly worn, and it is a ugly spot in the middle of YOUR dojo.

If you see someone whose belt is not tied properly, help him/her out.

If you see someone wearing jewelry in class, remind them that they've forgotten to take it off. Remind anyone to spit out their gum.

If you see someone who's got a ripped uniform, suggest that it might be time to buy a new one. Maybe, if they can't, you could offer to help out.

Why is it that we see all of these poor self-presentation issues in the American dojo, and yet, in Japan, there wasn't even anyone in the dojo who didn't consider the length of his/her toenails (to make sure not to inadvertently cut one of their classmates)?!

It's the Budo karate spirit.

Cut your toenails. Take off your jewelry. If you're a male, don't wear T-shirts under your uniform. If you are a female, wear a plain white one. Don't wear a tattered uniform. Don't wear a dirty one. Don't wear any uniform incorrectly. Learn to tie your belt, and develop a sense of pride that you've got it right.

Look in the mirror!

Is that a Budo karateka?

Not with a dirty uniform, not with an incorrectly worn one! Has that person in the mirror forgotten to trim his nails? Then he doesn't care for the well-being of his sempais, even!

You got it, that person is not a Budo karateka!

Dude, are you in your 100th day of training alone, barefoot in the mountains, like Mas Oyama did? Then, and only then, do you have an excuse to have a dirty, wrinkled or damaged uniform on.

Should you not come in to class one night simply because you failed to wash your uniform?

No, training is a higher priority, but it's your duty to plan ahead and prepare. A sweaty uniform that's at least hung on a hanger to dry is acceptable for training. The sweaty one left balled up in the back seat of your car is not.

Have some self-respect. Have some respect for your art. Have some respect for your dojo. Wear your uniform properly. Take care of it.

102. Oh My God, I Think I'm the Sinkhole! I Can't Seem to Figure My Way Out!

Remember *The Toes-Not-Heels Dojo*? (See #5.)
In the example, each dojo has 18 students:

Case A:	T T T T T T	Case B:	T H T H T T
	T H T T T T		H T H H T T
	T T T T T T		T T H T H T

We know that Case A is the Budo karate dojo, and case B is failing. Yet there's still an H-type student in the Budo karate dojo (Case A), right?

What if, all of a sudden, you realize that it's you?

"Oh, my god! I think I'm the H! I'm the sinkhole into which everyone's positive energy is falling away!"

If you realize this, GOOD FOR YOU! Realizing it is the first step towards fixing it.

Of course you DO have to then fix it, and you'll be empowered to do so now, because at least now you know what needs to be fixed.

But what if you realize you're the H — maybe your teacher or your sempais are annoyed with you! — and you CAN'T seem to figure out what needs to be fixed?

No problem!

Also, good for you!

But do ASK SOMEBODY!

If you don't know how you're being a nuisance and you take the proactive step of asking someone after class to help you figure it out, good for you! You're on your way!

This is the spirit of the Budo karateka.

103. The Importance of Consistent Training

We all have responsibilities in our lives other than our karate training. Sometimes they get in the way of our training. Other times, our own motivation suffers, in which case we can get in the way of our own training by failing to persevere.

All of this is to be expected . . . but never *accepted*.

Yes, we all have life difficulties. Yet, it's critical that we don't accept those challenges as valid excuses for not training. Even in the face of challenges, we should always fight to keep our training as consistent as possible. We should train regularly even if we didn't sleep the night before, for example. To give yourself the excuse, "I didn't sleep well last night, so I'm not going to train today," is to betray the Budo karate spirit.

The university or high school student who trains a couple of times a week even though he/she has exams that week will do better on his/her exams, even though intuition often tells that student not to interrupt his/her studying.

And there's another dimension to consistent training.

At what level do we train when we are training? Are there times when we train hard, and other times when we hardly train? Are there times that we follow instructions well in the dojo, and other times that we don't? Are there times when we rise to challenges, and other times that we pretend we didn't hear them?

If there is for you, you should know in no uncertain terms that you should fix this, immediately — in the one instant that it takes to adjust one's attitude — or, if you don't want to fix it, go find another dojo, an Americanized one where you'll feel more at home.

If you are going to bring your butt to the Budo karate dojo, you also have to bring your spirit. That, or stay away.

That means, train hard physically, but it also means that you continuously battle to replicate the attitude described in this book. Remember, if it all *dawns on you*, if you figure it out, it becomes who you are, and it's not something that you have to fight for.

But if it hasn't yet?

If you think it's okay to have a strong Budo karate attitude one day, and all that matters on a different day is that you're present in body, but not in spirit?

Wrong.

Please fix this.

Even if your entire karate experience is four hours per week, plus the five minutes that you happen to speak with your sempai on the phone, make sure all four of those hours, and for all five of those minutes, you are powerful every single second.

104. Bully vs. Victim

Karate training is the great equalizer.

Sorry, take one step back!

Budo karate training, rather, is the great equalizer. Americanized karate training falls short.

In the full-contact dojo, the bully-type personally tends to soften, and the victim-type personality tends to be emboldened.

Now, ask again, Mom and Dad, why contact fighting is important in the dojo!

From a Budo karate point of view, there is ONLY full-contact karate. Of course (!!!) we do a lot of training that's NOT full contact to prepare for that most intense of our exercises. No one wants anyone to be hurt.

But for me?

I'd far rather risk injury, and know Budo karate, than never take that necessary risk, and only know American "ker-rah-tee."

Mas Oyama built a style of karate that touched the lives of twelve million students during his lifetime. Do you think he would have achieved that if the only goal was to beat someone up?

Of course not, but it IS important to one's character development through karate training to experience, at some point, the full-contact fight. At the heart of the character-developing aspects of Budo karate?

You got it:

Full-contact fighting.

(Don't worry, parents, we'll take care of your kids! We didn't just pick this up yesterday! Budo karate is for men, women, and children. It's for the young and the old, the athletic and the not. All will be made healthier, even by participating in full-contact fighting, and especially if all students can grasp the concepts presented here.)

105. Dissent and Complaint

Dissent.

I've seen it in my first teacher's dojo (Mas Oyama's nephew, Sensei Seong Soo Choi, teaching in North Carolina in the '80s) and I've seen it, to a lesser extent, in my own.

Remember how I suggested in my introduction that negative cultural elements, such as Coke and the McDonald's hamburger, might piggyback on positive ones, such as democracy, when spreading from country to country?

Well, let me step in here and suggest that, in certain cases, the positive of one culture might also be a negative in certain situations in another. Take democracy. It can be the death of a dojo. I've watched it happen.

If a student rebels against his teacher, in the Budo karate way there's only one way, and that's the highway.

To follow, or not to follow, and no other options, or, *if there's something you inwardly question, to follow outwardly, SILENTLY and without complaint, until you either understand, accept, or conclude that you must leave.*

In America, however, it's possible for a disgruntled student (an H-type student, let's say, who's frustrated by being told to take a leap of faith that he/she's refusing to take) to voice his/her complaint to another like-minded student, and if enough students have enough behind-the-scenes chatter, it's possible for them to start to convince themselves that they can change the dojo, or even change their teacher.

Remember, though, that karate IS your teacher's karate in your dojo. If you don't like it, you only have one choice, and that's to leave. A really angry student might try to drum up support for his/her viewpoint, but that's why it's important, here, that I warn you of your responsibility in the Budo karate dojo.

In recent years, a black belt student of another instructor who is part of our organization, Kyokushin-kan, called me on the phone to complain about his teacher. "Poor thing!" I thought. He was angry because his teacher wouldn't give him a second dan, because his teacher (who's MY sempai!) thought he had a bad attitude. Well, guess what! He did have a bad attitude, apparently, because he was calling me, a virtual stranger to that dojo's hierarchy, to complain.

What was I to do, after all?

Our chairman, Royama Kancho, told us once how, when he was a young man, Mas Oyama expelled him from the dojo because he, Royama Kancho, had a disagreement with his teacher, Mas Oyama, and because he had made the mistake of voicing it.

And that *was* a mistake.

What's remarkable to us in the West, however, was that Kancho realized his mistake and left without complaint, practiced another style that did not compete with his teacher for three years, and then came back, humbly, to ask to be readmitted. Mas Oyama respected his commitment, and welcomed him back, after which he became one of Mas Oyama's most trusted students.

In my first teacher's dojo, I saw an attempt at a democratic action to change the dojo from within. It failed, of course. In my own dojo, I've seen disgruntled students complain behind the scenes (in the locker room, for example), and have been shocked to learn how, in certain cases, that student's classmates responded. In one case, they responded with sympathy! One H-type sempai responded to the complaint of his H-type koohai, "Yeah, Sensei was having a bad day today!"

I was amazed, and both students are now, of course, gone.

But I give you these stories—even the ones that are embarrassing for me!—so that I can tell you what your proper response is in the Budo karate system if you ever encounter dissent.

Angrily stamp it out.

Nip it in the bud, right then and there, on the spot. Scold, or even confront, the student who issues it, and refuse to hear another word.

"Gosh, Sensei was in a piss-poor mood tonight!" one (failing) student says.

"Yeah, of course he was!" responds the *Budo* karateka classmate. "Your attitude was so poor, he's got a right to be frustrated. Get with the program, dude, or don't come around here anymore!"

This is a correct response.

If it persists, discuss with one of your sempais.

Even if you're expelled from the dojo, you cannot succeed without your teacher, so you have to do something else (if you don't want to quit martial arts all together) that does not compete with your teacher until such a time as you adjust yourself to the point where you can return. What did Kancho Royama do during the years that he was expelled from Mas Oyama's dojo?

He trained hard, quietly, and, by doing so, adjusted himself until he was ready to come back and face his teacher. He didn't go away to teach his teacher. He went away to figure out his own shortcoming.

My first teacher once told me to fix my attitude or never come back to the dojo. Yet I knew that he was the one for me, and I left class that night and walked 40 miles, all night long, to his doorstep in the next city, where he lived, to bow to him and apologize. I was 17 years old, I had blood blisters the size of silver dollars on the soles of my feet, and it was then that he recommended me to his uncle, Mas Oyama.

The Japanese way is not always common sense to Westerners.

I got it right that day, but not because I was anything great. My NEED to remake myself through karate was great, and in that sense, I was lucky. My need was so great that I was willing to take that leap of faith.

Remember, in the dojo, it's your teacher's way or the highway.

Ironic that, that day, I took the highway right back to my teacher's dojo.

106. Addressing, or Discussing, Your Sempais: ALWAYS Use Their Title Correctly

We have, in the Japanese dojo, three honorific titles for our seniors, sempai (senior), sensei (teacher), and shihan (teacher's teacher). There is never a situation in which we address one of our seniors (anyone with a higher rank), or mention one of our seniors in the third person (that is, talking *about* one of our seniors while speaking with someone else), when we are not required to use their titles. The name itself is optional as long as it's clear from the context who's being discussed/addressed, but the title is not. You can call your teacher "Sensei," for example, but the "Ligo" part of "Ligo Sensei" is optional.

This means ALWAYS: inside the dojo or out, on the phone or in person, in a letter, in an e-mail, and so on. There is not an exception for cases when we are addressing or talking about someone of higher rank.

Please note:
1. Our senseis and our shihans are also our sempais because sempai means *senior*, but the term that we use should be the *most* honorific one our sempai has been awarded by *their* higher-ups. In your dojo it will be clear to you whether to use *Sensei* or *Shihan* for your

teacher(s). Everyone else (of higher rank than the speaker) should be addressed, or referred to, as *sempai*.
2. Mr. and Mrs. are also honorific titles, *-san* in Japanese (but unlike in English, all titles generally follow the proper name: "Ligo Sensei," for example, or "Amy Sempai"). Note that whereas you always use the title, you actually have a choice as to whether to use the person's first name or last name. Using the last name is more formal, so if there's any doubt, I would recommend "Ligo Sensei," for example, instead of "Nathan Sensei."
3. One does not refer to oneself with an honorific title. So, "Hi, I'm Ligo Sensei," or "Hi, I'm Amy Sempai," are never used, except by teachers in the West trying to educate their students in the proper terminology. This leads to a difficulty on the side of the Western instructor trying to create the proper system, because when I say "Hi, this is Nathan Ligo calling" (i.e. on the phone when calling a student), the proper response is "Osu! Ligo Sensei, how are you?" but instead, the Western student is often confused and thinks that I just gave him/her license to call me "Nathan."
4. One does not refer to their equals (same rank) or juniors (lower rank) by title. Again, another reason for confusion for Western students. I might say, for example, "Amy is teaching on Tuesday." That confuses the koohais sometimes because then they're likely to call her "Amy" instead of "Amy Sempai." The rule is simple, though: Use the honorific title EVERY time you speak with (or refer to) YOUR senior, but not when you speak with (or refer to) YOUR equals and juniors.

What if there's one student in your dojo who is your sempai because he/she'd already been training for a year when you began, but then he/she took a year off from training, and you passed him/her in rank? Remember that your sempai is everyone who started training even one day before you, so what are you to do if you get your first belt, but that student who started before you does not? This is another tricky situation for the Western student, so generally we go by rank. If you want to make an exception and address or refer to someone who has a lower rank than you as "sempai" because he/she has been training longer, you do have that prerogative. In Japan this generally occurs because the junior really *feels* strongly that that person helped to guide them, before they later passed that person in rank. The point is, though, we don't choose whether or not to address (or refer to) our seniors with their titles, but we may with our juniors-by-rank in that rare case.

107. Responding to All Types of Criticism

As you read below, please note that the first three cases are *strong student* cases, and the second three are *weak student* cases.

1. Strong Student Case A:

Teacher: "Nice job!"
Student: "Osu!" (Fiery-eyed, positive attitude, but never "Osu, thank you!" because that's not humble in the Japanese system, since "thank you" suggests you agree with the teacher's compliment.)

Strong (?) Student Case B:

Teacher: "Your karate is a bit off today, can you please fix it!"
Student: "Osu! Sensei, I'll fix it!" (Fiery-eyed, positive attitude. Immediately works on repairing the deficiency, and the mistake doesn't happen again.)

Strong (?) Student Case C:

Teacher: "Damn it, your karate is terrible today! You're in everyone's way! Are you trying to lower your dojo's average?"
Student: "Osu! Sensei, I'll fix it!" (Fiery-eyed, positive attitude. Immediately works powerfully on repairing the deficiency, and refuses to let it happen again.)

2. Weak (Attitude) Student Case A:

Teacher: "Nice job!"
Student: "Osu." (Blandly [*or* matter-of-factly], without fire and energy. Or an even smaller "osu" if the student really doesn't even want to be present, or no "osu" at all.

Weak (Attitude) Student Case B:

Teacher: "Your karate is a bit off today, can you please fix it!"

Student: "Osu." (Or a smaller "osu," or no "osu" at all. Note the missing exclamation point, and the missing "I'll fix it!" In addition to being weak, this student has now been rude. No attempt made to fix the problem, or, worse, gets MORE in the way now that he/she's been corrected.)

Weak (Attitude) Student Case C:
Teacher: "Damn it, you're karate is terrible today! You're in everyone's way! Are you trying to lower the dojo average!"
Student: No verbal response, angry or sad eyes. (Maybe a small "osu" because he/she knows that one is required, but no attempt made to fix the problem, and the student continues to get in the way, or, worse, gets MORE in the way, now that he/she's been scolded, because now he/she's feeling sorry for him/herself as well.)

* * *

Note that the strong student has a positive response even if his/her teacher's criticism is sharp. Note that when the criticism becomes derogatory (because the student should have known better), the attitude becomes even stronger, and the student makes an even more powerful correction. The only reason I included the question marks after "strong" was because in those cases the student had to be corrected in the first place. The responses were correct, but hopefully the strong student would avoid having to be corrected at all.

Notice that in the case of the weak student, though, the harsher the criticism becomes, the worse, or the weaker, the reaction becomes. This student would have gotten beaten up in the Japanese dojo, with the idea that he/she had better get with the program immediately, or not come back to the dojo, because this is conduct that's unbecoming, even to the white belt. Thus far, in my branch in America, I have not endorsed this kind of overt correction, yet as long as stern correction is subtle, go ahead. Please let that koohai know that his/her attitude is bad. I approve.

My first teacher, in America, used to bash us with a *shinai* (split-bamboo training sword for kendo) when we let him down. Our response was "Osu! Sensei, I'll fix it! (Please bash me again, bash me harder, if I let you down again!)"

And we loved him for it.

The Budo karate student of Japan also has the same attitude to a tongue-lashing. "Thank you, Sensei! Can I have another?"

Please try not to let yourself ever disappoint your teacher or sempai, but if you DO, and if your teacher/sempai lets you have it, the correct response is always the humble/determined/grateful one, never the opposite. The verdict is still out for me, in my own personal experience, whether the frequency with which I've seen the weaker reactions described above is a consequence of the fact that I work with at-risk kids though my nonprofit, or whether this is more of a broadly shared American, or Western, trait.

I only saw really bad attitude a couple times in Japan, and each time the student was bashed and thrown out of the dojo. So, please, just make sure your attitude is positive, even in the face of what could be painful criticism from your teacher or sempai.

See #16, *React Inversely to Hardship 3: A Visibly Angry, Frustrated, or Disappointed Teacher or Sempai*. Remember that if your teacher ever loses his temper with you, it's because YOU refused to fix a problem behavior that was negatively affecting the standard of the training. If you're gonna get mad, get mad at yourself. It's the weak student who consciously or subconsciously tries to punish the teacher (with a weak response and sad or angry eyes) for his or her own mistakes.

In one recent class, I heard myself telling a long-faced teen, "Hey! Brace up! I'm not on your case because I don't like you! I'm on your case because your performance is below par. Do what I'm asking you to do, and you'll see. The power to change how I respond to you is in YOUR hands, not mine." How reassuring it was that, in this case, I witnessed that student's eyes brighten, and he redoubled his effort to make the change I was asking of him! "Nice job! That's it!" I was able to say. "Good for you!"

108. Wouldn't You Rather Be Corrected for Doing Too Much, Rather Than Called Out for Not Doing Enough?

There's little more to say here than has already been said in the title. If you overdo something, in 9 cases out 10, it's because you're trying too hard, and that's at least a positive thing, right? If you under-do something, on the other hand, it's because you're not applying yourself enough.

Try this on for size:

Your teacher says, "Your stance is too deep! You're kiai-ing too loudly! You're saying 'Osu!' too often. You're learning too fast! You're volunteering too much; I want the other students to learn to volunteer too! Don't train so hard; I don't want you to hurt yourself!"

Since it's all about strength (physical, mental, spiritual), wouldn't you rather suffer this kind of criticism than the other kind, in which your teacher and your sempais consider your responses to be wimpy?

Remember that overcorrections show spirit and determination, and under-corrections show lack of commitment. Especially if you hear the same correction twice, it's a good idea to go nuts and correct in such a huge way that there's no doubt you're trying to comply with what your teacher/sempai is asking of you. See #12, *Hear it Twice? It's Life and Death.*

109. There's Nothing Wrong with a Bit of Ferocious Dedication to Your Dojo

On the contrary, *letting yourself go* to have a bit of ferocious dedication is the best way to make YOU the best you can be at karate.

You're aware of the ferocious dedication discussed in the news among soldiers who have fought together? You hear how a soldier about to leave the military reenlists instead, because he knows his unit is going back into harm's way?

Don't you think that kind of dedication ALSO makes the individual soldier stronger? Don't you think it makes them—at least by that degree—people of superior character?

And yet for the American karate student, this kind of attitude is rarely applied to the martial arts school. "This isn't something I *fight* for," one says, "this is something I *pay* for to get."

"Fool!" is my response, having trained in Mas Oyama's dojo and hearing HIS voice ringing in my ears.

Try this on for size! This is more what I'm used to hearing in the Budo karate dojo of Japan:

"No question, I'll train here and support this dojo forever! It's MY dojo, after all!"

"I'd even risk personal energy to make sure my dojo is well represented, and I'd do it with pleasure! Of course I would! These people are MY dojo family. Sensei, do you need me to fight in that tournament to show how strong our dojo is? Sensei, do you need me to put myself at risk, fighting with that overly proud student in our midst, to help pound the majority onto the correct path? I'm not sure I can beat him, but I'd do it gladly with all my might!

"Of course I would! I'd do it in a heartbeat! I understand that protecting the ideal that you're teaching is one and the same with protecting my own life, should the need ever arise. I know that without the successful *channeling* of your ideal, none of us will get it, none of us will be able to defend ourselves if we ever have to. If we're going to do the fantasy version, we'll pay for it if we ever have to fight to defend ourselves. [See #81, *To Fight for Correct Training Attitude IS to Defend your Life After All.*]

"Need me to volunteer to help around the dojo? It would be my honor! Osu!"

I've seen students overseas who would charge, headfirst, into a brick wall with all their might if their sempai asked them to. Of course a good sempai is not supposed to put his koohai needlessly at risk, so I've never see *that* happen, but this type of student, the Budo karateka, has set him/herself aside and accepted a ferocious sense of loyalty to *the Way*.

And don't you think he/she's stronger because of it?

Of course he is! Or course *she* is!

Such an attitude is certainly hard to come by in the American commercial environment.

Read #25, *Challenge vs. Command.* A hint! The weaker student will read that section and this one, and skip over them both, believing, "This couldn't possibly apply to me!"

Oh, but it does!

Your teacher is challenging every single one of you, not just "that other type of student"—ALL of you!—your teacher is challenging YOU to adopt a ferocious sense of loyalty to your dojo.

With it you've got Budo karate. Without it, you've got an imitation.

It was an educational moment for ME recently when I told a group of students that the members of my dojo's *Technical Committee Class* (currently four students that train with me on Saturday or Sunday mornings at 6 AM) had never once in one year missed a single class. I could see it in the eyes of this class of general students, "What? Really?" and I knew my suspicions were correct. Most of them were deciding on a daily basis whether or not to train that day or not. "Hmm, I don't feel good today, I'll train tomorrow," for example.

I realized the extent to which *that* group of American students were missing the point.

What are you going to do if someone tries to kill you with a baseball bat, and you're not feeling up to fighting back that night? Are you going to say, "Wait, hold on! Let me get warmed up! I think I should have a cup of coffee first."

I chuckle.

Of course you can't! Haven't you realized that strength in karate has to have nothing to do with how you feel in any one practice, or whether you feel up to it?

Learn this through ferocious dedication to your dojo.

How many hours per week do you practice? Six because you come to three classes, four because you come to two?

Good, then make sure you're ferociously dedicated to karate, to your dojo, and to your teacher, for those four or six hours. That's all that's required, that and powerfully deciding to apply yourself to the best of your ability, looking for additional ways to support your dojo outside of that minimum. Four hours is great if that's all you can do, particularly, if you're disciplining yourself to stick to a schedule so it has little to do with other things going on in your life.

Wanna take it to a higher level, though?

Then do that, but ALSO ask yourself daily if you can do more. If what comes back is even a hint of a "yes, probably, I could if I . . ." then grab hold of that impulse and run with it.

That's the strength of Budo karate growing within you!

If you deny those impulses, on the other hand, by turning your back on ferocious dedication, you're also turning your back on the exact strength you were hoping to acquire by practicing karate in the first place.

110. The BS Dojo

Do I need to define BS for anyone?

If anyone's really clueless, it's a nicer way to say something I shouldn't write here. Got it?

Okay, so . . .

We trained so hard in Mas Oyama's dojo that it set us up for a lifetime of seeing other martial arts schools around the world, and feeling completely justified in assessing, "Whew, this is BS karate!"

The point that seems to be hard for Westerners to grasp, however, is that there wasn't anything special about us. We were the students, so we were the energy and power in the dojo. It wasn't like everyone was a champion Olympic-class athlete! There were men, women, and children, young and old.

So what was it, you ask?

Why was our training so superior that so much karate around the world would look like a joke in the aftermath?

It was just the attitude with which the students trained, that's all. It was like all of them had caught a fever of "I want more and I'm not going to stop until I get it." Simply put, it was that all the students walked into the dojo with the attitude contained in this book.

So, read well, little ones!

None of this is hard. You don't have master any of this material; you just have to prioritize it. Rules are hard to memorize, but you can change your attitude in just one instant! Adopt the attitude of the Budo karateka, and karate in the West will never again be what it was!

I'm sorry to add one more perspective, also because it's another that exposes the challenges I have faced in my own dojo:

Look, folks! Sometimes I look at MY OWN dojo, and think, "Oh my God, this is BS karate!" And sadly, sometimes it is. It's a constant battle for the hearts and minds of the students. If the majority accepts the Budo mentality, we'll be golden, forever. I have a hunch that the reason why I've even seen the other case in my dojo is because my students, until now, haven't had access to this book. Until recently, the majority of my students have always come from disadvantaged backgrounds because of the work that I do for my community through the nonprofit that I run.

Here, we're currently making progress on both fronts!

Yet if half the students resist, "I don't want all of that other stuff," they might say, "I just want to learn karate!"

"Fool!" I would respond. "Without this, you're NOT learning karate! It's the attitude in this book that IS karate, after all!"

111. Stealing Karate: No Thieves Welcome Here, Please!

Rife within the American mentality is the notion, "I'm paying for this, so I can take from it what I want. I can do it MY way, and leave the rest alone."

But please be clear, you may NOT do it your way in the Budo karate dojo. It's your teacher's way or the highway. You work to adopt this training attitude or YOU ARE IN THE WAY.

In which case you should find another dojo.

Here, going through the motions to get what you want but resisting *the Way*, you are stealing from your dojo, and from a group of people who are battling to go ALL THE WAY.

112. Pronunciation, Enunciation

There are very few Japanese words that you'll need for training in the dojo. Of course you'll need numbers, to count with, from one to ten. You'll need the names of the techniques (and there's a bunch of those), and you'll need the names of kata. Those are all Japanese.

But other than that?

Don't worry, really, all of them come with time. To try to memorize them before you begin your training would be overkill.

I'll list the ones we use in my dojo:

1. Osu!
2. Osu! Arigatoo Gozaimashita!   Thank you very much!
3. Osu! Onegaishimasu!   Please extend this favor to me!
4. Sensei (Sempai) ni Rei!   Bow to Sensei (or the Sempai)!
5. Kamaete!   Assume (fighting) stance!
6. Naore!   Return to ready stance!
7. Yame!   Stop!
8. Mowate!   Rotate!
9. Otagai ni Rei!   Bow to your partner!
10. Hajime!   Begin
11. Kiairete!   Kiai!

What others? That should be about it. I have opted to have my students use "Osu! Sensei, I'll fix it!" instead of the "Osu! Shitsurei-shimashita! (Osu! I was very rude to make that mistake!)" we used in Japan.

The only point I wanted to make here is that it IS important to learn the correct pronunciation, and it IS important to say these words clearly. We all live in a world in which our attempt to imitate Japanese culture WILL, at some point, intersect with Japanese people.

And they do notice!

"Osu!" is long "o" like "Oh my god!" plus "su," like the name Sue, but with a silent "u." Since the "u" is silent, it might better be written "osse", but please note, this is NOT "oose", with the double-o, like "loose." We do not say "usse," we do not say "oshe." And yet I hear all of these on the North American continent, and people DO embarrass themselves when someone who knows (Japanese) hears them.

My advice for you?

Find someone who really knows — and someone who values telling you if you're wrong! Ask them to confirm that you're using your Japanese words correctly.

See #35, *Weak* Osu *Has No Meaning, Unheard* Osu *Might As Well Not Have Been One at All, Not Even Trying* Osu *Means You Might As Well be Home* for more on proper use of the word "Osu!"

113. Charging to the Front of the Curve

You are familiar by now with the *Toes-Not-Heels Dojo* of Budo karate (see #5), and of the importance of unanimous *fighting to be first* (Budo karate!) so as not to have a group that lags behind and weighs down an eager, but beleaguered one (Americanized karate). Look at the following diagram:

If we take the curve to represent strength and determination, look at all the students in Case A, all charging to the front of the curve! This is the Toes-Not-Heels dojo. This is a Budo karate dojo, as defined by the fact that all the students, except that one who lags slightly behind, are simultaneously fighting to be first.

These students are ferociously dedicated (See #109, *There's Nothing Wrong with a Bit of Ferocious Dedication to Your Dojo*).

But how about case B?

There are 3 T-type students in the room, but look at all those others who are taking their time!

Case A   Case B

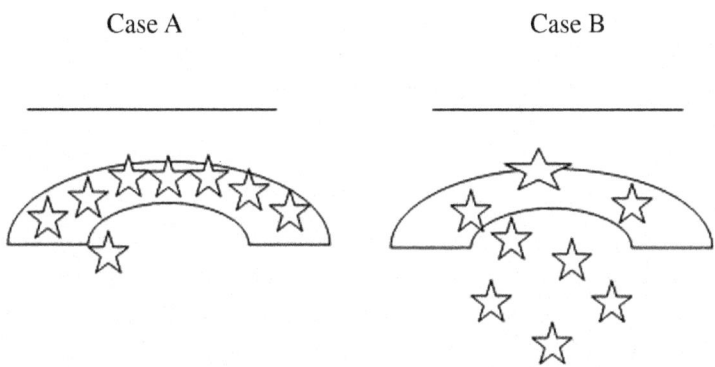

Since our most basic example given in #1, *Fight to Be First*, was an instruction by your teacher to "line up!" at the beginning of class, and if we take *in their final places in the lineup* to be the straight lines in the diagrams drawn above the curves, look at how much faster the students in Case A get to their places! (The stars now actually represent students' positions relative to their destination.) And look how slow the students of Case B would be to get to that same destination!

This is just another way of stating "Fight to be first," but it's so, so critical, I just want to give you every possible chance of understanding.

If every student in the room fights not to be the one who's last (or weakest, or missed the instruction, or sweats the least, or kiais the quietest), everyone stays at the front of the curve. This is the only correct attitude for even the beginning student in the Budo karate dojo. New students join the dojo, and, even if they haven't read this book and no one's told them how they're supposed to be, they will find themselves imitating the other students in the room, and, effortlessly, they'll find themselves fighting up to the front of the curve.

But if that's the case, consider the calamity it would be if that same beginning student entered a dojo in which all of his/her role models always hovered around performance levels of 50%, and maybe 60% on days when they felt particularly high-spirited. What if they constantly pissed and moaned about how hard and inconvenient it was to train hard? Of course, that's perhaps an unrealistic picture, but the point is that the newcomer is always shaped by the attitudes of the establishment. In the case of the Budo karateka, every student should fight to the front of the curve to make sure that the establishment is as strong as it can be.

114. You ARE the Dojo!

Oh, but YOU are the dojo, not the building that it's in, not your teacher!

Your teacher's job is to guide your energy down the right path, but it is NOT your teacher's job to coax you to have energy. Nothing feels better to me as a teacher than when certain students fight their hardest to impress me when I'm teaching. Nothing is more disappointing than when those same students have no fight in them those nights when I'm not.

It means their priority is all wrong.

It is certainly correct to try to impress your teacher with your fighting spirit. Please always do!

But you also have to remember that the best way to impress your teacher is to show that same fighting spirit, with even more ferocity, when your teacher is *not* around. If one of your sempais is teaching the class, he/she needs your energy as a role model *even more*. Your koohais need you as role model even more. YOU need, even more, to prove it *to yourself* that strength and spirit is YOURS, not something you're borrowing—or stealing!—from someone else, least of all from your teacher.

Remember the section about having an inverse reaction to hardship? (See #15, *React Inversely to Hardship 2: Turn On the Animal!*).

If your teacher is not in class, and your classmates are H's who are less enthused because your teacher is not there that night, *you* have to fight even harder! Fight for your dojo, fight for your teacher, fight for your classmates! But if you don't fight . . . something's wrong, and you should question your colored belt.

Perhaps you should have a white one.

Remember that *attitude* is the prerequisite for training. It's what you bring with you when you come, not something someone's going to teach you once you arrive.

115. Careful, or Your Dojo Will Weed You Out!

Did you understand that earlier section #45 that said karate IS what your teacher defines it to be, and that, "it's your teacher's way, or the highway?"

Understand that your teacher's goal is to channel his/her teaching, from his/her teachers above him/her, downwards through you, and on into your koohais of the future. It is a purely Western phenomenon, and definitely an American one, that students feel they can take a class and get only what THEY want out of it. If you enter a Budo karate dojo, understand that the only way to succeed is to align your goals with your teacher's. If your goal is divergent from, or less than, that of your teacher, you can only in the end have a contentious relationship with your dojo, and you can only, therefore, fail in the end.

In Japan, the student with the divergent attitude (who also, therefore, wouldn't learn what was being offered) was considered to have a *bad* attitude, and might even have been beaten in kumite until he/she either changed his/her thinking (the common situation), or quit (the rare one). In America, we prefer not to take that route, but I can assure you that if you are in the Budo karate dojo and trying to do it YOUR WAY, the system will beat you in small ways, and in bigger and bigger ways as you gain rank until you either adjust, or decide that karate's not so fun for you anymore.

I am next to heartbroken to consider many of the strong, able students I've lost during the years, many of whom I really liked as people, and who were really strong in certain ways, but who ultimately faded away.

The number one reason?

They grew in terms of kicks and punches, and kata, and kumite, but at that early stage of my branch's development before they had strong sempai role models, they failed to acquire—or perhaps I failed in my efforts to teach them!—the self-propagating powerful attitude of Budo karate as described in this book. Indeed, with more than one strong class of students, at different times in my history, I've had no choice but to push them—brown belts already, even!—to establish the proper attitude they should have been developing since blue belt, and in these cases, I've had to push them until karate wasn't fun for them anymore, if they still didn't get it. How could they have known what was at risk as they carried my branch down a path towards the establishment of the Americanized dojo, rather than the Budo karate one?

How could they have understood that the head of *that* dojo, I will not ever contentedly be?

I'd rather have one student fighting for Budo and be completely broke than have ten thousand who want to do it their way.

But never fear!

That's why I've written this book.

I can't help but think that if those students had read it, they would have been able to grasp what it was that they were missing. "Why is Sensei upset with me?!" I could see them thinking as brown belts, "I'm doing exactly what he used to compliment me for when I was a blue belt!"

And that, of course, is exactly the point.

To go from blue belt to brown belt, you have to learn many things, you have to develop in multiple ways, and that includes ways that are NOT just about kicks and punches. Your attitude also has to develop. Your ability to lead has to develop. Your dedication to the dojo has to develop. By the time you're a senior student it's no longer my job to keep the pace, it's YOURS—that is, *you* have to keep the pace that I originally set.

But if you've moved into a position of leadership in terms of rank, and you're showing yourself to be comfortable with a lesser pace for the future of the dojo that I started?

I'm forced then to wonder, am I, too, to remain, in the end, part of the American trend in which great instructors come from Japan and develop strong students who are ultimately unable to make followings of strong students themselves?

Please do understand that your Budo karate dojo will eventually weed you out if you don't acquire your teacher's way.

It is an extreme case, but I had one adult student early on in America who routinely hit his opponents too hard when it wasn't time for hard hitting. I told him to lighten up again and again, over a period of days and weeks, and then, finally, months. Particularly, I noticed, he was hitting the female students, and he was unaware of the extent to which he was hurting them. I tried and I tried to get through to him, but finally, one day, enough was enough—he was essentially assaulting weaker students—my training from Mas Oyama's dojo kicked in and I bashed him severely in kumite.

I am embarrassed that during the initial moments of the melee I lost my cool enough to try to punch his teeth out, and I am more thankful than embarrassed that I missed. I am not, however, particularly regretful that after I missed and realized how much trouble I could have gotten myself into, I changed my techniques to competition-legal ones, and drove him, with my punches and low kicks, right out of the dojo, until he was moaning and crying outside in a heap of defeat.

Two days later he hobbled back into the dojo with a much better attitude, and when he moved out of town a year or so later, I was sorry to lose him. He had gotten that much better. He had corrected his path.

I was lucky.

Knowing what I know today, I'm certain that I'll never again have to resort to such measures.

But please, do understand that that's how serious it is for you to allow your way to diverge from your teacher's way. It doesn't have to be that you're hurting someone. It can merely be that you're gobbling up the kicks and punches part of the training, but resisting any effort to be a leader for your juniors, and it just might be, in your teacher's mind, a *pound you out of the dojo* kind of shortfall. After all, that, too, IS hurting someone as far as I'm concerned. In that case, you would be working to prevent me from giving your koohais all that Budo karate should be, and THAT has the potential to injure people that you might not even have met yet.

It doesn't happen in the Japanese Budo karate dojo, because the student would be ashamed to not immediately align his/her own goals and methods with his teacher's, right from the beginning of training—that, or because one of his sempais would have bashed him first, like I had to do that day in my dojo without anyone those days to back me up. See #13, *Your Teacher Is Angry? It's Life and Death for EVERYONE, Especially YOU if You Feel Like Someone* Else *Was Responsible.*

In this country, America, *the unconquerable country*, it seems that students sometimes remain so individualistic that they resist even when being given the greatest of all possible gifts. I can take you to water, but I can't make you drink. If you continuously refuse to drink, however, you'll wind up so unhappy and so unpopular, and maybe even more battered and bruised than you want to be, that eventually you'll wander off and look, still thirsty, for somewhere else to drink.

Take a leap of faith, though!

Adopt the attitude described in this book, and I have no doubt that all of my students' karate, one day, will surpass my own, and when that day comes, we will celebrate together a future in which American karate can hold its own next to the strongest karate in the world.

116. Dojo Decorum and Sempai-Koohai Interaction
AS IF THEY WERE KATA

Even kata have a proper facial expression and a proper gaze.

Of course, in the West, we get to see karate students who make a great collection of faces when they do kata—snarling, tough-guy faces, for example!—but these are distortions that crept in, at one time or another, that may have served a purpose in the moment, but that have no final place in the practice of Budo karate. Budo karate, after all, is about self-defense, and any element in self-defense that's *extra*, and therefore unnecessary, ultimately detracts. Does a certain class of students need to learn how to *turn on the animal* (see #15)? Okay, so maybe let's snarl and make faces for a while to get over a hurdle, but then let's move on to something more pure.

The correct facial expression for practicing techniques is the relaxed but serious one. One's eyes should always be fixed on one's would-be attacker.

My intention here, however, in this section, is to suggest that Western karate students, for whom the decorum of the dojo and sempai-koohai interaction is so foreign, might well benefit by considering *every* element of decorum and dojo interaction as exercises that are just as regimented as kata.

Of course, even that takes a leap, because so many Western karate students incorrectly introduce so much variety into their kata that it's hard for us to grasp that they are meant to be done in just one formal way—note the facial expression dilemma cited above, for example! Yet I do think it will be at least easier to grasp this fact regarding kata than the fact that dojo decorum and interactions between sempai and koohai are also meant to be precise. Accordingly, the reader might use the parallel to gain clarity.

When you perform a formal exercise such as kata, there is only one way to perform it correctly, right? "But there's so much variety!" you might exclaim. "My teacher teaches it differently than your teacher! Some of my sempais do it this way, and some of my sempais do it that way!"

If that's the case, though, someone — or everyone! — still has a lot of work to do. There's only one correct way to perform any one kata.

So how do you define that one correct way?

There are three key elements. First of all, the way YOUR teacher teaches it IS the correct way . . . See #44, *Karate IS Your Teacher's Karate.*

The second is a memorized series of motions, and the third is perfecting each individual defense/counterattack so that it's the best possible one for the *mock* fighting situation at hand. And guess what, folks! There's only one perfect way in each case. As long as all students practicing a certain movement all have the same incoming attack in mind, there's only one way to do the defense/counter for the best effect. Hence, all mastered kata with the same attack/defense/counter in mind should be essentially identical.

But guess what else!

So should dojo decorum and interactions between sempai and koohai!

There's really only one way to do, not just your kata, but also nearly every second of the time that you spend in the dojo, or in the company of your sempais and koohais, and that includes all of the sempai/koohai interactions described in this book. Start with the rules of etiquette. There aren't variations on how to follow them. There's only one way.

Let's try to drop the variety, folks!

When you bow, there's only one way to do it correctly. There aren't situations where you do it one way, and other situations where you do it another.

When and how you answer with "Osu!"?

There's only one way.

How about the facial expression you should have in the dojo?

In the American dojo, there are all kinds. And yet your facial expression when practicing karate techniques should be serious and relaxed. That means snarling, smiling, teeth-baring, whispering, sideways-looking — all variations! — are essentially incorrect, albeit understandable in certain situations of extreme *physical* exertion.

Would you stop and whisper to someone else in the middle of a kata? Would you yawn? Would you pick your nose? Of course you wouldn't, but what might help you to grasp the concept here presented is that neither should you in the dojo, or while interacting with your sempais and koohais outside of the dojo. You wouldn't pick your nose in the middle of a kata, right? Don't do it in front of your sempais either!

Consider this example, and I think it will open your eyes.

You know from #10, *Complete Tasks That You've Been Assigned Promptly and Powerfully*, that you have to complete even the hardest tasks and challenges that your teacher or sempai gives you, OR communicate the fact that you haven't been able to—despite trying!—before your teacher or sempai finds that task or challenge un-accomplished.

Imagine that your teacher asks you to bring in a piece of equipment that you've borrowed from the dojo to practice at home, a bo staff, for instance.

Why not consider even this task a formal exercise?

So, with a proper facial expression, and proper eye contact, and from a proper fudo dachi, you respond properly, "Osu! Sensei, I'll bring it in tomorrow!" and your teacher has no doubt that you will in fact prioritize bringing in that piece of equipment when you come in the next time. So then you go home, and the first thing you do is to grab that bo staff and put it by the door so you're sure you won't forget it. It might be unbelievable for you, but why not consider THAT even to be part of a formal exercise that's supposed to be done perfectly? Yes, maybe no one's watching you at that moment, but you're taking your relationship with your sempai to be something to perfect, right, not something to take for granted? So in order to be perfect—not unlike in a kata—you have to be 100% sure that you get the job done.

The next time you go out to your car, it's the same thing: you take the bo staff out and put it in your car. Now there's no way you can forget it.

Now consider arriving at the dojo the next time. Your teacher's not in yet, so you put the bo staff you borrowed in among all the others and go about your business. Your teacher comes in, and goes about his/hers. Class starts, and you may or may not realize that part of the way through the class, your teacher is looking at you funny. Perhaps his/her temper is a bit short with you.

Why?

Because you didn't complete the task perfectly, as if it were a formal exercise like a kata. You didn't finish it.

Yes, it was correct to put the bo staff away and go about your business, and it would have been incorrect to run up to your teacher before he/she had a chance to put his/her bags down and take off his/her coat. But as soon as it felt to you like you wouldn't be disturbing your teacher, you should have jogged over to where he/she was, bowed in greeting and said "Osu!" and then told your teacher that you brought the bo staff in and put it with the others.

Your teacher will say, "Oh, right, thank you! Carry on. Have a good training! Did you see the ball game last night?"

Compare this to the above case in which you didn't complete the formal exercise of fulfilling the task that you'd been assigned by your teacher.

Now consider that every interaction, every moment of everything that you do in the dojo, has a correct way to do it.

Sure, it's okay to chat at times in low tones, sure it's okay to laugh and have fun when something happens that's funny (that is, in the proper circumstances), but consider, also, that if you want to perfect your Budo karate, just like in kata, you have to cut out all the extras. Just like extra motions or extra facial expressions don't fit in kata, extra motions, facial expressions, sounds, behaviors, don't fit within the Budo karate dojo.

Consider the student, the particularly weak child student, who gets angry and rolls his/her eyes when corrected or scolded by his/her teacher.

Did that extra and inappropriate facial expression fit in the dojo?

Of course not.

What about the student who yawns?

What about the student who doesn't answer "Osu!"?

What about the student whose "Osu!" is too weak?

What about the student who takes his/her time fulfilling an instruction?

What about the student who has to be told the same thing twice?

If your entire karate training experience were like a kata, all of these would be instances in which you blew it and lost your kata competition.

So, maybe it will help you to "get" dojo decorum and sempai/koohai interaction to consider the fact that all of it has a correct way that can be perfected, and that it's your job to try to perfect it.

Would you go to a kata competition and decide to do the kata your way, or in a less-than-serious way?

No way!

Neither, therefore, should you come in to your dojo and interact with your dojo-mates the way you want to, in a way that's less than what you know to be correct.

Make it all formal, and perhaps it will start to dawn on you that all of it is part of the training. The kicks and the punches ARE the important *what* of the training, because that's what you'll use to defend yourself if you ever have to, but the point is that in order to make your kicks and your punches perfect, you must first perfect the even more important *how*—your training attitude—and that means perfecting everything that you do in the dojo as if it were kata.

Emphasize kicks and punches, and perfect attitude will not come. Emphasize perfect attitude, however, and your kicks and your punches will be the best that they can be.

117. The Minimum Standard

It might be helpful for some to think about the concept(s) presented in this book in terms of *a minimum standard* of behavior in the dojo.

At least it seems to have helped several of my own students recently. "You are a colored belt now," I'll say. "It is a minimum standard for a color belt that you always answer with 'Osu!'"

Likewise, in the dojo, it is a minimum standard that you do all the things that you do in a powerful way. It is a minimum standard that you correct your technique when your teacher or sempai tells you *once*, or, at least, it is a minimum standard that you *don't make your teacher or sempai repeat him/herself* over and over again because you lacked the willpower to make the change. It is a minimum standard that you *follow the rules of etiquette*. It is a minimum standard that you *fight to be first* in all things, that you *respond to all challenges*, even the implicit ones issued by the T-type student training next to you, and that you decide resolutely to listen for the *how*, in addition to the *what*. It is a minimum standard that you understand that all things you do in the dojo, particularly following instructions, must be done *for effect*. In other words, it is a minimum standard that you SHOW your sempais and teacher, and that you SHOW your koohais for whom you must act as role model, that you are powerful, that you *own the techniques you've been shown*, and that you are, first and foremost, humble.

In an earlier section of this book (see #48), we went through similarly and rephrased many of these directives in terms of "I won't let myself be the one who . . ." I won't be the one who doesn't do something in a powerful way, for example. I won't be the one who makes my teacher or sempai tell me the same things over and over again. I won't be the one who doesn't apply and enforce a minimum standard to my participation in the dojo. I won't be the one who doesn't fight to understand and embody the concept(s) presented in this book. I won't be the one who lowers my dojo average by being lazy or complacent. I won't be the one who doesn't fight to show my ferocious sense of loyalty to my dojo, to my teacher, and to Mas Oyama's Budo karate.

We could go on, and on.

But please, understand that the single concept presented here in this book, the Budo karate ideal, is a minimum standard. It's an attitude, not something you have to learn, unless you are a young child, an at-risk child, or a child with a learning disability.

Budo karate, folks!

Not the dumbed-down Americanized version.

Join me, and there will be nowhere we cannot go!

118. Panicking? One Look Back at Cultural Differences

I hate for there to be a LAST concept in this book, because there is not one of least importance, least of all this one. Yes, I have grouped the first dozen or so at the very beginning because I consider them the most important for following my chain of thought throughout all of the rest of this book. But the same does NOT mean that the 100 or so sections that follow are LESS important.

This last point is NOT least important, especially if it might help to repair any damage sustained to your confidence as you've read.

I have done a lot in this book to convince you, the Western student of Budo karate, that you are disadvantaged simply by being of a different culture from the one in which Budo karate came to be. Furthermore, I have done a great deal of describing situations in which Western (American) students have failed to grasp the lessons being offered.

But don't worry too much. On the contrary, let this encourage you.

Remember, first, that that's why I've written this book, and, second, that Western students who read it will be that much better off than those who don't. Clearly, *you're* reading — certainly if you've made it this far! — so you should be confident that you're going to be one of the ones that gets it . . . all of it!

There's no question that *I'm* looking forward to teaching students of the future who have been thus prepared!

Consider where you are on the following spectrum in terms of your natural inclination to grasp the Budo karate mentality.

10	9	8	7	6	5	4	3	2	1	0
Japanese			New Generation Japanese			Westerner			Disadvantaged Westerner	

My hypothesis is that the Japanese student, for whom Budo is an inherent part of one's cultural identity, is more able to grasp the concepts described in this book than the average Westerner. Indeed, this first group, at the far left of the above spectrum, might not need to *grasp* these concepts at all. For this group, I think it's more likely that if they train hard—if their training *squeezes* them—it will be Budo that comes out all on its own.

You will recall from my introduction, however, that even Mas Oyama believed that there was a new, younger generation of Japanese who were more and more influenced by Western (American) pop culture, for whom these ideals, central to Budo, were becoming harder and harder to grasp. You'll note this group on the above scale in the 5 through 8 range.

Next there's you, the Western student of Budo karate, and last, there's those of you who are disadvantaged, even in your own country, in terms of being able to follow strong, mature, proactive routines. You will recall that in my personal case, I have a great deal of experience working with disadvantaged youth, since it is within the mission of my nonprofit organization to do so.

So where are you on this spectrum?

Well, if you have read this book, my guess is that you are probably at the higher end of the *Westerner* block on the above scale. You are probably the 4.5 or the 5.

That's why I'm continuously encouraging you to *take a leap of faith*. Mas Oyama would have you in the 8's and 9's, of course (in terms of understanding, not nationality!), which means you have to take a big leap, but even in that light, don't panic! Let's look again.

What defines the 6's and the 7's in this case?

Mas Oyama would tell you that it's their desire to resist traditional thinking, which would stand to make them resist, of course, Budo. Perhaps they don't want it.

So how big of a leap is it for you, after all?

Consider how important *wanting it* can be to the student who endeavors to learn. Presumably, you, the Western student who signed up to take karate classes, wants to learn it the right way, right? And now that you've read this book, you're starting to grasp what *the right way* is!

So good for you! You're on your way!

For that matter, let's rework our spectrum:

10	9	8	7	6	5	4	3	2	1	0
Japanese			Westerner Who Wants It & Reads This Book			New Generation Japanese		Disadvantaged Westerner		

Remember that one of the reasons Mas Oyama was ragging on American pop culture was because it was lowering the standard of his own average Japanese student. Maybe, if we look again, we can consider that the biggest division on this scale is not whether you're Japanese or Western, but rather, instead, whether you *want* to learn it correctly or not. The new-generation Japanese aren't so eager; they have to be *won over* just like our own disadvantaged youth. But you're reading this book, so you're one of the ones that wants it, right?

Try this on for size!

Maybe, the first scale I presented above, in which you were in the 3, 4, 5 range, *does* apply for the Westerner, but maybe that's only the Westerner who doesn't understand what Budo is, the one who doesn't understand the cultural difference, the one—dare I say—who hasn't read this book. Maybe, then, the second, reworked spectrum, the one in which you have suddenly been elevated to the 5's, 6's and 7's, applies to the Western students who *have* read this book or who have trained in an authentic Budo karate dojo, the ones who both want it, AND who understand clearly what it is they're supposed to want.

So don't be dismayed. Be encouraged!

Sure, I have done a lot of discussing of Western (American) students who were resistant. But those are the 1's, 2's and 3's, right? Or, they were ones who might have wanted it, but who didn't understand what it was they were pursuing. That wasn't you. That was just discussion to make you understand how you differ from those who will not be successful!

Just make sure that you are one of the ones who is pursuing Budo karate, not just karate as you, based on *your* cultural understanding, believe karate to be. Make sure that your dojo's majority is leaning in that direction—fighting for it—and you'll be fine.

Your generation—whether you're men, women or children, young or old—will be the one that puts your country's Budo karate on the map.

Remember the meaning of "Osu!"?

Persevere in the face of hardship and you will fulfill your goals and ambitions. Now that you know what the challenge is, your pursuit will be that much easier.

Epilog

The Establishment of *Budo Karate Culture*

As you have seen, the Budo karate dojo must possess a specific culture. Much of what that culture is stems from Japanese culture, but not all Japanese people are inherently Budo-inclined. Westerners, of course, are inherently *not*.

I would like to ask that the Western reader stop for a moment, here at the end, and consider the fact that while you are fighting, day in and day out, to learn KARATE—"the kicks, the punches, the kata, and the fighting ability," let's say—your teacher might be fighting, day in and day out, to teach BUDO KARATE, which might have quite a different definition from the one you're familiar with. I remind my students that if, for them, karate is kicks and punches, that's not what I'm teaching, and that's exactly why they're not progressing as fast as some of their classmates. I remind them that I am teaching *Budo karate*, which we might, for this particular purpose, define as "the MANNER with which one learns the kicks and punches of karate." If you learn that proper manner in my dojo, your karate will be one hundred times better in the end. If you try to ignore it, your karate will be worth very little: some sweat spilt, some calories burned, months or years passed, but little else.

Imagine me as a math teacher, asking my students to use math to solve a math problem, but, instead, they insist on trying to solve it with writing. They necessarily fail the test, right? It's the same in the dojo. If I ask a student for MANNNER and METHOD, and he/she gives me *kerrrahtee* (Americanized kicks and punches without trying to learn manner), that student necessarily fails.

Remember that to be successful in the Budo karate dojo, you must align your priorities with your teacher's.

If you join your teacher, in this case, and fight to establish the *Budo Karate Culture* in the closed environment that is your dojo—the one described by this book!—the kicks and punches, kata and kumite that you came looking for will be yours for the taking. In fact, you'll surprise yourself, because the kicks and punches of the *Budoka* are ten times greater than those of the hobbyist. Resist the effort to establish this *Budo Karate*

Culture, on the other hand, and not only will you deny yourself that wow moment when you realize you've far surpassed your wildest expectations, but you ALSO won't have learned kicks and punches, or kata or kumite, that are worth a damn.

Consider the individual *moments* of the karate training that show a dojo's culture to be Budo.

How about the students answering their teacher or sempais with a powerful "Osu!", one that expresses the meaning that it's meant to convey? If it's there, if it occurs regularly in your dojo, you've got Budo, and your kicks and punches are on the road to being spectacular. But what if the "Osu!" is lacking? If it is, the culture in your dojo is not correct, and you will not gain the *kicks and punches* proficiency you hope for without joining forces with your teacher to shift that culture across the cultural divide.

Ask yourself the obvious:

Is it YOU that doesn't put your heart and soul into your voice each and every time you express the power word "Osu!"?

Is it YOU whose performance is less than the one described to be optimum in this book?

If it's you, the power is in YOUR hands, to either make the change that will take your dojo to a more authentic level to become BUDO rather than BS (see #110, The *BS* Dojo), or keep the dojo reduced to a level in which those who resist strength, confidence, and ambition might feel themselves to be more at home.

How about hearing your teacher's every instruction, and SHOWING that you're making an effort to enact it? How about the *implicit* challenge issued by someone in your proximity training harder than you, and your either responding to that challenge by upping your intensity to match it (the Budo Karate Culture), or pretending instead that that challenge doesn't apply to you (the Americanized karate culture)?

All of these—count 'em! 118!—passages in this book represent MOMENTS in which you either define your karate to be Budo, or degrade it to something less.

Remember that you don't have to be perfect, because powerful effort to grasp what you haven't yet grasped is also a proper Budo attitude! If on the other hand, though, you think you're applying yourself to make an attitude change, but are still consistently failing to get there, perhaps it's time to reevaluate? Remember that it's not necessary to BE first; it's just important to consistently FIGHT to be. But please DO understand that the

Budo karateka strives for success *in order to attain it in short order.* He/she doesn't strive for success to become comfortable (habitual?) in the *striving for, and yet falling short of,* the goal.

At the new Ligo Dojo (in Chapel Hill), I have a few students that are left over from an earlier era (on Parrish Street in Durham), in which THOSE students learned karate in a substantially different culture from the one that's developing on quite a different path at the new location. In that earlier culture—one that developed in which so many of the students were, for one reason or another, "at risk" due to our nonprofit function—it never became the norm for students to behave powerfully, for example, even on days when they didn't feel powerful. There were simply too many students in the dojo who were too accustomed to defeat . . . there were too many present whose culture taught them to *console* each other in falling short, rather than providing the backbone of the strong role model needed to surround a challenged student and show him/her that there's a better way. In that environment, I actually watched some students take backwards steps; those who weren't accustomed to buckling *learned to buckle* from a majority who were more comfortable buckling.

My current students who are left over from that era are doing a heroic job of conquering, in themselves, the remnants of that culture in which *their* earliest karate was shaped. In other words, they are succeeding where many others before them failed to become part of a succeeding *Budo Karate Culture.*

And so I remind them, those times that they still perform a motion with little or no demonstration of an awareness of my having instructed them to do it differently the last time they did it, that that deficiency is not necessarily *in them,* so to speak. It might not be *their* inherent deficiency. The deficiency, rather, is in the culture in which their karate was born. "Defeat that weaker culture!" I tell them, "there's no call to be down on yourself! Simply overcome! Become part of this new, true *Budo Karate Culture* we're now finally in this new environment succeeding to build!"

"But isn't it the teacher's job to create the proper culture?" you might ask.

Yes, absolutely, it is.

And in the case of *this* particular teacher, I am aware that, facing insurmountable odds, I did fail many of that particular, earlier group of students by failing to win over the hearts and minds of that disadvantaged majority. Ultimately, it is MY responsibility.

The power to drink the water I lead you to is in your hands alone; the *responsibility* of trying to convince you to drink is indeed in mine.

Of course every culture has its pluses and its minuses, and of course we should embrace the positive of any culture to which we're exposed!

But what about the negative side?

Is it not our duty to identify whatever it is that's deficient, even in our own culture, and try to defeat it in ourselves? Of course we will always be at-risk for demonstrating the worst that our culture is, but isn't it a grave error, in the end, to say, "I am my culture and I cannot change"?

Don't we always, as individuals, have the power to decide to change?

As Budo karateka, we must make it so.

Otherwise, we admit defeat and remain disenfranchised from those who will experience true success.

My own confidence is not founded on any notion that I do everything right. On the contrary, it's founded instead on a rock-solid conviction that I am, myself, at risk of making life decisions that are based on the worst that my own personal culture is, rather than on the best that the culture I aspire to develop in myself can be if I refuse to let down my guard, and continue to fight for it. My confidence is based on a notion that because I'm aware, I'm therefore *on guard* in situations in which the norm—for our Western culture!—is to take our cultural tendencies and inclinations for granted as *the way things are*.

In the dojo—in MY dojo!—dare to join me in this struggle?

Do, and I guarantee you, you will not be disappointed.

Appendixes

Appendix 1 : The Dojo Oath

In the Japanese Budo karate dojo, every class ends with a recitation of the Dojo Oath. Of course, in Japan it's done in Japanese. One senior student (or the instructor) leads, and virtually shouts out — think military-like tone — a prescribed portion of each line, and the entire class, then, echoes it back. The senior student goes on to the next section, and so on, until the class has repeated all seven lines of the Oath. I have included it here in English, broken up by line into the portions that it should be broken up into during the recitation. Since, on the first line below, all that's written is "The Dojo Oath," this is the first portion that the leader recites, before the class echoes it back. "One," the number by itself comes next (and all by itself), and then each line in its turn should be shouted out and echoed back. The end of each segment should be inflected upwards, conveying energy, power, determination, and excitement. Think, here, the difference between "OSU!" and "osu," where one is powerful and embodies the word's meaning, and the other is weak and betrays it.

The oath was written by Mas Oyama with the help of Eiji Yoshikawa, the author of *Musashi*, the fictionalized account of the life of Japan's most famous historical Budo-ka, Miyamoto Musashi.

The Dojo Oath

One
We will train our hearts and bodies
For a firm and unshaking spirit.

Two
We will pursue the true meaning of the martial way
So that in time
Our senses may be alert.

Three
With true vigor
We will seek to cultivate a spirit of self-denial.

Four
We will observe the rules of courtesy
Respect our sempais
And refrain from violence.

Five
We will follow our heart's true path[3]
And never forget the true virtue of humility.

Six
We will look upwards to wisdom and strength
Not seeking other desires.

Seven
All our lives
Through the discipline of Kyokushin Karate
We will seek to fulfill the true meaning of the Way.

---

[3] The Japanese version reads, "We will follow the way of Buddha," which isn't appropriate for the Western dojo. I've used before, "We will follow our religious principles," but now that I'm older, I think that inappropriate, too, in the secular environment the Western dojo must remain. (We cannot ask students to adhere to their religious principles because some students might not adhere to any, per se.) Hence "adhere to our heart's true path," meaning "follow our conscience"—which is actually the Confucian way (Confucianism is a philosophy, not a religion), teaching that all people desire to do right—is the translation I've chosen to endorse here. What an uplifting, optimistic viewpoint, after all! Follow your conscience! Have faith in your ability to choose right over wrong!

Appendix 2 : A Sample Complex Exercise Chart

Listed are complex exercises you might be learning if you were at my dojo. It is a sample chart, meaning that at your dojo, you might create one that varies to match your dojo's curriculum.

According to principle #6, *Take Responsibility for Learning Even Complex Series of Motions in Just One Class, Even When Shown Just Once,* you should know each and every one of these after exposure in just one class. Yet this chart gives you three chances. Note the three columns after each exercise? I recommend you use this chart and put an X in the first column after you've practiced the complex exercise in one class, a second X (in the second column) when you've seen it in a second class, and a third one when you've seen it for the third time. In this way, you can keep track of how embarrassed you should be if you're continuing to bring "I don't know it yet" back to your teacher class after class. If you don't know it after the first time, ask a sempai to help you after class, or before the next one. At my dojo, I usually exempt white belts from this requirement, but they often voluntarily rise to the challenge. This chart will help them do so.

Of course the very complex exercises are for higher ranks. I have starred or double-starred (with * or **) the items in the list to which adult and teen white belts at my dojo will have had significant exposure by the time they're testing for their first belt. Students at other dojos shouldn't panic about all the double-starred items, as these are exercises unique to MY dojo (with these titles, that is), whereas your dojo will surely have its own set of similar complex exercises you're accustomed to referring to with alternate terminology.

Many of the items listed in the two *advanced* kata sections are a listing of what black belts and/or instructors participating in Kyokushin-kan seminars in Japan will be working on. Remember that YOUR Kyokushin dojo might have a list that varies.

Basic Kyokushin Kata			
Taikyoku sono Ichi*			
Taikyoku sono Ni*			
Taikyoku sono San*			
Pinan sono Ichi*			
Pinan sono Ni			
Pinan sono San			
Pinan sono Yon			
Pinan sono Go			
Yantsu			
Gekisai Sho			
Sanchin*			
Naifanchin Shodan*			
Kihon no Kon (a kata for the bo staff)**			
Oshiro no Kon			
3-step Kumite, 1-step Kumite, Kumite Drills			
Pinan Bunkai 1 and 2 (Pinan sono Ichi)*			
Pinan Bunkai 3 and 4 (Pinan sono Ni)*			
Pinan Bunkai 5 (Pinan sono San)*			
Pinan Bunkai 6 (Pinan sono San)			
Pinan Bunkai 7 and 8 (Pinan sono Yon)			
Pinan Bunkai 9 and 10 (Pinan sono Go)			
3-step kumite with jodan uke defense**			
3-step kumite with chudan soto uke defense**			
3-step kumite with gedan barai defense vs. punch**			
3-step kumite with gedan barai defense vs. mae geri**			
3-step kumite with chudan uchi uke defense**			
"Cut-to-the-corner" defense vs. gedan mawashi geri**			
"Cut-to-the-corner" defense vs. mae geri**			
"Cut-to-the-corner" defense vs. ushiro geri**			
"Cut-to-the-corner" defense vs. straight punch**			
Oshiro no Kon Kumi Bo*			

Advanced Kata			
Gekisai Dai			
Juu no Kata sono Ichi			
Juu no Kata sono Ni			
Saifa			
Garyu			
Kanku			
Seienchin			
Seipai			
Sushiho			
Tensho			
Bassai-Dai			
Naifanchin Nidan			
Advanced Weapons Kata and Weapons Bunkai[4]			
Shushi no Kon			
Shushi no Kon Kumi Bo			
Ryubi no Kon			
Terukawa no Tonfa			
Tawada no Sai Sho			
Tawada no Sai Dai			
Kinhon with Jo (five types)			

---

[4] This book is not a technical manual, but I will make one brief note as to the role of training with the traditional weapons of Japan in the Budo karate dojo. We do not presume to teach the student how to fight with weapons. Studying their use, however, provides an unrivaled insight into the origin and application of our karate (as a weaponless art, since karate means "empty hand") techniques. Hence we study the use of Japan's traditional weapons (bo, tonfa, sai, jo) in order to deepen our understanding of karate. However, before leaving it at that, one should also consider that the only way to truly study a martial art is to take its practice very seriously, and consider its use in actual self-defense. Therefore, even though we don't teach weapons to teach our beginning students how to fight with them, if we *do* practice with weapons at all it's the student's responsibility to train with them with a degree of seriousness that suggests in the next moment we might actually have to use them to defend ourselves. To repeat: we do not teach weapons anticipating that our students will learn to fight with them, but if our students don't practice with them *as if they actually will*, their training is substandard for the Budo karate dojo.

Appendix 3 : A Sample What/How Chart

In the Budo karate dojo, it's important to develop a sense for *how* your teacher has asked you to do each and every thing that you do in the dojo. Of course, if the majority is already doing one thing correctly—that is, according to your teacher's standard—you may not have heard a verbal expression of *how* your teacher wants you to do that thing. However, if your dojo's majority (or you as an individual) are falling below your teacher's standard in the performance of any single motion, routine, tradition, or exercise, you will likely have heard your teacher tell you—hopefully not too many times!—*how* he/she wants that thing done better.

If, for example, when the teacher asks the students to "line up!" the majority are routinely failing to find straight lines, you likely will have heard your teacher remind you, "Straight lines, please!" a number of times. Of course, the trick is to recall, each time your teacher announces an exercise, routine, tradition, or motion, exactly *how* you have heard your teacher say he/she wants you to do it. I have found that having a chart can help a new group of students to adopt this type of thinking. Here's a sample, but you can make your own. Whether you're a teacher or a student, you can continue this chart to match the needs of your own particular dojo.

Remember that the *how* in your chart has little to do with the general instructions for executing that particular *what*; it's rather the specific *how* that your teacher has told you verbally lately because you (or your class) is falling short of doing it according to your teacher's standard. Be sure to see #2, *It's the* How, *Silly, Not the* What. This will all become clear to you as you read the chart. *Loudly*, for example, the first *how* for #1, "Answer with 'Osu!'", would be there because (and only if) the teacher has been discontent with how loudly you (or the dojo) have been answering with "Osu!"

The What	The How
1. Answer with "Osu!"	Loudly, promptly, always, any time my teacher or sempai addresses me directly or the whole class, even when instructions come in the form of gestures.

The What	The How
2. Line up!	Quickly, powerfully, by rank. Make sure lines are straight, and particularly that distances behind and in front of me are the same as distances to my right and left. Keep these lines! Fix my koohais if they get out of place.
3. Straight punches during kihon.	Powerful, tight fists, keep pulling hand pulled back tight, keep eyes focused on target. Keep stances lowered. Focus on abdomen during exhale. Make sure to punch the correct target.
4. Following instructions.	Promptly, powerfully. Listen to all of my teacher/sempai's words, and pick out the *how* he/she wants me to do the *what* he/she is asking me to do.
5. Naifanchin Shodan (or any kata).	Deep stances, powerful focused techniques, make sure I'm looking in the correct directions.
6. Kumite.	Keep my guard up at all times. Make sure I'm at the proper distance so that I'm locking my arms out when I throw the majority of my punches. Take it easy on those weaker than me, fight hard with those bigger/stronger than me.
7. Your Item:	How you've been encouraged by your teacher to do it:
8. Your Item:	How you've been encouraged by your teacher to do it:

Appendix 4: The Techniques of Mas Oyama's Kihon Series

The first forty minutes of each and every 2-hour class taught at Mas Oyama's dojo during the (nearly) two years I was there consisted of 36 repetitions of each and every one of these techniques, done in this order and from the stances given. The first six were silent and for warm-up, and the following 30 were done full power and with kiais. If we did fewer of any of the techniques (i.e. fewer than 36), I give those numbers beside the listing in parentheses. After each section of the kihon I provide some tips on learning the vocabulary. *Kihon* means basics, or basic techniques.

closed-handed techniques (from right foot forward sanchin stance)

1. seiken chudan tsuki — middle section punch
2. seiken jodan tsuki — upper section punch
3. uraken shomen uchi — back fist to face
4. uraken sayu uchi — back fist to side
5. uraken hizo uchi — back fist to spleen
6. seiken mawashi uchi — roundhouse strike
7. seiken ago uchi — forefist strike to the jaw

Tsuki means punch, and *Uchi* means strike. Notice first that all of these techniques are either punches or strikes by looking at the *third* word in each technique's name. Now look up and down the list at the *first* word. Note that all of the techniques use either *seiken* (forefist) or *uraken* (back fist). By learning only four terms, therefore, you've already got 2/3 of all the vocabulary needed. By understanding the pattern, you'll have another big boost. Now look at the middle column, the *second* word in each technique's name. Here you have some learning to do, but it will help you to understand that each one of these words describes either the *target* or the *path* of the technique. *Ago* means jaw, for example, but *mawashi* means circular.

techniques in kiba-dachi (from horseback-riding stance)

1. shita tsuki — uppercut (6+20)
2. hiji age ate — vertical (rising) elbow strike (6+20)
3. hiji ate — horizontal elbow strike (6+20)

There's punch, again, *tsuki*. *Shita* means *from below*. *Hiji* means elbow. *Ate* (two syllables please, i.e. *a-te*) is another word for strike. (I'm not sure why we did fewer repetitions for these three techniques in kiba dachi, but I promised to report when that was the case!)

> knife-hand techniques (from left foot forward sanchin stance)
> 1. shuto gammen uchi—knife-hand strike to the face
> 2. shuto sakotsu uchi—knife-hand strike to the collarbone
> 3. shuto sakotsu uchi komi—driving knife-hand strike to the collarbone
> 4. shuto uchi uchi—inside knife-hand strike
> 5. shuto hizo uchi—knife-hand strike to the spleen

Shuto means knife-hand, and *uchi* means strike, so you've got 2/3 of the vocabulary for this series already. Add *komi* to *uchi* and you've got *driving strike*. The *second* words, the center column, so to speak, once again refer to the target or the path of the techniques. *Gammen* is face, *sakotsu* is collarbone, etc.

> blocking techniques (from right foot forward sanchin stance)
> 1. jodan uke—upper block
> 2. chudan soto uke—outside middle block
> 3. chudan uchi uke—inside middle block
> 4. gedan barai—low block
> 5. chudan uchi uke gedan barai—simultaneous inside middle block and low block

Uke means *block*, and that one exception, low block, uses *barai* which means *sweep*. Otherwise the first words, the first column, so to speak, define the level of the blocks. I recommend that students start to learn *jodan*, *chudan*, and *gedan* with *chudan*, because *chu* sounds like chew and you have to have something in the middle in order to chew. *Soto* means outside, *uchi* means inside. We already had *uchi uchi* in the *shuto* techniques: *inside strike*.

geri (kicking techniques)

1. mae keage — forward leg lift (6+10 right leg first, then 6+10 left leg)
2. uchi mawashi geri — inside crescent kick
3. soto mawashi geri — outside crescent kick
4. hiza geri — knee kick
5. mae geri — front kick
6. kin geri — groin kick
7. yoko keage — sideways leg lift (6+20)
8. yoko geri — side kick (6+20)
9. kansetsu geri — side kick to the knee (6+20)
10. ushiro geri — back kick (6+20)
11. mawashi geri — roundhouse kick

Geri clearly means kick, and nearly all of these techniques are *geri* (kicks). Two of them are *keage*, which means *leg lift (or rising leg)*, since these aren't generally thought of as offensive techniques. Once again, the *other* words here all describe the target, the direction, or the path of the kicks. Note *soto* and *uchi* again (inside and outside).

enkei gyaku tsuki (round house block and punch)

1. enkei gyaku tsuki (6+10)

Mas Oyama's enkei gyaku tsuki, which doesn't quite fit with the rest of kihon (it's not stationary like the rest), was always, nevertheless, always the finale of the kihon series in all classes taught at Mas Oyama's Honbu Dojo.

Appendix 5 : Our Moment in History (For the Kyokushin Instructor)

It's 2013 and it's been 19 years since the death of our founder, Mas Oyama.

From one massive *organization* governing all, Kyokushin has evolved into a *style* of karate that may be taken up by anyone. Large swaths of it are still governed by international organizations that battle for prominence, just as small swaths of it are likewise governed by smaller organizations. The *independent dojo*, in the West, has come to be. For all of these entities, however, big or small, the question that we all struggle to answer is whether to preserve that which we witnessed of Kyokushin during Mas Oyama's lifetime, or whether to allow it to evolve. Which elements should we fight to keep unchanged, and which ones would Mas Oyama himself have allowed to change with the times?

I can provide perspective here that may help some of you to sort out the answer to this question.

First, it's necessary to understand that during Mas Oyama's lifetime, Kyokushin WAS always evolving. Part of the reason why it became great is that Mas Oyama allowed it to change with the times. In that sense, to stop Kyokushin's evolution is to diminish Kyokushin's greatness. To make Kyokushin, for all time, exactly what it was *at the moment in history that you witnessed it during Mas Oyama's lifetime* is to stop a vital part of what made/makes Kyokushin great. The important question that we all face, therefore, is, "Do we, as individuals, dare to allow something to evolve whose evolution was originally overseen by Mas Oyama himself?"

Before attempting to answer that question, however, we should also understand that there were certain elements of Kyokushin, even during Mas Oyama's lifetime, that did NOT evolve, and some, in fact, that DEVOLVED and became weaker than they had once been, also under Mas Oyama. Our important question, therefore, becomes three questions:

1. Which elements of Kyokushin do we improve upon looking forward (into realms where Kyokushin has not yet gone)? 2. Which elements do we leave untouched? and, 3. Which elements do we improve upon by looking backwards (to a time in its history when Kyokushin did it better)?

One thing I can say unequivocally is that whichever of us get the answers to these questions right are going to be the ones that history will show to have continued Mas Oyama's legacy.

The greatest piece of advice I can offer here would be to ally yourself with someone (an elder) who is exceptional at what they do, as a teacher and as a leader, yes, but also one who KNOWS because he/she was there to witness the evolution, the devolution, and those elements that remained static during the breadth of Mas Oyama's lifetime. As fate would have it, there is not another American who spent more time in daily contact with Mas Oyama than I. Of course there were some who had sporadic contact with Mas Oyama over many more years than I did, and there are a few Japanese who later became Americans, such as Shihan Kenji Fujiwara, who spent longer sustained periods of time in Mas Oyama's tutelage. However, before you allow that statement to make you think me haughty, the point that I seek to make here is only this:

I have had more contact with Mas Oyama than most Westerners, so, trust me—and *DON'T TRUST EVEN ME* as a definitive source, one who KNOWS what Kyokushin was in its entirety, enough to judge what elements of Kyokushin should be maintained, which ones should be regained, and which ones should be improved upon. I was only 23 years old when Mas Oyama died.

When at all possible, find someone older and wiser (than I) who was there, in close contact with Mas Oyama, for more of Kyokushin's history that I was. Find someone you feel comfortable following, and follow that person like your life depends upon it, OR, since it's not possible for everyone to just pick up and move to Japan, make sure that the person you're following, like me, for example, is doing his/her best to follow someone else who KNOWS better, and is delivering the fruits of that learning to you.

In my case, that person is Kancho Hatsuo Royama, and of all the things I am thankful for in my own personal Kyokushin experience, the greatest, hands down, is that I have lucked into finding someone that I can follow with all of my heart. As you will see, unless you're one of the unlucky few who find themselves with the responsibility of being the leader of many, karate is not Budo without someone to follow, and even more so, without someone to follow *with all of your heart*.

We have, in Kyokushin's history, an element that might be referred to as *degrees of separation*. There are those who learned from Mas Oyama, those who learned from students of Mas Oyama, and those who learned from students of students of Mas Oyama, and so on. Whereas in some countries around the world, we have seen instances where each degree of separation, each generation, is greater than the last, the unfortunate case for the North American continent has always been that each generation of Kyokushin has been LESS than the previous one.

It has always been the North American dilemma.

Indeed, I consider it my duty as an uchi deshi (personal student) of Mas Oyama to spend my lifetime, if necessary, trying to sort out the answer to this very problem. Why do the Eastern Europeans get better at karate with each degree of separation, while we in America get worse?

My own theory is a still-developing one, and those who would think me bold for suggesting that I have anything to say on the matter at all should also be assured that when looking for the culprit, I spend as much time, if not more, looking inward *at myself,* trying to identify my own shortcomings, as I do looking outward, comparing Kyokushin in Japan to Kyokushin on the continent on which I live. I can state the following, though, unequivocally — and stating it will lead us back to the core focus of this book, and to the replication of Mas Oyama's Kyokushin in the Western Dojo.

The attitude with which the Western, and particularly American, student of Kyokushin tends to BEGIN his/her training differs substantially from the attitude with which the Japanese student, and students of many other nationalities around the world, begin their own. Here, maybe, is a good opportunity to challenge the Western beginning student of Budo karate, and, because I have a vested interest, the American one.

Make YOUR generation the one that turns the tide!

Make YOUR generation the one that surpasses that of your teacher by making sure that your successors, your own koohais, are set on the right path to surpass you.

But be careful!

And hopefully, if you read this book, you'll start to see that there are certain pitfalls into which the Western student might fall in an attempt to follow the same piece of advice that a Japanese student of Budo karate would follow in a completely different way.

In this case, the Japanese student, taking loyalty to his/her teacher for granted, understands that "surpass your teacher" means "honor your teacher at all costs, and learn the best of what your teacher has to offer, so that you might pass it on, and someday even improve upon it, should you gain the strength and wisdom to do so." It is following this route, the Japanese one, that Kyokushin has continued to develop in many countries around the world, where it's the norm for each degree of separation to become stronger than the last.

"Realize that it's your duty to surpass your teacher," to the American student, however, tends to mean something completely different.

"The way to surpass my teacher is to identify ways that I can do better than my teacher, ways that I can cut corners that my teacher didn't cut to get ahead, ways in which I can show my teacher's ways to be inferior, so that my koohais, today, will see that my way is superior, and maybe even, one day, I can push my teacher aside, and do more than he/she's done."

We don't realize it, and no student likely does so on purpose, but this, paired with an also incorrect, despairing notion that "we can never possibly catch up with our teachers who had firsthand contact with their far greater teachers," is perhaps exactly why American Kyokushin, for one, tends to stair-step downwards. The beginning Kyokushin student, therefore, would do well to understand that both are incorrect.

You CAN surpass your teacher if you do it by HONORING your teacher. You canNOT surpass your teacher who is honoring his/her own teacher by dishonoring your teacher, and trying to get ahead without him/her. In Japanese culture, honoring one's teacher is taken for granted. In American culture, one's right to *take* success from those who are successful is equally taken for granted.

The problem is that Budo karate, being a uniquely Japanese entity, is better mastered through an approach mimicking the culture that created it, rather than through a culture that in many ways runs contrary to it. Remember that Mas Oyama considered American culture the antimatter to Budo karate's matter. Look at the first students of Mas Oyama that he sent to the U.S. to teach Budo karate to Americans. Look at how great their students were.

But what about those students' students?

What about the next generation after that?

Approach Budo karate, as a beginner, though the lens of Bushido-influenced Japanese culture, and you just might be one in the generation that reverses the trend. Does this mean committing ritual suicide through disembowelment, as the samurai would do, if you fail?

Of course not.

It just means having the proper fighting attitude each and every time you step into the dojo.

It is my hope that this book will help you to find that proper attitude.

Appendix 6 : Could It Be That It's NOT Desirable to Replicate the Way Things Were in Mas Oyama's Dojo?

Yes!

Of course it's possible that there are *some* elements of *the way things were* in Mas Oyama's dojo when I was there that it would be better not to replicate—and in fact I've endeavored, already, to leave that tiny minority *out* of the current presentation. After all, if you've read Appendix 5 just above, you'll understand that we are left with the responsibility of picking and choosing among the elements of Mas Oyama's karate to determine what's best for Kyokushin's future.

But how about this, the totality of Mas Oyama's sempai/koohai system, Mas Oyama's *specific one* that's been so much the focus of this book?

The truth is that having experienced some elements of the sempai/koohai system as presented by Kyokushin-kan International (Kancho Royama's current organization), I have come to believe that there ARE some things that Kancho Royama's branch division of the original Kyokushinkaikan does better than Mas Oyama's world headquarters dojo did during the small window of time that I was living and training there. Remember that Budo karate is always YOUR teacher's karate, and Kancho Royama, when he was *Shihan* Royama, branch chief in Saitama under Sosai (chairman) Mas Oyama, would have done *some things* differently than his teacher due to his relative degree of separation and independence.

There is always some content and method variance from teacher to teacher, from dojo to dojo, from branch to branch, and certainly from county to country.

What I'd like to suggest here, however, is merely this:

The content I've provided in this book, whereas it might not be perfect in all ways, would be a MAJOR step up for the level of Kyokushin in the West, were the majority of Western Kyokushin students to adopt it.

Is it perfect?

No, but is what we currently have?

Far from it!

Remember that's it's our duty to admit that we're not perfect so that we will have a better chance of discovering the ways we might improve.

Think about Kyokushin in Eastern Canada and the extent to which it was shaped by Shihan André Gilbert. Consider the extent to which much of US Kyokushin was shaped by then-Shihan Tadashi Nakamura or then-Shihan Shigeru Oyama.

The same might be said about every country's Kyokushin.

I lived and trained for two years in Hungary. And no one would deny that no individual had a larger impact on Kyokushin in Hungary than Shihan Kalman Furko, unless perhaps it was *his* teacher, Shihan Howard Collins, who introduced Kyokushin to Hungary in the first place.

But surely there is some difference between each Shihan in these cases! They all have their differences, so which one is better? Which one is right and which one is wrong?

No one can deny that the split that occurred in the US between Mas Oyama (Honbu) and, first, Shihan Tadashi Nakamura, and, second, Shihan Shigeru Oyama, has had an enormous impact on those of us who learned from them or their early students. For better or for worse, we have all learned that even greats such as these break ties with their teachers in Japan, and some of us have learned — whether it's true or not — that it's even possible in America for instructors to become somehow greater in the public eye because of it. There is no question that Kancho Royama's philosophy for the development of Kyokushin is one of globalization and cooperation, even between would-be rival organizations. Is the fact that the US trend is so grounded in fortification and isolationism, therefore, a product of the conflict we watched play out as our own role models broke with their teachers, over and over again, and then had to defend their choices in the aftermath? How many instructors do you know who have bounced around more than once from one teacher to another, or from one organization to another?

In America, is it not all of them?

What about in other countries? What about in Japan?

We know that Kancho Royama followed his teacher, Mas Oyama, from the time he was a teenager until Mas Oyama died some 30 years later. We know that he struggled to support Matsui, his koohai — because Mas Oyama asked him to! — for an entire decade before he finally decided that enough was enough.

The important point that I hope to illustrate here is that we learn from the things our teachers do that are great, but we also learn from the things our teachers do that aren't so great. Of course we see how well they do or don't handle themselves when they face misfortunes that are no fault of theirs, but who are we to judge, in all cases, whose fault their misfortunes were?

In Mas Oyama's case — in *MY* teacher's case! — I feel certain that he would tell us today to make sure that we learn from his mistakes, not by replicating them out of a sense of "Mas Oyama did it that way so it must be the best way," but rather by ensuring that we don't make the exact same mistakes.

In every country — and particularly America! — there is still so much that we have to learn. In some cases — like America, for example — there are some things that we have to *un*learn. There are some lessons that we've learned, in other words, that we might have to correct. Sometimes those lessons, too, are so ingrained in our understandings of what karate is that we're not even aware that there might be another way.

It's important, here, I think, to open our minds, and ask why karate in the US, and to a lesser degree karate in the West, remains forever so far behind what has become the international norm.

Appendix 7: A Photograph That Should Inspire Us

I love this picture of the earliest of Mas Oyama's students that he sent to America to teach Kyokushin: (from left to right) the young Shihan Tadashi Nakamura, the young Shihan Shigeru Oyama, and the young Shihan Seiji Kanemura. I'm partial to it, in this case, because they look so skinny, and so young. In this picture, they might as well be kids compared to how they've gone down in history.

I ask you, though, what made these three skinny kids so great in the eyes of a generation of American Kyokushin karateka?

Of course, they were Mas Oyama's students; that was a plus in their favor. Other than that, though? Was it that they are Japanese? Are they savants? Were they born being karate masters? I don't think so. I think they had a great teacher, and I think other than that they had a great training attitude, and, from it, a great sense of commitment to their art. They trained hard, that's the biggest thing. Can you and I be like them? Can you and I surpass them?

(Special thanks to Richard Scibilia for the use of his father's photo.)

I'd like to suggest that we must try. I'd like to suggest that we must get over the idea that we never could.

These three greats made great students, in the 1970s and 1980s particularly, but when we look at Kyokushin worldwide today, can we really be content with the state of Kyokushin in America?

How can we possibly?

My suggestion is that any one of you guys (or girls) half my age can be as great, and even greater than, these three guys if you train with the proper attitude. If you train hard, you can be more successful, even, than them.

Remember that it's our duty to honor our teachers, and to battle with all of our heart and soul to match them, but it's also our duty to identify, finally, what mistakes our teachers may have made, learn from those mistakes, and make sure that we don't make those same ones.

Would any of these great teachers really want us to live forever in their shadow? Would my teacher, Mas Oyama?

I feel certain that he would not.

Does it not, in fact, dishonor our teachers to hold them up to such a height that we take for granted that we can never achieve something that they failed to achieve?

I know that Mas Oyama would be pleased that we honor him, but he'd be disappointed if we didn't battle to soar on past him and accomplish things that he failed to accomplish during his lifetime, even if we have to band together to do it. Of course, it's very unlikely that I might in too many ways in the case of Mas Oyama, but what were some of the things that he did NOT accomplish during his lifetime?

I know for a fact that he was never content with the current state of Budo karate in America.

Is it not our duty to try to finish what he started?

LIGO DOJO OF BUDO KARATE
A 501.c.3 Public Charity Nonprofit

All proceeds from this and other Nathan Ligo titles support The Society for the Betterment of the Human Condition through the Training, Instruction, and Propagation of Budo Karate (d.b.a. Ligo Dojo of Budo Karate and Ligo Ink). Readers who want to know more, or wish to make a tax-deductible contribution, can find information online at:

www.ligodojo.com

Contributions go directly to make self-esteem- and discipline-instilling karate training available to young people who might not otherwise be able to participate.

Available through
your online bookstore

Hungarian Rhapsody:
A Kyokushin Adventure

A Novel by Nathan Ligo
available in paperback / $14.95
ISBN-13: 978-0615576206

*This title contains adult themes
and is not intended for children.*

Available through
your online bookstore

Mightier Than the Sword:
A Kyokushin Karate
Coming of Age Story

A Memoir by Nathan Ligo
available in paperback / $21.95
ISBN-13: 978-0578077291

*This title contains adult themes
and is not intended for children.*

www.ingramcontent.com/pod-product-compliance
Lightning Source LLC
Chambersburg PA
CBHW071901290426
44110CB00013B/1232